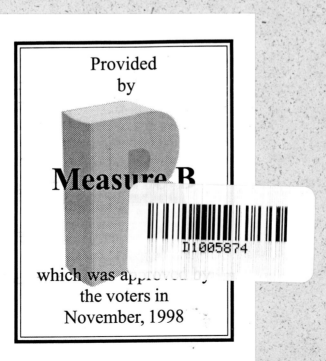

ROGUE
MESSIAHS

ROGUE
MESSIAHS

TALES of

SELF-PROCLAIMED SAVIORS

COLIN WILSON

HAMPTON ROADS
PUBLISHING COMPANY, INC.

Cover design by Susan Shapiro
Cover art by Anne L. Dunn and PhotoDisc

For information write:

Hampton Roads Publishing Company, Inc.
1125 Stoney Point Road
Charlottesville, VA 22902

Or call: 804-296-2772
FAX: 804-296-5096
e-mail: hrpc@hrpub.com
Web site: www.hrpub.com

If you are unable to order this book from your local
bookseller, you may order directly from the publisher.
Quantity discounts for organizations are available.
Call 1-800-766-8009, toll-free.

Library of Congress Catalog Card Number: 99-91473
ISBN 1-57174-175-5
10 9 8 7 6 5 4 3 2 1

Printed on acid-free paper in the United States

This book was originally conceived as a collaboration with my two sons Damon and Rowan. This finally proved impractical, but I am grateful for Damon for helping me with research, particularly on David Koresh, Ervil LeBaron, and Rock Theriault. He also suggested the title. I am grateful to Maurice Bassett and Ted Browne for helpful comments, and to Howard Dossor for duplicating the typescript. It was also Ted Browne who presented me with Savage Messiah, and so introduced me to the case of Rock Theriault.

Thanks also to my wife Joy, who read the typescript and made some invaluable suggestions.

ANALYTICAL TABLE OF CONTENTS

The final assault on Waco. The mass suicide of the Branch Davidians. Why do normal people join such cults? Koresh as seducer of under-age girls. How Marc Breault became a follower; his disillusionment. Koresh is found dead. Early life of Vernon Howell. The dominant five percent. Sex and the adolescent. Seduction of Lois Roden. Conflict with George Roden. Koresh takes over Mount Carmel. The quarrel with Marc Breault. The end.

Sabbatai Zevi, the Messiah of 1666. Excitement all over Europe. The news of Zevi's apostasy. The Jewish expectation of the Messiah. Zerubbabel of Judaea. The Maccabees. Jesus of Nazareth. The Essenes. Jesus did not regard himself as the Son of God. He foretells the end of the world within his lifetime. This fails to happen. Simon Bar Kochbar. Moses of Crete. Christ of Gevaudon. Serene of Shirin. Aldebert of Soissons. Eudo de Stella. Tanchelm of Antwerp. The Christian Church as oppressor. The Brethren of the Free Spirit. Klaus Ludwig and sexual liberation. Sabbatai Zevi, mystic and kabbalist. The massacre of Polish Jews in 1648. Sabbatai's eccentricities. He marries Sarah. Nathan becomes his disciple. Nathan's gifts as a publicity agent. Sabbatai's triumphant progress to Smyrna. Arrested in Constantinople. Is converted to Islam. His supporters remain loyal. His maniacal outbursts. His death at the age of fifty. Nathan and Sabbatai. Messiahs and disciples are involved in a symbiotic relationship.

Three: The Psychology of Discipleship 42

The professor from America. Jim Jones and group marriage. My *Six Years With God*. Jeannie and Al Mills become disciples of the People's Temple. Jones's "miracles." Jones's increasing paranoia. He tries to take over the flock of Father Divine. Beating the disciples. His promiscuity. "Do you want to have sex with Father?" The size of his organ. The Beating Board. Bad publicity. Congressman Ryan asks the federal authorities to intervene. The investigative team travels to Jonestown. Jones orders their executions. Mass suicide of the cult. Jones's character and background. Colonel Olcott and thaumaturgy. Paul Brunton and *Secret India*. Bernard Masson writes to Brunton. Jeffrey Masson and "my father's guru." Masson's spiritual experience. Brunton and UFOs. His disciples are advised to move to South America. At Harvard, Masson realizes Brunton "was simply a charlatan." A fake miracle detected. Brunton's death. "Wake up, Bernard!" The disciple's craving for spiritual evolution. William James on "the will to believe." James's breakdown. The career of Madame Blavatsky. The Tibetan Mahatmas. *Isis Unveiled*. Madame Blavatsky denounced. Returns to London. W. B. Yeats joins the disciples. Yeats and wishful thinking. Shelley's old Jew. Yeats and magic. Fairies.

Four: The Messiah as Killer 72

Auguste Comte tries to overthrow religion. He founds his own religion. The case of Jeffrey Lundgren. Early failure. He becomes a Mormon priest. He moves to Kirtland. Joseph Smith and the Mormons. The Book of Mormon as a forgery. Murder of Joseph Smith. Founding of Salt Lake City. Lundgren announces that he has seen angels. He swindles the church. Increasing paranoia. He purchases rifles. The Avery family. The Kirtland massacre. Living under canvas. Intercession. The bodies are found. Lundgren sentenced to death. Why did Lundgren commit murder?

Five: A Taste for Power 89

The LeBaron family. Dayer sees a ghost. Joel becomes the Prophet. Ervil's power mania. He is dismissed by Joel. Murder of Joel. Ervil walks free. Verlan becomes Prophet. Firebombing of Molinos. More murders. Assassination of Rulon Allred. Failure to kill Verlan. Ervil flees. His arrest and trial. His death in prison. Arturo LeBaron becomes Prophet. Murder of Arturo. Heber conducts a purge. The four o'clock murders. The killers arrested. Murder of Natasha. The trial of the LeBarons.

ROGUE

MESSIAHS

INTRODUCTION

On March 20, 1995, soon after seven a.m., commuters on the Tokyo subway began to experience a tickling in the throat and a soreness in the eyes and nose; soon they smelled a stench like a mixture of mustard and burning rubber. Within minutes, dozens of people were choking or falling to the ground.

It was happening all over the Tokyo underground system. No one had any idea what was causing it. Fleets of ambulances ferried gasping or unconscious passengers to hospitals—the figure finally reached 5,500. Many seemed to be paralyzed, and a dozen would finally die. Yet it was not until mid-morning that a military doctor made a cautious and incredible diagnosis: the victims were suffering from poisoning by a nerve gas called sarin, once used by the Nazis in their death camps.

The police had a strong suspicion about who was responsible: an immensely wealthy religious cult known as Aum Shinrikyo, or Aum Supreme Truth, led by a forty-year-old guru who called himself Shoko Asahara. During the past six months police had received dozens of phone calls accusing the cult of fraud, abduction, and brutality. Things had come to a head a month earlier, when a sixty-eight-year-old lawyer named Kiyoshi Kariya had been kidnapped in broad daylight, grabbed by four powerfully-built men, and bundled into the back of a van. Kariya's sister had been a cult member who had absconded, and Kariya had received a threatening phone call, demanding to know where she was. After Kariya's disappearance, his son found a note that read: "If I disappear, I was abducted by Aum Shinrikyo." A police investigation began, but failed to find either Kariya or his body.

Now Aum Shinrikyo was the chief suspect in the gas attack. In spite of his protest ("We carry out our religious activities on the basis of Buddhist doctrine, such as no killing"), police raided Asahara's headquarters on the slopes of Mount Fuji. Most of the cultists had left, taking crates of documents; but the police found a huge stockpile of chemicals like sodium cyanide and peptone for cultivating bacteria. But the cult insisted, through its spokesmen, that this was all for legitimate peaceful purposes. On April 23, the cult's chief scientist, Hideo Murai, was murdered in front of a crowd of reporters and TV cameramen, stabbed repeatedly in the stomach by a small-time crook named Hiroyuki Jo, who then demanded, "Isn't anyone going to arrest me?" Police quickly obliged.

But where was the guru? He had vanished without a trace. On May 5, two months after the sarin attack, a bag left in the toilet of the Shinjuku station burst into flame. Alert staff doused it with water, but not before it had begun to emit choking fumes. Police discovered later that it would have given off clouds of hydrogen cyanide gas, called by the Nazis Zyklon B, which would have been sucked through the ventilators onto the platform.

One of the chief suspects was a young cultist called Yoshihiro Inoue, the guru's intelligence chief. He was caught driving a car that contained chemicals for manufacturing high explosives. This left no one in any doubt that the cult's protestations about love and peace were false. On May 16, there was another huge police raid on the Mount Fuji headquarters; this time they found a secret room, inside which a large, bearded figure sat cross-legged on the floor in the meditation posture. He admitted: "I am the guru. Don't touch me. I don't even allow my disciples to touch me."

I followed the subsequent trial closely through press clippings sent by my Japanese literary agent. A few weeks before the sarin gas attack, my wife and I had taken a train to Shinjuku station and eaten at a pleasant little restaurant nearby, so we could visualize the scene on that March morning. But the trial, followed by Asahara's conviction for murder, failed to answer the question raised by the killings: why had a wealthy and steadily-expanding cult decided to commit mass murder? I had already written most of this book, so regarded myself as something of an authority on prophets of the millennium. Yet at the end of the trial, there was still no obvious answer to this question: why had a man who had everything decided to throw it all away?

Asahara, whose real name was Chizuo Matsumoto, had been born blind in one eye and partially blind in the other. He was raised in a poor home, but had been a brilliant pupil at school. He thought of becoming a radical politician, like Mao Tse Tung, then began to meditate and claimed that one day he felt the kundalini mounting his spine. The 1980s in Japan were rather like the 1960s in Britain and America, a period that Asahara's biographers have called "the rush hour of the gods." Asahara founded a yoga school, which became so profitable that he opened several more. Then he went off to the Himalayas to meditate and had himself photographed with the Dalai Lama, who told him he had the mind of a Buddha. (After Asahara's arrest, the Dalai Lama was deeply embarrassed by this gaffe.) There in the Himalayas, Asahara claims he experienced enlightenment and achieved psychic powers.

Back in Tokyo he changed the name of his yoga school to Aum Supreme Truth (*Om* or *Aum* is a Sanskrit syllable pronounced during meditation) and was soon surrounded by hundreds of followers. Since he assured them that large cash donations would hasten their spiritual enlightenment, he was soon a wealthy man. Brilliant young students from the universities began to join the sect; one of them, Hideo Murai, invented a kind of electric cap which,when placed on the head, would raise the level of consciousness.

But desertion roused Asahara to a kind of frenzy. One disciple who announced he was leaving the sect was told he was in need of physical as well as psychological help, and ordered to drink large quantities of freezing water. He went into shock and died. Another disenchanted disciple, Shuji Taguchi, was strangled; his body burned. Another was attacked when he had returned home to his family; his skull was smashed with a hammer. The cult members also murdered his wife and child.

Asahara practiced sex with selected female disciples, and swore them to secrecy. But, as so often happens with rogue messiahs, his followers were ordered to be celibate.

During the 1990s, Aum Supreme Truth began to spread all over the world. There had probably not been such a successful cult since Ron Hubbard's Scientology. The post-Communist Russians were particularly sympathetic to it, and at the time of writing, Aum Supreme Truth continues to be a powerful movement in Russia.

World success made Asahara think in terms of world power. In 1993, his chief engineer, Kiyohide Hayakawa, was instructed to try and buy an atomic bomb. (In fact, during 1994, Hayakawa made eight trips to Russia trying to buy a nuclear warhead.) When he failed, the cult tried to buy a rural area near Tokyo, where there were deposits of uranium. And when this also failed they decided to buy land in Australia. It was half a million acres of scrubland called Banjawarn Station, which the cult bought for $400,000, in cash, after which it paid a further $110,000 for mining rights. There they began testing nerve gas on sheep whose skeletons were later found by police.

It would seem, then, that as the cult's success increased, so did its paranoia. This may seem strange, but in the course of this book, the reader will begin to find it glaringly familiar. It seems to have escalated sharply after the interest the police took in the disappearance of Kiyoshi Kariya, and this "persecution" in turn seems to have triggered the decision to launch the sarin attack. It certainly made no sense. What possible point could there be to gassing hundreds of people in the Tokyo subway system? Such violence was bound to lead to the kind of backlash that had destroyed so many other cults.

Is it possible to even begin to understand this apparently insane behavior?

In fact, as we shall see, the behavior of "rogue messiahs" tends to fall into a number of well-defined patterns.

To begin with, we have to recognize that these "messiahs" are driven by two basic human needs, power and sex. Of course, there are probably very few human beings on the face of the planet of whom this is not, to some extent, true. But when these needs expand beyond certain limits, it is as if they cease to obey the normal laws of nature, just as superheated gases behave quite differently from gases at ordinary temperatures. This is when these needs result in such behavior as the attack on the Tokyo subway or the mass suicides in Jonestown, Guyana, and Waco, Texas.

Of these two potentially explosive forces, sex and power, let us begin by considering the first. And because there is nothing more boring than trying to discuss sex in the abstract, let me speak in frankly personal terms.

At the time of my own sexual awakening, in early adolescence, the sheer intensity of the drive was a permanent nuisance. I felt like that man in the joke who has to strap his penis to his leg to prevent a permanent bulge in his trousers. Even the sight of women's underwear in a shop window or on a clothesline was enough to cause a rush of adrenaline.

One day when I was about twelve, a girl came around the corner on a bicycle, and her dress blew up in a gust of wind, showing a pair of blue knickers. She smiled with sly amusement, obviously quite unembarrassed, but for me the sensation was like being kicked in the stomach. The image came back to me for weeks afterwards, and it seemed unfair that God should fill the world with these infinitely alluring creatures, but reserve them for older men. What about all the sex-starved twelve-year-olds?

The starvation was to last for many more years, in fact, until I was almost nineteen. Although I was an "intellectual," always reading, studying literature, science, and later philosophy, and deriving enormous pleasure from them, that basic sexual hunger always formed a background to what I was reading or thinking.

My first sexual encounter was quite unlike the feverish daydreams of adolescence. There was no intense ecstasy, no overwhelming sense of ultimate fulfillment. She was a girl from a slum section of my home town, who gazed at me admiringly as I was selling tickets for a gambling machine in a fairground. When I asked her if she wanted to buy one, she asked me if I wanted to sell myself. I was nearly nineteen, she was fourteen. It was she who took the initiative in sex; I was too shy and awkward. The second time we met, she unzipped my trousers and critically examined my erection. And two days later, in a field, she made me lie on my back, removed her knickers, and very slowly, with gasps of pain, lowered herself onto me, then moved up and down. A few seconds later I had to tell her to move off quickly.

We made love about six times more that day, and what amazed me was that there was no ecstasy, no sense of revelatory discovery.

And as we walked together through the country lanes on our way back to the bus, I felt oddly relieved that it all seemed so ordinary and commonplace. Suddenly, it was perfectly obvious that sex was an illusion.

Yet although I had felt it was almost an anticlimax to see her naked from the waist down, I noticed that once she was again wearing her skirt, the old desire to see what lay underneath it was as compelling as ever. The illusion simply re-formed. One evening when we had made love on the rug in a house where we were babysitting, and when I afterwards felt a total lack of desire (almost a new experience), I noted that it flooded back instantly when she pulled on a pair of flesh-colored knickers.

It was experiences like these that made me aware that sex is a kind of confidence trick. The sight of a girl in her underwear was enough to make me salivate like a Pavlov dog, yet there was no way to satisfy this desire. Undressing and making love to the girl was no answer, for that was quite different. It was settling for something far less exciting than my glimpse of the girl whose skirt blew up on the bicycle.

It seemed to me that the position of the male is rather like that of a prince who falls in love with a magician's daughter. Every time he gets her into a corner and tries to steal a kiss, she turns into an ugly, cross-eyed chambermaid. Finally he persuades her father to allow them to marry. But on their wedding night, after he has turned off the light, he is seized by a sudden suspicion, and turns it on again. Then the guard outside the door hears him shout: "Oh no, not you again!"

This, I feel, is an accurate assessment of the truth about sex. This is why the Roman physician Calenus wrote: "*Post coitum omne animal triste est*," meaning, all animals feel sad after sex. We are vaguely aware we have been swindled, that someone has switched the gold brick for a lead one, but are not sure how the trick was accomplished.

All this explains why, after that first love affair, I never again felt envious of lovers like Casanova and don Juan. I could see that the main difference between us was that they had been swindled more often.

Of course, sensible people come to terms with this, just as they come to terms with the interest they have to pay when they change foreign currency at the bank. Besides, loving is not simply about sex; it is also about tenderness and protectiveness and mutual affection. I was later to find that having a wife and children was more than ample compensation for being unable to find the girl on the bicycle. Realism also helps: the recognition that she never existed and cannot exist.

What has always fascinated me is what happens when males refuse to recognize this, and try to catch that will o' the wisp in a butterfly net. That sounds absurd, since no one but a fool would even try. But it is not. When we understand why it is not, we can begin to understand the strange kind of insanity that drives so many "messiahs," and why so many of them pursue sex as a form of salvation.

Just as beauty is in the eye of the beholder, so the most important part of sex takes place in a space behind the eyes. That is why human beings, unlike other members of the animal kingdom, are capable of masturbation. They can create a sexual fantasy in their heads and bring it to fruition in orgasm. No animal can do that, even the chimpanzee, our closest relative.

What is even stranger is that this "mental sex" can reach an even greater intensity than sex with a physical partner. Victorian engineers learned how to make superheated steam, and Victorian pornographers learned to create what might be called "superheated sex." The bellows that blows the fire to white heat is called "the forbidden." The Marquis de Sade, imprisoned in the Bastille, with no way to feel alive except by blowing his imagination to a white hot glow, was the first to try to catalogue every form of "forbidden sex" in a vast work called *The 120 Days of Sodom* that encompassed incest, pedophilia, bestiality, torture, even murder.

This explains why those who try to catch the sexual will o' the wisp in a butterfly net are not, contrary to common sense, wasting their time. Sexual perversions can produce greater intensity than "normal" sex. But they also have dangerous side-effects. Like heroin, they are addictive, and entail a kind of slow poisoning. In effect, they create a form of sexual insanity.

A few years ago I entered into correspondence with an American serial killer named Danny Rolling, and wrote an introduction to his autobiography, *The Making of a Serial Killer*. Rolling's career illustrates the process I am describing. As a child, he was introduced by a friend to the practice of peeping through windows and watching women undress. He was caught at it, and relations with his father, an egotistical bully, reached breaking point.

In his teens he was called up for service in Vietnam, but was discharged from the Army when he was caught with drugs. The strained relations with his father, who had been a war hero, grew even worse.

Rolling experienced a religious conversion, and married a fellow church member. But when he was again caught peeping through windows, his wife divorced him. On the day he was served divorce papers, he committed his first sex attack, breaking into the home of a young woman who was alone and raping her. He felt such remorse the next day that he went back to apologize. But when he saw two muscular, grim-looking men leaving her house, he changed his mind.

Soon after this Rolling committed his first armed robbery and was sent to prison. The brutality there hardened him. Free once more, he now experienced a compulsion to commit rape. He admits that what he most enjoyed was the surrender of the terrified girl; it was balm to his ego.

Back home again, Rolling spent his evenings peering through the bedroom window of a pretty model named Julie Grissom. But on the day he was dismissed from his job in a restaurant for absenteeism, he reacted again as he had reacted to the divorce papers: broke into a woman's home (Julie Grissom's, this time), tied up her father and eight-year-old nephew at gunpoint, then raped her. He left after stabbing all three to death.

At this point there was a curious development. Rolling became convinced that he was possessed by two demonic entities, one a rapist and the other a murderer. It sounds like a typical excuse, but he has written to me about it, as well as describing it in his autobiography, and I have no doubt he is telling the truth as he sees it. Certainly, he had nothing to gain from a lie; he was on death row in Florida when he wrote to me.

After the triple murder, he traveled around the country, living by burglary and committing more rapes. Then, in August 1990, Rolling went on an orgy of murder and rape on the campus of the

University of Florida at Gainesville, causing an exodus of terrified students. His victims were four female students, but he also stabbed to death a male student, simply because he happened to be in the same apartment as one of the victims.

Soon after that, Rolling was arrested while trying to rob a grocery store. A routine blood test revealed that he was the Gainesville serial killer.

Danny Rolling's career is an example of what I mean by trying to capture a will o' the wisp in a butterfly net. His activities as a Peeping Tom and his teenage addiction to pornography led to over-expectation of what sex can provide. He found marriage unsatisfying, but finally achieved satisfaction in rape and the sense of control it brought. From then on, only "superheated sex" could leave him fully satisfied.

Rolling's sexual violence never developed into actual sadism. I suspect that is because he was caught scarcely a year after he had begun his career of sex murder. Most habitual sex killers become increasingly sadistic. Ted Bundy, executed in 1989, also began life as a Peeping Tom and a devotee of pornography. Then he graduated to breaking into the rooms of the girls he had observed and kidnapping them; the murders followed after a night of rape. Bundy's girlfriends would later testify that he developed a need to tie them up before sex; the compulsion was to make them look like helpless victims. He was caught after committing more than two dozen murders in four years (police believed the actual number could be closer to fifty). In his final confession, Bundy admitted that he could not bring himself to describe what he had done to his last victim (a twelve-year-old girl) because it was too horrible.

Here we have a clue to what drives "messiahs" to behave in an increasingly demented manner until they seem to invite catastrophe. They are addicts whose fix is illusion. The psychological kick Bundy and Rolling got from feeling themselves in total control of a terrified girl, rogue messiahs get from their power over their disciples.

So "superheated sex" is only one ingredient in this poisonous cocktail. Even more addictive is the craving for power and control. What was important to Danny Rolling was not simply raping the victims, but forcing them to repeat such litanies as "Do it harder,

Daddy." He was attempting to choreograph reality into his fantasy.

Am I suggesting that human beings would be better off if they felt no interest in sex? Obviously not. Knowing that sex is an illusion need not prevent us from enjoying it. When we go to the cinema, we are being subjected to a double illusion: we know that we are looking at shadows on a screen and we know that the story and characters are fictitious. That does not prevent us from enjoying the film. But if a member of the audience began firing a revolver at the screen villain, we would realize that he has allowed himself to be taken in to a dangerous extent. This is what happens to sex criminals like Danny Rolling and Ted Bundy.

Before we go on, it needs to be explained that five percent of any animal group is dominant. I first learned about this from the writer Robert Ardrey, who told me that one of the most closely guarded secrets of the Korean war was there were no escapes of American prisoners. The reason emerged after the war. Instead of keeping the Americans all together in one prison camp, the Chinese observed them closely, then selected all those who seemed to have any kind of drive or enterprise, and confined them in a separate compound. The Chinese quickly noticed that these dominant prisoners were precisely five percent of the total, or one in twenty. When these had been confined separately, the other ninety-five percent became passive and made no attempt to escape.

It seemed that this had actually been known for a long time. Zoologists had always recognized that five percent of all animals are dominant. And when Bernard Shaw asked the explorer H.M. Stanley in 1900 how many men could take over leadership of his expedition if he fell ill, Stanley replied "one in twenty."

In fact, Stanley himself belonged to a very small percentage of humans zoologists call "king rats"—people so dominant that they automatically become leaders of every group. They are probably five percent of the dominant five percent. Most rogue messiahs belong to this group.

It would be a mistake to assume that all the dominant five percent are potential great men or men of genius. They include every foreman in a factory, every sergeant in the Army, every member of a professional football team. Great men or men of genius are a far smaller number, perhaps five one-hundredths of one percent.

When we examine this five one-hundredths of a percent, we discover something that distinguishes many of them from the rest of the dominant five percent. Nearly all dominant people require other people to acknowledge and express their dominance. The sergeant needs his platoon, the actor his audience, the politician his electorate. But the five one-hundredths of a percent seem far less dependent on people. It is true that a Plato, Beethoven, or Einstein wishes his achievement to be recognized by his fellow humans. But he still cares more about the creativeness itself than about fame. Similarly, a St. Francis or St. Theresa seems to care more about God than about other people.

Such men and women are obviously the most interesting part of the dominant five percent. They are, in fact, the most interesting members of our species. The rest of the dominant five percent are obsessed by their personality, and the impact it makes on other people. You might say that, on the other hand, the five one-hundredths of one percent are trying to escape from personality; they seem to have a curious craving for the impersonal.

I suspect that some of the messiahs in this book have had their glimpses of impersonality, such as Paul Brunton, "Brother Twelve," Aleister Crowley, perhaps even Asahara, who claimed that he had experienced enlightenment in India. But, as we shall see, the problems of being a guru tend to drag them down into the realm of personality and the craving for control.

This brings us to one of the most curious manifestations of dominance: the problem of the "Right Man."

The term was invented by the writer A.E. Van Vogt, who also uses the term "the Violent Man." Such a man will never, under any circumstances, admit that he is in the wrong. Confronted with evidence that he is wrong, he will fly into a violent rage and lash out with his fists.

Van Vogt became aware of the phenomenon through studying divorce cases in which the husband had behaved in an outrageously unfair way, treating his wife and family as if he were a mad dictator. Such men were often flagrantly unfaithful to their wives, yet would burst into a rage if their wives even smiled at another man.

The odd thing was that colleagues of such people were usually unaware of this paranoid behavior; they found him sociable and normal, a "nice guy." It was only in the privacy of his family, where he felt he had total control, that this kind of man would behave like some Eastern potentate.

The Right Man is characterized by a deep and nagging sense of inferiority, a feeling that he is ultimately inadequate to meet the challenges of life. He conceals this from his peers, doing his best to seem balanced and normal. Marriage often brings him his first real sense of conquest, of being the one who gives orders. The feeling is so intoxicating that it becomes a drug to which he becomes addicted.

Right Men are frequently unfaithful because they need to repeat the experience as often as possible, the sheer exultation of being the conqueror, of possessing and dominating yet another woman. (The act of lovemaking is in itself an act of conquest, even if the woman herself is highly dominant, for she has placed herself in a position of surrender.) He flies into a rage at the least sign of contradiction or opposition from his family, for he needs them to soothe the deep-lying sense of inferiority, and to sustain the fantasy that he has created.

This also explains why, if his wife leaves him, the Right Man experiences total collapse, often to the point of suicide. His wife has shattered the foundation of his tower of self-delusion, and revived his worst nightmare of being trampled and destroyed by life.

We can see that the Right Man has enclosed himself in an illusion of superiority. His wife and children are co-opted to support this illusion; the slightest sign of doubt or reluctance on their part provokes a screaming tantrum or physical violence.

When Right Men also happen to possess real power, like Hitler or Stalin or Mao Tse Tung, they are perfectly capable of ordering the deaths of millions of people. The slightest show of opposition (as when the Russian *kulaks* objected to being forced onto collective farms) fills them with murderous rage; it seems self-evident to the Right Man that such people deserve to die.

It may seem odd that men who have achieved political power should need to be sustained by the delusions of the Right Man, which spring from weakness. But the delusions are inherent in his character. They are due to a combination of fear and the need for self-assertion. Hitler started off as an unsuccessful artist who then projected the blame for his failure onto the Jews. Once the Right Man has a scapegoat, someone he can blame, he becomes involved in a vicious circle of hatred and self-justification. Once he has made a long-term commitment to these paranoid fantasies, turning his back on them would be a form of self-destruction.

The divorcees described by Van Vogt are obviously not as extreme as this, but the basic mechanism is the same. When a Right Man marries, he is inclined to feel that he has bestowed himself on someone who is not really worthy of him, and who should prove her appreciation of his uniqueness by serving him with selfless adoration; since few wives look upon their husbands with this degree of hero worship, he soon begins to regard her with irritation and hostility. Children of such a marriage are potential rivals for his wife's love and attention, so he treats them harshly.

The trouble is that being the master of this small dictator-state is bad for his character. His craving for admiration is so ravenous that even if he happened to have thousands of admirers, the thirst would still remain unquenchable. It springs from a basic sense of inferiority, a lack of self-esteem, that sticks in the unconscious mind like a splinter. He seldom mellows with age; in the domestic arena, his behavior is likely to grow more and more outrageous.

Most of the rogue messiahs in this book are "king rats" who are also Right Men. They combine the Right Man's craving for domination with the serial killer's urge for the ultimate sexual fulfillment. And when these two illusions enter into combination, the result can be deadly.

But the psychology of discipleship is just as bizarre. It is basically the psychology of wish fulfillment. In the skills of self-deception disciples are, if possible, even more adept than their masters. They want to find someone in whom they can believe as unreservedly as saints believe in God, and on to whom they can transfer all their longings for a golden age and a life without moral responsibility. They are like romantic women looking for the ideal husband, and once they have found him, nothing will convince them that he is anything less than perfect.

Introduction

That is why this book is not simply about Right Men, but about disciples who seem to enjoy being bullied. It is as a study in the behavior of disciples that the cases of Sabbatai Sevi, the seventeenth century Jewish messiah, or Paul Brunton or Rudolf Steiner, are just as significant as David Koresh or the Rev. Jim Jones. For the same reason, that is why Georges Gurdjieff and P.D. Ouspensky are included here, although neither were Right Men. Gurdjieff knew that disciples can create a sticky web in which the guru becomes entrapped.

In most cases, the guru is unaware that his disciples serve as a catalyst in his disintegration. Even among genuinely great men, there have been few who have escaped the corrupting influence of power, and most "messiahs" are far from being great men. To offer them unlimited control over a horde of admirers is like giving an alcoholic a pub for his birthday.

Finally, it should be emphasized that this book is not intended to be simply a study in corruption. In my first novel, *Ritual in the Dark* (1960), the hero is engaged in writing a book called *The Varieties of Human Self-Delusion*. The present book is probably the closest I have come to actually writing that fictionalized book. But it is about more than human self-deception. It seems to me that the most significant case in the present book is the story in chapter 6 ("How to Transform Reality") about the man who could transport himself to Mars. John Carter, the Mars traveler, illustrates far more than the disciple's usual ability to tell himself lies. He has somehow learned to use the unconscious mind to back the power of the conscious, and to turn fantasy into his own reality.

In this case, that may seem a dubious achievement, since it made Carter into a less efficient scientist. But the case also provides a dazzling insight into the hidden powers of the human mind. The philosopher Edmund Husserl recognized that perception is intentional. When you "see" something, it is as if you have thrown a spear at it. If you fail to put energy into the throw, you simply do not see it, as when you look at your watch without paying attention, and have to look a second time to see what time it is. Husserl recognized that perception is a creative act. It is like a football game: you have to participate, you are not allowed to be a spectator.

The case of John Carter seems to demonstrate that the power of intentionality is more creative than even Husserl recognized. Flying to an imaginary Mars may be the least of its achievements. We might, for example, be capable of flying to a real Mars without leaving the room. . . .

Man is an evolutionary animal, the only animal who feels a continuous need to change. This book is about the curious forms this need can take.

ONE

SEX AS SALVATION

Early in the afternoon of April 19, 1993, CNN began to broadcast pictures of the final assault on the Branch Davidian compound in Waco, Texas, where David Koresh and his followers had been holding police and federal authorities at bay for fifty-one days. Koresh, who claimed to be the Son of God, had been wanted for questioning by the Bureau of Alcohol, Tobacco, and Firearms (ATF) because he and his followers had been stockpiling weapons and explosives. On February 28, heavily armed ATF agents had attempted to take the compound by surprise. But they were the ones who were taken by surprise as gunfire erupted through the walls of the main building, killing four agents and wounding sixteen others.

Throughout March and early April, the surrounded cultists expressed defiance. On a number of occasions, their leader agreed to surrender, then changed his mind at the last moment. To the worldwide audience that watched the siege daily on television, it seemed obvious that David Koresh was enjoying making fools of the authorities. Magazine articles about the thirty-three-year-old rock guitarist talked about his harem of wives (which included under-age girls) and hordes of children, while ex-disciples described his self-glorifying sermons, which sometimes went on for as long as sixteen hours. The result was that most people were impatient with the "softly softly" tactics of the authorities, and looked forward to the day when Koresh would be standing in court and sentenced to a long term of imprisonment.

So on that April morning, when the ATF and FBI agents decided to break the siege with tanks, there must have been few people in the worldwide audience who did not look forward to the prospect of Koresh getting his comeuppance. It all began when an armored vehicle rolled up to the main building in the compound, and a loudspeaker asked those inside to surrender. The answer was a barrage of bullets that bounced off the armor. The vehicle rolled forward and tore the corner off the building. Meanwhile, other tanks, with metal tubes attached to their "noses," began demolishing other buildings, while CS gas was pumped in through the tubes. Then the vehicles withdrew and waited.

In Cornwall, I and my eldest son Damon had been following the siege intermittently since lunchtime (England being six hours ahead of Texas). It was of more than casual interest to us, because in the previous year, we had collaborated on a book called *Cults and Fanatics*, in the course of which we had both become fascinated by the psychology of "messiahs." Now we watched as, after six hours of stand-off, the first wisps of smoke began to drift up from the buildings. It looked as if some of the shooting had started a fire, perhaps igniting the CS gas. In a few minutes, flames were bursting out of upstairs windows. We expected to see cult members rushing out of the doors with their arms up, as the attackers obviously did; instead, there was silence, broken by the sound of explosions, as the place turned into an inferno. In less than half an hour (half past midday in Texas) it was obvious the siege was over. A few people, the CNN newsreader said, had escaped from the burning buildings, but apparently Koresh was not among them.

This abrupt climax of the seven-week siege left us feeling slightly stunned. We knew the compound had been full of women and children, and in the past week or so, had seen British relatives of cult members expressing their anxiety on television. Now it was all over, without the arrest of Koresh or his Mighty Men (armed guards). It seemed oddly anticlimactic. Already commentators were criticizing the federal authorities for launching the attack, and President Clinton for authorizing it, and asking why there had been no fire trucks present. Later, at a public hearing, these accusations reached a climax with the accusation that the authorities had murdered the defenders by deliberately igniting the CS gas.

In fact, on September 2, 1999, the FBI finally admitted, after six years of denial, that its men had fired flares into the compound.

The U.S. Attorney General, Janet Reno, made this admission with obvious annoyance and embarrassment, clearly aware that she was supplying ammunition to groups who saw Koresh as a martyr.

The accounts of the nine cult members who had escaped the siege suggest that, even if this is true, the martyrdom was to some extent self-chosen. They said that it was Koresh who had decided that his followers would die rather than flee. Many corpses were lying face down, a position typical of death by smoke inhalation; others had died of cyanide, or gunshot wounds. As had the Reverend Jim Jones in Guyana in 1978, it looked as if Koresh had decided on mass suicide.

The surviving cultists nevertheless insisted that the federal agents had fired first on the day the siege began, and that bullet holes in the metal door proved that the bullets had come from outside. This door later disappeared, adding plausibility to the notion that the cultists had been defending themselves.

All this came long after. What baffled me at the time was why so many apparently "normal" people had decided to leave their homes (some from England and Australia) and follow Koresh, this skinny, long-haired Texan, who made the improbable assertion that he was King David as well as the Son of God. What was equally baffling was what could motivate a man to declare that he is God, in the face of the self-evident fact that he is nothing of the sort. There have been plenty of cults founded by men who claim to have been taken to Venus in a flying saucer, or on a journey to the center of the "hollow earth"; but at least they made their fantasies sound plausible. A man who claims to be God seems to be inviting raspberries.

As the evidence about Koresh began to emerge, the problem became more, and not less, puzzling. At first, it looked as if he was a straightforward con man. When he had first joined the Branch Davidian sect as an odd job man, he lost no time in seducing its leader, sixty-eight-year-old prophetess Lois Roden, explaining that he had received a revelation that he was to become the father of her child. Whether she believed him or not, she became his secret mistress, and was soon convinced she was pregnant. From then on, Koresh maneuvered until he took over the cult.

Revelations about Koresh's later sexual behavior reinforced the con man theme. Soon after the affair with Lois Roden, he announced that God had told him to marry a fourteen-year-old girl named Rachel Jones, daughter of cult members Perry and Mary Jones. Not long after he seduced another fourteen-year-old girl, Karen Doyle, daughter of another convert. When her father found out, he was furious. But Koresh explained that he had been equally shocked when God told him that he had to "give his seed" to Karen. "I begged God not to make me do this."

Karen first learned about God's command when she was asleep in a bus used as a dormitory, and felt a tap on her shoulder. Koresh whispered to her that God had ordered him to give her his seed, and Karen whispered back, "I will do whatever the Lord wants." So Koresh climbed into bed with her. At the time, his first wife, Rachel, was on a visit to California.

Twelve-year-old Michele Jones was his wife's sister, and Koresh drove to California to bring her back to Texas. As he explained it, he was again an unwilling participant in the seduction. Halfway back to Texas he experienced a powerful urge to undress Michelle and make love to her. He stopped the car, walked up the road, and asked God: "God, what's happening to me? I mean I wanted to fuck her—that's all I could think about." God helped him overcome his lust and Koresh drove her back to Texas.

There, reading a passage in the Song of Solomon about a girl with no breasts, he realized that God was indicating that Michele was to become his wife. "So I go right to Michele and I climb into bed with her. She thinks I'm trying to get warm. I reached for her underwear to take 'em off. She didn't know what I was doing so she struggled. . . . But I was too strong, and I was doing this for God, and I told her about the prophecies. That's how she became my wife."

Koresh explained to his male followers that they should not envy him because "None of you men know the pain I endure to do God's work." The women wore him out, he complained. "I get tired, I suffer." His sufferings would eventually father twenty-two children.

A book called *Preacher of Death* by Martin King and Mark Breault fills out the picture. Breault was a leading disciple who had become disillusioned, and defected. When he met Koresh, Breault was studying to become a minister. In 1986, Koresh's father-in-law,

Perry Jones, introduced himself to Breault as a journalist specializing in religion. When he told Breault that he thought his son-in-law had "inspiration from God," Breault agreed to meet the prophet.

Koresh turned up with his wife Rachel and baby son Cyrus. He seemed friendly and sympathetic, and Breault immediately liked him. In Breault's apartment, Koresh launched into a three-hour Bible class. He had an amazing gift of fluency and conviction. His central point was that God always worked through prophets, and that God had granted him special insight into the Book of Revelation. To Breault, this sounded plausible. At the end of that three hour session, relatively short by Koresh's usual standards, he was willing to follow him anywhere.

Why should a young man with a promising career in the ministry abandon everything to follow an underweight messiah with a strong Texan accent? Reading Breault's description of the meeting, it all becomes clear. Koresh presented himself as an open, friendly but intense young man—he was 27—who differed from others only in the depth of his biblical knowledge, and his conviction that God had chosen him as His instrument for a special revelation.

Similarly, Hitler's architect Albert Speer recorded that he was converted by Hitler under parallel circumstances. Expecting a ranting maniac, he was surprised to find that Hitler spoke gently and reasonably, and said many things about Germany that Speer perceived as true. Once intellectual assent has been given, the rest follows naturally. All human beings long for powerful conviction, for ideas that seem to offer them a new and more meaningful way of life. When Breault decided to follow Koresh, he felt that it was the ideas he was following; the fact that their mouthpiece was an intense but unthreatening individual made it seem natural and inevitable. Breault's account makes it clear that Koresh was no mere Tartuffe, relying on a mask of piety, but an intellectual con man of awesome plausibility.

Once in the movement, Breault became Koresh's confidant and right-hand man, so the relationship remained, to a large extent, one of equals. Breault went to Hawaii, his home, and made some powerful converts, including his best friend, Steve Schneider. Once he had accepted Koresh as a prophet, it was not difficult to accept that he was in some sense the Son of God. And once Breault had gone this far, it became easier to accept the greatest stumbling block to regarding Koresh as a messiah—his obsessive seduction of teenage cult members. Koresh explained that he simply wanted them to receive his holy seed, to build up the future generation that would inherit the earth. The whole process was so gradual that there was no point at which Breault felt that he was trying to swallow a camel.

Breault's disillusionment began when he witnessed Koresh's brutality to his three-year-old son, Cyrus. Koresh had ordered the child to acknowledge that another cult member was his true mother; when Cyrus refused, Koresh beat him for twenty minutes on his bare bottom with a wooden paddle, then made him sleep in a garage that was (Koresh claimed) infested with rats. When the child still refused to deny his true mother, Koresh starved him for two days until he was too weak to hold a glass of water. Koresh was clearly a person who would not, under any circumstances, allow his will to be thwarted.

Further disillusionment followed when Koresh delivered a sixteen-hour sermon whose content was the declaration that all the women in the compound belonged to him. (Endless sermons and harangues are one of the basic techniques of brainwashing.) Judy Schneider, the wife of chief disciple Steve Schneider, was seduced while Steve was abroad on a recruiting drive, and was soon pregnant. Steve was at first shattered, and even thought of murdering the prophet; but the thought of what might happen to his wife if he failed finally deterred him. The seduction of Judy served a double purpose; it subdued Steve, who had always felt ambivalent about the prophet, and it persuaded all the other married women in the compound that they ought to follow Judy's suit.

It was when Koresh started making advances to another recent convert, with whom Marc Breault was in love, that Breault decided it was time to leave. It happened in California, after Koresh ordered him to humble himself and lick the dust. Breault answered back, and was ordered to return to Texas. Instead, he flew back to Australia, and there set about de-converting other Branch Davidians. When Koresh heard the news, he rushed to Australia, where there was a confrontation. Koresh won hands down, with a performance that included gazing at the heavens and declaring that he was being crucified all over again. Breault beat a tactical retreat. But soon after his exit, the police arrived—Breault had asked his brother to call them if he was not home by ten—and Koresh left hastily by the back door and caught the next plane back to America.

It was largely due to Breault's efforts that the Bureau of Alcohol, Tobacco, and Firearms finally decided to take action about the enormous cache of weapons and explosives that Koresh was known to have stored at the Waco compound, and the siege of the Branch Davidians began. When it ended on April 19, police found over a million rounds of ammunition still unspent in the underground arsenal of the compound. Seventy-two bodies were recovered from the ashes. All Koresh's twenty or so "wives" and fourteen of his twenty-two children died in the fire, four of them shot through the head.

A man had been seen running away from the burning buildings, and there was speculation that Koresh had escaped. But almost two weeks after the siege, his body was identified through dental records; he had died of a gunshot wound in the head, apparently self-inflicted.

Confronted with a case like this, we are inclined to ask the obvious question: was Koresh simply a confidence man, or did he, to some extent, believe what he said?

The answer is: both. And when we understand how that is possible, we have achieved one of the basic keys to the whole messiah phenomenon.

The first thing we need to know about Vernon Wayne Howell (who became David Koresh) is that he spent the first part of his life looking for security. Born illegitimate (in 1959) to a fourteen-year-old girl, brought up by a harsh step-father, educationally disadvantaged— he was dyslexic—bullied because he was small—he was once even raped by older boys—he was a shy and not particularly outstanding child. His refuge from his problems lay in religion—his school was affiliated to the Seventh Day Adventists—and he read the Bible as other children read Batman, and spent hours on his knees praying.

By the age of twelve he had learned the New Testament by heart. Then life suddenly changed. His teacher entered him for a race on the school sports day. Vernon had never seen himself as the sporting type, and had avoided physical competition. But he had spent a great deal of time racing against his brother on the farm, and could take off like a whippet. He won the race (and several others) and the congratulations were an intoxicant. Suddenly he was asked to join teams; he became the school sports hero. Determined to maintain his new status, he went in for body building, taking an enormous pride in his physical strength. By the time he was thirteen, the shy, quiet boy had become a leader.

In retrospect, it is obvious that Howell belonged to the group described in the introduction as "the dominant five percent," the one-in-twenty in all animal groups that has "leadership qualities." In fact, it later became clear that Vernon Howell was a "king rat."

All human beings possess a longing to change, to evolve; we hate nothing more than "marking time" in a life of boredom and frustration that offers no opportunity for change. We are all born with the craving for control over our lives, and when a child learns to crawl across the room, pull himself up on a chair and reach for a box of chocolates, he experiences his first flash of the delight of conquest. But in the dominant five percent this craving has the character of an obsession, which drives them like a spur. Howell was obsessed by dominance to the point of being a "control freak."

Biologists have also noted that evolution seems to occur in spurts, not in some slow, continuous process of development, like a steady uphill climb. This is also true for the individual: our personal growth is less like a gradual slope than a hillside out of which a series of steep terraces have been hacked at intervals. We scramble up a slope, sweating, panting and slipping backwards, then suddenly find we can pause for breath on a kind of plateau and survey the scenery. In that moment, we are overwhelmed by a sense or relief and achievement.

What happened to Vernon Howell when he won the race was like clambering up on to a terrace. Once a member of the dominant five percent has experienced the intoxication of leaving his old self and his old frustrations behind, he feels as if he has received a revelation. He has glimpsed the possibility that life can be a series of triumphs.

It is at this point that the dominant individual, particularly the male of the species, finds himself facing one of the most troublesome problems of his intermittent development: sex. As the hormones begin to flow, the adolescent is plunged into a permanent state of sexual desire, tormented by a craving to perform indecent acts on every girl he sees. He wonders if his parents realize that he has suddenly turned into a kind of Frankenstein monster. As he watches a television advertisement showing a woman in her underwear, he wonders if the advertisers realize that these images affect adolescent males as the smell of raw meat affects a starving tiger. In past centuries, society took care to reduce the levels of sexual stimulation by making women conceal their bodies in modest garments, and did its best to convince young men that the desire to know what lay underneath these garments was prompted by the devil. All this began to change in the nineteenth century, when literature and art mounted an offensive against the old Puritanism, insisting that sex should be treated as a normal part of everyday life. Little by little, the bastions crumbled, until by the beginning of the twentieth century, the reformers had won, and it was possible to publish things that a century earlier would have been regarded as criminal pornography.

Under the circumstances, young males could no longer be expected to believe that their perpetual furtive interest in naked ladies was a proof of damnation. But that still left the problem of how to live with it. Young women might wear short skirts and revealing blouses, and stay out dancing until two in the morning, but they still experienced nothing like the male's indiscriminate desire to commit sexual malpractice on every member of the opposite sex. The truth is that, except in rare cases of nymphomania, a woman tends to see a man as a potential husband and breadwinner, and she wants a mate who is stable, protective, and reliable, not a series of lovers.

Fortunately, most men are willing to settle for this state of affairs. The religious rearguard proved to be mistaken when it prophecied moral decline and the disintegration of the family, for basic human instinct guarantees that the majority of men settle down with a wife, and father children exactly as in the Victorian era.

But the attitude of men had changed. Since, in spite of the new morality, the majority of women remained as inaccessible as if they wore chastity belts, they had to learn to come to terms with the fact that the strength of the male sexual urge is greater than any useful purpose that it serves. If the desire to have a harem of mistresses is immoral, why has nature made it so powerful?

The answer, of course, is that the life force has hit upon the device of ensuring the propagation of the species by making us see the opposite sex as mysterious and forbidden. This element of "forbiddenness" causes the male to regard sexual experience—particularly with a new partner—as a "conquest," an "achievement," comparable to genuine problem-solving. In fact, as already noted, the problem evaporates with the sexual excitement, leaving the man with a sense of having been the victim of a confidence trick. If he is intelligent, he will do his best to readjust his sense of reality, and to bring a certain skepticism to bear next time the impulse cries "wolf." If he is unintelligent—and highly dominant—he may go on pursuing the mirage for the rest of his life, and wondering why it brings an increasing sense of frustration.

This was Koresh's problem (and, as we shall see, the problem of most other "messiahs" of the past century). As a teenager, his natural charm and dominance made him popular with the opposite sex, and he lost interest in religion. Then, at nineteen, he had an affair with a sixteen-year-old girl, who bore his child. He wanted to marry her; she felt he was unfit to raise a child, and left him. The blow to his ego was painful, and in the emotional turmoil, he turned for solace to the religion of his childhood, and became a born again Christian in the Southern Baptist Church. But now that he was religious again, the strength of his sexual impulse began to worry him; he turned to his pastor, explaining that he was a compulsive masturbator. The pastor told him that if he prayed to Jesus, he would be given strength. When this failed to happen, he decided that the Southern Baptist Church lacked a true link with God, and returned to the Seventh Day Adventists.

Howell fell in love with the daughter of his new pastor, and while he was praying for guidance, seemed to hear God's voice telling him that she would be given to him. When he opened his eyes he saw his Bible open at Isaiah 34, which declared that none should want for a mate. Convinced that this was a sign, he went to the pastor to tell him that God had given him his daughter for a wife. The pastor threw him out, and when he persisted, he was expelled from the congregation. (The girl herself seems to have agreed with her father.) One indignant member accused Howell of never thinking above his belt buckle.

This conflict between his natural dominance and his inability to get his own way became a torment, undermining his self-belief. For the potential "king rat," there is no more agonizing pain than being unable to find a way to give expression to the force he feels inside him. All the dominance and conviction in the world cannot make up for having no marketable talent, no ready-made niche in society. So Howell wandered from place to place, doing odd jobs. One day he found his way to Mount Carmel, near Waco, in Texas, and joined the Branch Davidian sect as an odd job man; for a long time he was the dishwasher. He later described himself as "the camp bum, the loser that did all the dirty jobs." He was also disliked by most of the others because of his arrogance and egotism.

By comparison, Lois Roden, the head of the sect, was everything Howell had dreamed about. Still attractive at sixty-eight, she was a famous TV evangelist, a friend of the rich and famous, who spent much of her time traveling around the world. She was also a favorite of the feminist movement, since she had announced that God was female, and began the Lord's Prayer "Our Mother, who art in heaven."

For a long time, she shared the general view of the new recruit, and made Howell live in a small unfurnished room to try to cure his conceit. Her view began to change when, two years after his arrival, he told her that the Lord had revealed to him that he had been chosen to father her child, who would be the Chosen One. When Roden's son George, who expected to replace his mother as president, found out, he did his best to eject the interloper. His mother, convinced she was pregnant, defended Howell. The power struggle ended abruptly when Howell announced that God had ordered him to marry a fourteen-year-old named Rachel Jones. For a while, George was placated. Then his fury erupted again, and he opened fire with an Uzi machine gun. Fortunately, his aim was bad; but Howell and the few followers who had succumbed to his burning conviction decided to leave Mount Carmel.

For the next two years, Vernon Howell and his disciples—there were about twenty-five—lived in the "wilderness," that is, they set up camp at a place called Palestine, and lived rough. But while his followers coped with lack of running water and sanitation, Vernon was off on "recruiting drives," in California, in Israel, even in Australia. He was hurled bodily out of a Seventh Day Adventist church in San Diego when he interrupted the service to announce that he was the Messiah. But although many potential converts began by regarding him as a madman, some of them ended by being swayed by his incredible flow of words, or by his insistence that they would be damned unless they followed him. The settlement at Palestine grew; so did the number of his underage mistresses. When disciples had a teenage daughter, she usually became Vernon's "wife."

Back in Waco, George Roden—his mother was now dead—was showing signs of the paranoia that tends to afflict religious fanatics. George announced that he was God, and ended prayers with "In the name of George B. Roden, amen." And although Vernon and his followers were ninety miles away, in Palestine, George brooded constantly on humiliating the impostor. In 1987, he devised a bizarre challenge. An eighty-five-year-old woman named Anna Hughes had died at Mount Carmel. George dug up the body, installed it in the chapel, and challenged Vernon to a contest: whichever of them could raise Anna Hughes from the dead was the true prophet of God. George had the satisfaction of seeing Vernon decline the challenge and slink away. But when Howell told his lawyer what had happened, the lawyer was delighted; George Roden had laid himself open to the charge of abusing a corpse. Vernon hastened to tell the police what had happened.

They were cautious, realizing that getting mixed up with religious cranks could be a time-wasting experience. They explained that they would need a photograph of the corpse. Vernon agreed to supply one. But since that meant that he would have to enter Mount Carmel by stealth, he decided that he might as well make the best of the opportunity, and try to evict George. He and his followers bought weapons. On November 3, 1987, a team of commandos wriggled through the undergrowth at Mount Carmel towards the chapel, rifles slung on their backs. A dog spotted them and barked; George Roden rushed out with his Uzi and began to blaze away. Vernon and his eight commandos blazed back, none of them succeeding in hitting anything. The sound of firing brought the local police, and everyone was arrested, except one Mighty Man who managed to escape.

Vernon and one of the Mighty Men—he happened to be a millionaire—were released after paying $100,000 bail. To George Roden's fury, Vernon seized the opportunity to tell his version of the incident on the local television news. Roden now made his fatal mistake; he wrote letters to the Texas Supreme Court threatening to strike everybody down with AIDS and herpes unless they sentenced Vernon to a long spell in jail. Instead, George himself was sentenced to six months for contempt of court. And when he appeared in court as a witness against Vernon and his Mighty Men, and explained how he intended to raise Anna Hughes from the dead, the jury lost no time in acquitting Vernon and his commandos.

Fifteen months later, George Roden ceased to be a problem when he was sentenced to life imprisonment for murder. The story of how this came about is an interesting demonstration of the contagious nature of messianism. One day in the summer of 1988, an ex-alcoholic named Dale Adair came to see Vernon Howell and Marc Breault, declaring that he wanted to get back to God. Vernon harangued him for three days, trying to convince him that he, Vernon, was the Messiah. Suddenly Adair's eyes glazed over, and he stared towards heaven. "My God, my God. After all these years I understand. I'm the Messiah. I'm the David. Now I know why I've suffered all these years."

"Dale lost his sanity right before our eyes," said Breault, who does not explain how he distinguished between Dale Adair's madness and Vernon Howell's normality.

Adair hurried to George Roden to tell him that he was the Messiah, but Roden was unconvinced, putting the claim to the test by seizing an axe and splitting open Adair's skull. Roden was convicted of murder, and since he owed thousands of dollars in taxes, Mount Carmel was put up for sale. Vernon's followers raised the money, and later that year, Vernon Howell—he now was calling himself David Koresh—at last became owner of the Waco compound. From the time he had arrived there as Lois Roden's disciple, it had taken him eight years to gain control.

Within five years he was dead. And, with the benefit of hindsight, we can see that this was almost inevitable. From the beginning Vernon Howell was on a collision course with reality. He would have found it intolerable to stand in the dock, to be jeered at in the media as a religious crank, to be sentenced to life imprisonment for murder. When he ordered his Mighty Men to fire through the doors at the Federal agents, he knew he had opted for martyrdom and suicide.

But although his convictions about himself ran counter to reality, it would be an error to assume that he was in some sense insane. What Koresh was defending so frantically was his sense of self-esteem, a problem we all recognize as central to our lives. Even the most modest and shy person has a need to feel that he or she is not a total nonentity. To feel worthless is to be incapable of any kind of development. As we have already noted, the craving for some kind of personal development is the most basic urge of human beings.

This is why Koresh's most dangerous moment was when he became the owner of Mount Carmel. He was now the unchallenged leader of more than a hundred followers, including a dozen or so heavily-armed guards. Every night he renewed his sense of conquest as he possessed his underage wives. He told Marc Breault with pride that most men imagine that an adolescent girl would lack passion, but that his own experience was that they could become as sexually excited as any adult woman.

Yet even this was not enough to soothe his fear of becoming a victim, a failure. His ego needed continual boosts to maintain his self-esteem. He had to announce that he alone had a right to all the women in the compound, although he admitted to Breault that non-stop sexual activity was leading to impotence. When Breault objected to his own girlfriend joining the harem, he had committed the ultimate sin of defying the master; this was why he was ordered to kneel down and eat dirt. He rebelled and left, yet admits that he found it difficult to begin thinking for himself again, after years in which every decision was made for him.

For the messiah, every follower is a kind of wife, and when a wife deserts him, he feels the ground crumbling under his feet. When he realized Breault had left, Koresh called an emergency meeting and launched a manhunt. But it was too late. Breault was determined to bring about the downfall of his former "master." He wrote letters to the police, to state authorities, to members of Congress. His greatest coup was to organize the visit of an Australian television team to Waco. Unaware that Breault was behind it, Koresh allowed the team into the compound because he hoped for favorable coverage; but the program, when it went out in April 1992, left no one in any doubt that Koresh was a child molester and a highly dangerous man.

In May 1992, the *Waco Tribune Herald* began an investigation into the Branch Davidian sect. One result of their revelations was a decision by the Bureau of Alcohol, Tobacco and Firearms to launch an investigation into the sect. In February 1992, the ATF decided to lure Koresh away from the compound and place him under arrest.

Unfortunately, Koresh was tipped off by friends in the police department, and declined to be lured away. So on Sunday, February 28, 1993, ATF agents knocked on the door of the main building of the Waco compound and were cut down by gunfire from inside.

In effect, David Koresh had decided not to relinquish his own version of reality, even if it meant dying for it. In retrospect, his choice of the name Koresh seems oddly appropriate: it is the name of the fourth horseman of the Apocalypse, the pale rider on the white horse, and signifies death.

TWO

THE MILLENNIUM COMETH

At the beginning of 1666, the whole of Europe awaited the greatest event in human history: the coming of the Messiah who would lead the Jewish people back to their former greatness. This messenger of God was a forty-year-old Jew named Sabbatai Zevi, who lived in Smyrna, but who was soon expected to overthrow the Sultan of Turkey, then ride into Jerusalem on a dragon. After that he would destroy his enemies in battle, and become King of the World.

Even Christians began to worry as Jews told them: "We shall soon be your masters." For several years now, Puritans had been announcing that the year 1666 would be beginning of the Millennium, and now it began to look as if they might be right. In his diary, Samuel Pepys recorded that a Jew in London was taking bets at ten to one that this new messiah would be King of the World within two years, and had already laid out £1,100 in wagers.

In many major cities, this expectation was already causing chaos. Commercial centers came to a halt as Jews ceased trading and prepared themselves for the Last Judgement. In Amsterdam, Jews danced in the streets. Many prepared to have the bones of dead relatives dug up and transported to the Holy Land, for letters from Constantinople described how the Messiah could raise the dead. In Hamburg, people sold their houses and land in preparation for the Millennium. In Poland, crowds raved about how the Messiah would take them to heaven on a cloud, and whenever an unexpected cloud appeared in the sky, they stood and gazed expectantly. The news spread throughout the settlements of the Jews in Russia, and even reached as far as America. In Prague, one of the largest and most important Jewish communities, the excitement caused a backlash among Christians; many Jews were attacked, and the Prague carnival featured a mocking parody of Jews in a blissful state of messianic ecstasy. Yet nothing could dampen the spirit of expectation, not even the news that the Messiah had been arrested and thrown into prison by the Sultan he was supposed to overthrow. Stories told how Sabbatai had simply walked through locked doors, and his chains had dissolved and fallen from him.

Then, towards the end of the year, joy changed to dismay as incredible rumors began to spread. These declared that not only had Sabbatai been unable to escape from the Sultan's prison, but that he had converted to Islam. At first, many believed that the stories were malicious Christian inventions. But more precisely detailed accounts by fellow Jews destroyed this hope. They told how Sabbatai Zevi had been taken before the young Mehmet IV and told that he must either convert to Islam or be impaled alive, and how the Messiah had at once thrown his Jewish cap on the ground and spat on it, then allowed a white turban to be placed on his head.

Oddly enough, the Jews were not as shattered by this report as their critics expected. The sheer scale of the expectation had made them more aware of their religious identity. Some even continued to believe that Sabbatai was deliberately testing their faith. Apparently his chief disciple, Nathan Ashkenazi, continued to believe in him. But even those who accepted that Sabbatai had feet of clay continued to feel that the expectations of 1666 could only be a prelude to great events that would change their lives. The enormity of the disappointment forced them to confront the basic question: was the expectation of the Messiah an illusion, or would God send them a true leader one day? It was the faith that triumphed, and, according to one Jewish historian, Gershom Scholem, caused a basic change in Jewish consciousness. So in a sense, it could be argued that Sabbatai Zevi was not entirely an impostor.

The Jews had been awaiting the Messiah for just over two thousand years, since the armies of King Nebuchadnezzar had dragged off the people of Judah to Babylon in 587 B.C.. Messiah (*mashiakh*) meant the Anointed One, and he would lead the Jews out of exile, establish their national independence, and bring universal peace. Since then, there had been many messiahs, but none had lived up to expectation.

When the Jews came back from their fifty-year exile in Babylon, a man called Zerubbabel became governor of Judea, and because he rebuilt the Temple, was widely believed to be the Messiah. But Zerubbabel had no ambitions in that direction, and ignored the hints of the prophets Haggai and Zechariah. Two centuries later, the incredible conquests of Alexander the Great led many Jews to believe that he was the Messiah; but he died of a fever at thirty-three.

For two centuries, Jerusalem was ruled by Egyptians, then by Alexander, then by a Syrian dynasty called the Seleucids. The latter admired the Greeks, and at one point they outlawed Jewish culture and placed a statue of Zeus on the altar of the Temple. But a family of priests called Maccabee led a rebellion and drove out the Syrians. Judas Maccabeus' triumph soon fostered the belief that he must be the Messiah; but he was killed in battle in 161 B.C., and the leadership passed to his brothers, who were also killed.

Within a century, the Maccabees were squabbling among themselves, and the Romans seized the opportunity to take Jerusalem. They were even more impatient about the Jews and their fanatical religious beliefs than the Syrians had been, and the result of their oppression was a rash of militant messiahs: Simon, Judas of Galilee, an Egyptian whose name is not certain, but who led an army of thirty thousand within sight of Jerusalem before they were scattered, and a man called Theudas, who claimed to be a magician who could make the River Jordan divide, but failed to enchant the Roman sword before it cut off his head.

The only messiah of that period who is remembered today was called Jeshua, better known by the Greek form of his name, Jesus. Oddly enough, it is probable that Jesus of Nazareth did not think of himself as "the Messiah." When his disciple Peter remarked, "They call you the Christ, the Messiah," Jesus advised him to be silent. The claim obviously embarrassed him. And this was because the Jews expected the Messiah to be a warrior like Judas Maccabeus, who would drive out the Romans. Jesus was too realistic to expect to end the Roman occupation. His teaching was quite different. Study of the scriptures had led him to believe that the world would end within the lifetime of people then alive; there would be wars, famines, and earthquakes, and the dead would be brought back to life. The sun would be turned to darkness and the moon to blood, and the stars would fall from the sky

The message by which we remember Jesus—love one's neighbor and do unto others as you'd have them do unto you—was already a part of the Jewish religious tradition. More than a thousand years of oppression—the Jews had been enslaved by the pharaoh Rameses II as long ago as 1250 B.C.—had developed a spirit of pacifism and submission to the will of God; so Jesus's injunction to love your enemy was merely a restatement of the Mosaic teaching.

Nowadays, an increasing number of scholars believe that Jesus was a member of the Essenes, a religious order that withdrew to caves at Qumran, near the Dead Sea and lived rigidly ascetic lives. It has even been seriously argued that Jesus did not die on the cross, but was given a drug, from which he later recovered, and that he lived on into his mid-sixties.

Whatever the truth, it is certain that the story of the crucifixion and subsequent resurrection played an important part in establishing Jesus as the most convincing Messiah so far. It is important to bear in mind that his followers believed that the end of the world was only a few years away. It is also important to recognize that Jesus did not regard himself as the Son of God; as an orthodox Jew, he would have been profoundly shocked by any such suggestion.

In the years following his reported death, Jesus had two main groups of followers. One, the Messianists (or Nasoraeans) believed he was still alive, and would soon lead an army that would destroy Rome. The others, led by the converted Jew, Paul, called themselves Christians, and held a more pacifistic doctrine. One of the most fundamental beliefs of Judaism was that the sufferings of the Jews were caused by the sin of their forefather Adam. Paul announced that this "original sin" had been canceled out by the death of Jesus on the cross, so that anyone who became a Christian was now redeemed. This doctrine suited gentiles as well as Jews, which is why Paul spent so much of his time traveling far and wide and making converts. But this in turn meant that the Christians were far more scattered than the Messianists, and would sooner or later fade into a minority sect.

That this failed to happen was due to a historical accident. In 66 A.D., thirty three years after the crucifixion, Jewish rebels rose up against the Romans and seized the Temple, in which daily sacrifices were made to the Emperor Nero. Under Nero, the Roman army was disorganized, and his suicide in the following year complicated the situation. But when the general Vespasian became emperor in 70 A.D., he sent his son Titus to subdue the Jews. The temple was besieged and burned; more than a million rebels were slaughtered. The last fortress, Masada, fell in April 73, and the slaughter of its thousand-strong garrison marked the end of Jewish resistance—and hopes of Jewish independence.

Most of the Messianists perished in the rebellion, which left only Paul's Christians to preach the message of Jesus's Second Coming, and the imminent end of the world. Now both the Christians and the Jews centered their hopes on the coming of the Messiah, although the Jews continued to believe he would be a member of the House of David and would lead them to military victory, while the Christians expected Jesus to return and initiate the end of the world.

Before 100 A.D. it was clear to everyone that Jesus's prophecy was not going to be fulfilled. But by that time, Christianity had become so widespread that this made no difference. The expectation of the end of the world was now transferred to the Millennium itself—the year 1000 A.D.—and the word Millennium became a synonym for the Day of Judgement. Christianity achieved its greatest triumph so far on 313 A.D., when the Emperor Constantine—as bloodthirsty and vicious a maniac as any of the Roman emperors—declared it the official religion of the empire.

The next Jewish Messiah came close to ending the tradition. Simon Bar Kochbar rose up against the Romans in 132 A.D., when he heard a rumor that the Emperor Hadrian intended to rebuild the Temple. The rumor was only partly true: Hadrian only meant to build a temple dedicated to Jupiter on the site of the Temple. But it led to the greatest Jewish uprising since the Maccabees. When the celebrated Talmud scholar Rabbi Akiva greeted Simon

Bar Kochbar with the words: "This is the King–Messiah," Kochbar himself seems to have been convinced. He collected guerrilla bands and turned them into a highly disciplined army, trained with the same thoroughness as the Romans. The struggle was violent and bloody. At first his success was remarkable; Jerusalem fell, and town after town surrendered to his army.

As his garrisons were wiped out one by one, Hadrian sent for one of his most formidable commanders, Julius Severus, from Britain. Recognizing the difficulty of defeating a guerrilla army, Severus took a sledgehammer to crack a nut, and destroyed village after village—985 of them—as well as destroying fifty rebel strongholds. His tactics finally worked; Bar Kochbar was surrounded in the fortress of Bethar and killed. Hadrian had Jerusalem renamed Aelia Capitolonia, and forbade Jews to live in it. The revolt had lasted three and a half years, and its total failure caused such deep disappointment that the very idea of a Messiah became unmentionable.

It was three hundred years before another messiah arose. He came from Crete and called himself Moses. Like so many later messiahs, he convinced his followers that he could perform miracles. If they gathered on the seashore, he told them, he would emulate his great predecessor and cause the waters to part, so his army could walk across dry shod. As he raised his arms above his head and ordered the waters to separate, his followers strode forward, and kept walking, even as the sea rose up to their waists, then their shoulders. At this point the sensible ones turned back; others were dragged down by the weight of their equipment and drowned. By the time the army reorganized on the beach, Moses of Crete had vanished.

Many messiahs were undoubtedly mental cases, suffering from psychotic delusions. In 589 A.D., a man went insane after being surrounded by flies in a forest near Arles, France; two years later, he dressed himself in animal skins and made his way down to Gevaudon, in the Cevennes, declaring that he was Christ, and that he had the power to heal the sick. (In fact, the power of healing, known as thaumaturgy, is by no means uncommon.) He began to accumulate an army of followers, which reached three thousand, and towns they approached were asked to acknowledge that he was the Christ, which most of them did to avoid trouble. Approaching the town of La Puy, he quartered his army in halls and churches, and sent naked messengers to announce his arrival to Bishop Aurelius.

When the bishop saw these emissaries turning somersaults, he had no doubt that they were inspired by the devil; so hiding his disgust, he sent some of his men to welcome the man who called himself Christ. They bowed as if to kiss the messiah's knees, then dragged him to the ground and stabbed him to death. Without their leader, the followers quickly dispersed, although the messiah's mistress, a woman who called herself Mary, was tortured to make her reveal the diabolic secrets that had given the Christ of Gevaudon his power. But St. Gregory of Tours, who records the story, adds that the messiah's followers continued to believe in him until the day of their death—another familiar phenomenon, as this history will show.

The rise of Islam was a major factor in discouraging messianic movements, not because the Muslims suppressed their Jewish and Christian subjects, but because they were unusually tolerant of other religions, as their Prophet had taught them to be. So far, messiahs had appeared in times of social unrest and religious persecution. Now the chief persecutor was the Christian church itself, which regularly burned and massacred pagans and heretics; the Muslims simply absorbed them and allowed them to practice their religion. When a messiah named Serene arose in Syria (probably named after his town of origin, Shirin) in 720, and led an army towards Palestine, he was not even punished by the caliph Yazid II; he was merely handed over to the rabbis for punishment. Like most messiahs (including Jesus), Serene was opposed to the strictness of the rabbinical law—another theme we shall find recurring down the ages—and gathered support from those who also felt that their religion had lost the true spirit of divine inspiration in mechanical observances.

Twenty years after Serene, about 742, a messiah called Aldebert, who came from Soissons, announced that he was a saint; his followers built chapels for him which he named after himself. He claimed to own a letter from Jesus himself. Pope Zachary was so worried about "Saint" Aldebert's influence that he tried hard to capture him, and, when that failed, excommunicated him. Adelbert went on for at least two more years, and seems to have died of natural causes.

Three centuries later, another messiah called Eon or Eudo de Stella was less lucky. He gathered hordes of disciples in Britanny, and organized his followers into a Church with archbishops and bishops. Unlike Jesus of Nazareth, he had no hesitation in declaring that he was the Son of God. 1144 A.D. was a good year for a messiah to acquire followers, for an appalling winter caused multitudes to starve. Eon's followers lived in the forest, and ravaged the countryside, living mainly by plunder. But in 1148, he was finally taken prisoner by soldiers of the Archbishop of Rouen, and imprisoned in a tower, where he was starved to death. His followers refused to renounce him, and his "bishops" and "archbishops" were burned alive in the now traditional Christian spirit.

One of the most remarkable messiahs of the twelfth century, Tanchelm of Antwerp, was already dead by then. He seems to have started his career as a monk, then become a diplomat working for Count Robert of Flanders, trying to persuade the Pope to hand over some of Utrecht to Count Robert. The Pope refused, and when Count Robert died, Tanchelm's career as a diplomat came to an end. He became a wandering preacher, making his headquarters in Antwerp.

Tanchelm seems to have possessed what all messiahs possess: tremendous powers as a preacher and orator. We also have to remember that a large part of his audience would be ignorant peasants who had never heard a really good preacher. As Tanchelm addressed them in the open fields, dressed as a monk, the audiences reacted like modern teenagers to a pop idol. Tanchelm denounced the Church for its corruption, and told them that if the sacraments were administered by sinful priests, they would fail to work. So many were convinced that the churches were soon empty. And when Tanchelm told his followers not to pay taxes to the church (called tithes), they were delighted to follow his advice.

Was Tanchelm a charlatan, or did he really believe he was a messiah? He certainly felt that he had a right to live like a king. He dressed magnificently, and was always surrounded by a large retinue, including twelve men who were supposed to be the twelve disciples. One day he announced that he would become betrothed to the Virgin Mary, and held a ceremony in which he and a sacred statue were joined together in front of a vast crowd, whose members offered their jewelry as an engagement present.

With so many followers, the Church could do nothing about Tanchelm; he held Utrecht, Antwerp and large areas of the countryside. Finally, about 1115 A.D., he was killed—like the Messiah of Gevaudon—by treachery, being stabbed by a priest who had been allowed to approach him. But his influence remained as powerful as ever, and it took another "miracle worker," Norbert of Xanten (who was regarded with favor by the Church) to finally "de-convert" his followers in Antwerp and restore power to the Church.

How did these "messiahs" become so powerful? To begin with, all of them had the gift of preaching. But it was more than that. As we have seen, the Christian Church, which began as a poor and persecuted organization whose leaders were thrown to the lions, suddenly became the official religion of Rome in 313 A.D., under the Emperor Constantine.

As soon as they gained power, the Christians began to behave far worse than their enemies, destroying pagan temples, burning heretics, and squabbling amongst themselves. In effect, the Church became the supreme dictator. And the poor, ordered to go to church every Sunday, groaning under heavy taxes, and forced to pay to have their sins forgiven, became increasingly disenchanted with their spiritual masters. But there was nothing they could do; the Church exerted the same iron grip as the Nazis in Germany or the Communists in Stalin's Russia.

This is why the rebel messiahs found an eager audience. Like Jesus, they attacked the establishment and declared that the law was less important than the spirit. Besides, there had always been a strong tradition of mysticism in the Church. Mystics were men who had experienced moments of overwhelming joy and illumination in which they felt they had seen God. The mystics taught that every man has a divine spark, and that therefore, in a sense, every man is God—or contains a fragment of God. They also believed that all nature is an expression of God; in fact, some (called pantheists) believed that nature *is* God. One of the greatest of the early mystics, Dionysius the Areopagite (around 500 A.D.) taught that God is a kind of emptiness or darkness, and can only be reached by recognizing that God is not knowledge or power or eternity, or anything else that the mind can grasp, but that God is beyond all words and ideas.

So although many of the great mystics spent their lives as members of the Church, they did not believe that the Church was essential for "salvation." Man can know God directly, without the need for priests and sacraments. Some of them, like the thirteenth century Meister Eckhart, came dangerously close to being excommunicated, or even burned at the stake. (Eckhart was tried for heresy but died before he was condemned, which he later was.)

It was only one step from this belief that man has direct access to God to the belief that there is no such thing as sin. If man is truly free, then he has choice, and if he chooses to reject the idea that something is sinful—for example, sexual promiscuity or incest— no authority has a right to tell him he is a sinner. Preachers of this doctrine were known as Brethren of the Free Spirit.

One popular story of the Middle Ages was about a rich merchant whose wife began to spend a great deal of time in church. When her husband heard rumors that the church consisted of adherents of the Free Spirit, he decided to follow her one day. Wearing a disguise he walked behind her into an underground cavern where to his surprise the service began with a dance, in which everyone chose his or her partner. After that, the congregation ate food and drank wine. The husband began to understand why his wife preferred this to the local Catholic church; the service was better.

When the priest stood up, he announced that all human beings are free, and that provided they lived in the spirit of the Lord, they could do what they liked. "We must become one with God." Then he took a young girl and led her to the altar. The two of them removed their clothes. Then the priest turned to the congregation and told them to do the same. "This is the Virgin Mary and I am Jesus. Now do as we do." The girl lay down on the altar, and the priest lay on top of her and, in full view of the congregation, commenced an act of intercourse. Then the congregation each seized his dancing partner, and lay down on the floor.

In the chaos that followed, the wife did not notice as her husband took hold of her hand and pulled off her wedding ring; she was totally absorbed in her partner. Realizing that no one was paying any attention to him, the husband slipped away.

When his wife returned home, he asked her angrily how she dared to give herself to another man, even in the name of religion. She indignantly denied everything, demanding whether, as the wife of a wealthy merchant, he thought she would behave like a prostitute. But when the husband asked her what had happened to her wedding ring, she went pale. Then, as he held it out to her, she realized that he had seen everything, and burst into tears. The wife was beaten until she bled, but she was more fortunate than the others, who were arrested by inquisitors and burned at the stake.

The story may or may not have happened, but such congregations actually existed. They began to multiply not long after the year 1200 A.D., and soon spread across Europe. The Free Spirit movement declared that God is within us all, and that therefore the Church is unnecessary—in fact, it is the Whore of Babylon. The great poets are as "holy" as the Bible. Sex must be an acceptable way of worshipping God, since it brings such a sense of divine illumination. In his book *The Black Death*, Johanne Nohls gives this account of the Brethren:

"The bas reliefs . . . in French churches . . . represent erotic scenes. In the Cathedral of Albi a fresco even depicts sodomites engaged in sexual intercourse. Homosexuality was also well known in parts of Germany, as is proved by the trials of the Beghards and Beguins in the fourteenth century, particularly the confession of the brethren Johannes and Albert of Brunn, which are preserved in the Griefswald manuscript. From these it is evident that the Brethren of the Free Mind did not regard homosexuality as sinful. 'And if one brother desires to commit sodomy with a male, he should do so without let or hindrance and without any feeling of sin, as otherwise he would not be a Brother of the Free Mind.'

"In a Munich manuscript we read: 'And when they go to confession and come together and he preaches to them, he takes the one who is most beautiful among them and does to her all according to his will, and they extinguish the light and fall one upon the other, a man upon a man and a woman upon a woman, just as it comes about. Everyone must see with his own eyes how his wife or daughter is abused by others, for they assert that no one can commit sin below his girdle. That is their belief.'

"Other curious doctrines, such as that incest is permissible, even when practiced on the altar, that no one has the right to refuse consent, that Christ risen from the dead had intercourse with Magdalena, etc., all indicate the deterioration and confusion of moral ideas caused by the great plagues, particularly that of 1348."

The comment about Christ and Magdalena is of particular interest in the light of the assertion in *The Holy Blood and The Holy Grail*, and Barbara Thiering's *Jesus the Man*, that there is strong historical evidence to support the view that Jesus was married to Mary Magdalene and fathered children by her. The Brethren of the Free Spirit were undoubtedly aware of this esoteric tradition, and regarded it as justification for their doctrine of promiscuity. As Jack Gratus remarks in *The False Messiahs*: "Sexuality and messianism are related both in theory and practice."

In short, according to the Brethren of the Free Spirit, every man is his own messiah. The Church did its best to stamp out these beliefs by sword and fire, but it still took three centuries. Even when the Free Spirits had been wiped out, the ideas continued to exert influence. Around 1550, a man named Klaus Ludwig, who lived in Mulhausen in Germany, formed a church in which members were initiated by having sex with a stranger. Like so many messiahs, Ludwig said he was Christ, the Son of God, and that these things had been revealed to him. The sacrament was another name for sex. Man was bread and woman was wine, and when they made love, this was Holy Communion. Children born out such communion were holy. And the members of his congregation could not be killed. Ludwig's sermons ended with the words "Be fruitful and multiply," and the congregation made haste to undress and obey.

Ludwig taught that sexual desire is the prompting of the Holy Spirit, so that if a man feels desire for any woman, he should regard it as a message from God, a viewpoint with which David Koresh obviously concurred. If, of course, the woman happened to be a member of Ludwig's "Chriesterung" (or Bloodfriends), then it was her duty to help him obey the will of the Lord, even if she was another man's wife.

Ludwig told the Bloodfriends to observe great secrecy and to behave like other people. But no doubt some of his congregation were eager to make converts of husbands with attractive wives. Like the congregation in the medieval story, the Bloodfriends were found out and put on trial, although Ludwig himself escaped. One member of the sect's Council of Twelve Judges admitted that he had celebrated Holy Communion with sixteen different women. Three Bloodfriends were executed in 1551, and the others were reconverted to a more conventional form of Christianity.

Sabbatai Zevi, the most successful messiah since Jesus of Nazareth, was born seventy-five years later, in 1626. A Turkish Jew, the son of a rich merchant of Smyrna, he was trained from an early age by rabbis, and developed a strongly religious inclination. His teachers also seemed to have instilled in him a deep feeling that sex was sinful; at the age of six he dreamed that his penis had been burned by a flame, and thereafter seems to have been "tortured by nightmarish dreams," says his biographer Gershom Scholem. A brilliant student, Sabbatai completed his studies by the age of fifteen, and thereafter plunged into a life of solitude and prayer. He also studied the Kabbalah (the Hebrew mystical teaching) on his own. At the age of sixteen he began to observe a fast which lasted for six years. He already felt that he had been chosen by God for some remarkable destiny.

His nervous parents decided that an arranged marriage might be the solution; Sabbatai allowed himself to be led to the altar, but refused to consummate the marriage, and his wife eventually divorced him. A second marriage ended in the same way, for the same reason.

Gershom Scholem acknowledges that Sabbatai was a sick man, suffering from an extreme form of manic depression. States of exaltation and ecstasy were followed by periods of suicidal gloom when he found it impossible to focus his thoughts. This condition continued for the rest of his life. His neighbors seem to have regarded him as some kind of a madman.

The first great change in Sabbatai's life came in 1648, when he was twenty-two. News from Poland told of appalling massacres of Jews. Under the leadership of the notoriously cruel Bogdan Kmelnitsky, the Cossacks of the Ukraine, also noted for their savagery, rose against their Polish landlords, and showed particular vengefulness towards the Jews, who served them. All kinds of atrocities took place: some

Jews were skinned alive, some were buried alive, some had their hands and feet chopped off. Pregnant women were disemboweled, women raped before their husbands, children killed in their mothers' arms. A hundred thousand Jews died, and thousands fled to other countries, including Turkey. Ironically, the book of the Kabbalah called the *Zohar* declared that 1648 would be the year in which the dead would be restored to life.

Sabbatai seems to have been shattered by the stories of atrocities, which he probably heard from the lips of witnesses. At some point, he experienced the revelation that he was the Messiah. This was accompanied by a curious phenomenon: his body began to exude a pleasant, scented smell. Reproved by a doctor for using scent, Sabbatai stripped naked to prove that the smell emanated from his skin, then revealed to the doctor what he had so far only confided to his family: that he was the Messiah. The smell was proof that the Lord had anointed him.

At some time in 1648, Sabbatai scandalized all his fellow Jews by standing up in the synagogue and pronouncing the Holy Name of Yahweh (Jehovah) which was strictly forbidden under Jewish law. Soon after this, he began to attract followers who regarded his fits of mania as evidence that he had been chosen by God.

By 1651, his fellow Jews were sick of his strange behavior, and expelled him from Smyrna. Sabbatai and his followers went to Greece (where he had been born) and made a powerful impression among the Greek Jews. Many of these were Marranos from Spain, that is, Jews who had been forcibly converted to Christianity, and who were crippled by a sense of guilt. There must have been a wonderful sense of release in listening to this messiah who told them that even now, God was in the process of changing and revising his own Holy Laws—for example, that the name Yahweh must not be pronounced aloud.

Sabbatai's eccentricities were outrageous. On one occasion he bought a large fish, dressed it up as a baby, and put it into a cradle; to those who inquired, he explained that it was a symbol of the coming Age of Pisces, when the Jews would be freed from bondage. Worse still, he invited the rabbis of Salonika to a feast, and while they were eating, took a Scroll of the Law into his arms as if it were a woman, and carried it off to a marriage canopy. This suggestion of sexual intercourse horrified the assembly, and the rabbis lost no time in expelling Sabbatai from the city. After that he was expelled from Constantinople for declaring that the Ten Commandments had been abolished.

The Sufi mystic al-Junayd said that "God brings upon those that love him a kind of sudden and supernatural madness, in which a man may speak and act against the directions of religion which He has revealed from Heaven." Scholem feels that this explains Sabbatai's astonishing declarations that such and such a law could be ignored, or that certain transgressions were now sanctified. In fact, when he was his normal self again, Sabbatai was deeply shocked by the things he had done and said in his manic state, and even sought help in expelling his "demons."

In his absence from Smyrna the expulsion order had apparently been lifted, and he returned there and stayed until 1662, when he moved to Jerusalem. He now had a devoted band of followers, who supported him in style. He seems to have owed his influence as much to sheer charm as to his strange doctrines; when in his "normal" state he radiated kindness, and gave freely—it was his disciples' money—to charity.

For some odd reason, Sabbatai now decided he needed a wife. He heard about a beautiful Polish courtesan named Sarah, who had often declared that she was destined to be the bride of the expected Messiah. Sarah had been six years old at the time of the pogroms in Poland, and had been placed in a convent. It was said that she and her brother had later traveled around Europe and indulged freely in sexual activity. When Sabbatai heard that she was in Leghorn, in Italy, he sent twelve of his followers to ask her to marry him. She agreed, and the marriage between the thirty-eight-year-old man and the twenty-two-year-old girl took place in 1664.

It was during this period that Sabbatai began to preoccupy the thoughts of a young man called Nathan Ashkenazi, the son of a devout Sephardic Jew of Jerusalem. Nathan's history resembles in many ways that of Sabbatai. He was a brilliant student at the rabbinic school, and was married at the age of twenty. Then he began to fast and meditate on the Kabbalah, and was rewarded with visions of angels. "I saw visions of God all day long and all night." One ecstasy lasted for a whole day. As a result of his new fervor, he became spiritual director to many Jews in Gaza (his wife's home) and soon acquired an awesome reputation. Nathan seems to have possessed such a degree of insight that he was able to read the minds of those who came to him, and whisper their sins in their ears.

Everything we know about Nathan suggests that he would have been a far more appropriate Messiah than Sabbatai. He was a visionary, an intellectual, and a man of tremendous energy and purpose (Sabbatai was relatively weak-willed.) Yet it seems that one of his visions revealed to him that Sabbatai was the Messiah—this was in March 1665—but for some reason he kept this to himself, merely revealing that he had been vouchsafed a vision of the Messiah. This created considerable excitement, and many people came to see him to learn more.

Now comes perhaps the strangest part of the story. Sabbatai was in Egypt, on some kind of mission for his fellow Jews of Jerusalem; when he heard the news about Nathan's vision, he decided to go and see him on his way home. The meeting took place in April 1665, and Sabbatai seems to have told Nathan that he had come to be cured of his strange attacks of depression and exaltation. He was staggered when Nathan told him that he was the Messiah. His first reaction was to laugh. "I used to be a messiah, but I abandoned it." But in the week that followed, Nathan convinced him.

They went on a tour of the tombs of Jerusalem and Hebron, and Nathan listened to Sabbatai's life story and became increasingly convinced that he was the Anointed One who was expected. Sabbatai remained dubious.

The next crucial event is even more mysterious. Sabbatai fell into one of his bouts of melancholia, and went home. But Nathan, in his capacity as spiritual director of the local Jews, went to the synagogue, and sank into a kind of trance in which he began to call upon various individuals to repent of their sins. Then a "voice was heard"—whether it spoke through Nathan's mouth is not clear—ordering them to "heed Sabbatai Zevi." When Nathan came round, the assembled rabbis asked him what it all meant, and Nathan announced that it meant that Sabbatai was the Messiah, and worthy to be King of all Israel.

Sabbatai, recovered from his depression, visited Nathan, and was told what had happened. Now, at last, he himself began to be convinced. He had spent much of his life in psychological torment; now he began to believe that the answer lay in accepting his destiny as the Messiah. Three days later, as he went into his manic phase, he suddenly lost all doubt. In the synagogue, his face "shining with radiance," Sabbatai stood before the congregation, which saw his majestic demeanor as proof that he was the Messiah. Apparently he stood there for three hours, and ended by choosing twelve of the rabbinic scholars as representatives of the twelve tribes of Israel.

Soon after this, Nathan had another vision, in which he saw a handwritten book, from which he was allowed to copy a page, declaring that the Messiah was Sabbatai Zevi, and that he would be rejected and persecuted by a "mixed multitude"—a phrase suggesting "children of Satan." Like many other documents that have claimed divine origin, this "vision" became one of the basic scriptures of Sabbatai's followers.

The Messiah, surrounded by a host of believers, now settled down to playing his role in earnest. As a great day of religious fasting approached, Sabbatai had a revelation and announced that the festival would be abolished and celebrated as a feast. He then rode to Jerusalem with a band of forty followers, and after riding around the city seven times, created further scandal with his usual eccentric behavior, uttering "blasphemies" and encouraging his followers to eat forbidden kidney fat, which he blessed. The rabbis once again expelled him.

Meanwhile, Nathan was revealing formidable gifts as a publicity agent, writing letters to Jewish congregations all over Europe and the Middle East, announcing the advent of the Messiah, and comparing him to Simon Bar Kochbar. The tremendous sensation caused by these letters was due to their sheer conviction, and to Nathan's highly developed literary faculty. But it was also true, as pointed out earlier in this chapter, that there was already a mood of messianic expectation, among Christians as well as Jews. Christians noted that the number of the Beast in Revelation was 666, and felt that it was inconceivable that the year 1666 could pass without some earth-shaking event. But since the prophecies also declared that the Millennium could not take place until the Jews had become united in Palestine, many Christians felt that the arrival of a Jewish Messiah would be the first step towards Armageddon. There were rumors of great armies on the march in the Middle East.

This explains why, when Sabbatai decided to return to Smyrna, as a first step in his mission to become King of the World, his progress caused wide excitement, and he was greeted everywhere by huge crowds. Aleppo, for example, treated him with ceremonial reverence. As the news of this progress reached Europe, Jews danced in the streets, and many sold all they had to prepare for Heaven on Earth, where it would be unnecessary to pursue a trade or work for a living.

Meanwhile, Sabbatai had arrived quietly in Smyrna in September 1665 and to begin with, conducted himself with unusual decorum, giving the impression that he had turned over a new leaf. His manic depressive illness was in its quiet phase. But by December, when a delegation of admirers from Aleppo arrived to pay homage, he was again in his manic phase, and his feverish exaltation again swept everyone away. There was an outbreak of what we would now call mass hysteria; dozens of people began to prophecy and see visions; pillars of fire were particularly popular. Stories of miracles began to circulate.

When the orthodox rabbis met to decide what to do about the menace, Sabbatai ordered a day of public prayer, which the majority of Smyrna's Jews observed. Sabbatai attended the synagogue dressed in magnificent robes, leading a procession that would have been worthy of a Pope; as usual, he pronounced the forbidden name of God aloud, and blessed the believers with a royal scepter. On December 14, he proclaimed himself the Messiah, and went on to distribute royal titles among his followers, with the implication that they could take possession of their kingdoms immediately after the Millennium. Smyrna went into festive mood. Visitors poured in from surrounding towns and cities, and delegations arrived to offer homage.

Totally convinced that God would intervene to ensure the success of his mission, Sabbatai now embarked for Constantinople, preceded by letters that reported signs and miracles. Constantinople was soon in the same state of feverish expectation as

Smyrna. The commercially-minded saw the opportunity of profit, and began churning out letters full of even more preposterous reports, which were sold to gullible enthusiasts. Even Constantinople's Christians shared the excitement.

The ship carrying the Messiah was having problems; bad weather extended the voyage from the usual two weeks to more than a month. Meanwhile, rabbis hostile to Sabbatai told the Grand Vizier, Ahmed Koprulu, that a false messiah was on his way, and that his aim was to overthrow Sultan Mehmet IV. The Vizier was not greatly alarmed, since it was obvious that the Messiah had no army. But he was concerned about the disruption of the commercial life of the city by all this religious excitement. So Sabbatai's ship was met far out at sea, and on February 8, 1666, he was brought ashore under arrest.

Everyone expected him to be immediately executed. But when he was brought before the Grand Vizier (the Sultan was out of town), his charm and obvious intelligence again served him in good stead. His Arabic was perfect, and the Vizier was a cultured man who loved the language. When he asked Sabbatai if it was true he was a messiah, Sabbatai replied that he was simply a Jewish scholar collecting money for the poor. But the behavior of the believers— they had sent deputations to the Vizier—made it clear that this was not entirely true. Large sums of money were paid by the faithful to ensure the Messiah's comfort and to obtain visiting rights.

Meanwhile, outbreaks of "prophecy" were occurring in Constantinople, just as earlier in Smyrna, and crowds filled the city, hoping to see the imprisoned Messiah. The Vizier, having no time to devote to his prisoner (he was busy provisioning a fleet to invade Crete and eject the Venetians) and concerned at the increasing excitement, had Sabbatai transferred to a fortress on the other side of the Dardanelles, in Gallipoli. Visitors flocked there, and Sabbatai went into one of his manic phases and issued new laws and commands. He was virtually holding court.

Far from losing strength, the messianic movement continued to grow. The "prophet" Nathan was expected to arrive from Gaza any day, and there was a general feeling that the Messiah's imprisonment was a minor episode that would end in the triumphant accomplishment of his mission.

Instead, there was totally unexpected disaster. The cause was the arrival of a Polish rabbi named Nehemiah Kohin, who wanted to indulge in theological argument. Some sources declare that he believed himself to be the Messiah, but the likelier version of the story is that he was a narrow and literal-minded man who was impervious to Sabbatai's charm, and who proceeded to attack his pretensions to being the Anointed One.

Sabbatai seems to have made the mistake of defending himself. After three days of increasingly acrimonious argument, Nehemiah flung himself out of the room, shouting angrily at the guards that he wanted to become a Muslim. He was taken before the Sultan (or, more probably, one of his officials), where he renounced Judaism and "took the turban." The motive of the conversion soon became apparent when he went on to lay all kinds of charges against Sabbatai Zevi, from sexual debauchery and trampling on the holy books to the intention of overthrowing the state. He obviously felt that he would stand a better chance of ruining Sabbatai as a Muslim than as a Jew. After that he returned to Poland, where he "repented" and returned to Judaism.

On September 15, 1666, Sabbatai Zevi was brought to Adrianople, where the court had moved. Excited Jews laid carpets in the streets, convinced that this was the moment when the Messiah would dethrone the Sultan. When a Frenchman made a mocking remark, one of the Jews told him: "Before long you will be our slaves, by the power of the Messiah."

Sabbatai was taken before the Privy Council, with the Sultan watching from a latticed alcove. There are conflicting accounts of what took place, but the likeliest is that Sabbatai had been told in the utmost detail how he would be tortured to death if he refused to renounce Judaism. Under these difficult circumstances, he displayed his usual weakness and passivity. He declared that he was not the Messiah, and that he wanted to become a Muslim. One account has him throwing down his Jewish cap and spitting on it before he allowed the turban to be placed on his head.

Most reports also seem to agree that he described his disciples in uncomplimentary terms. The Sultan graciously accepted the convert, giving him the new name of Mehemit Effendi, and the post of gatekeeper at fifty ecus (or silver dollars) per month. He was then taken to the bath, and clothed in "robes of honor," after which he was presented with three purses each containing 500 ecus, as well as other generous gifts. The apostasy of such a famous "Messiah" was quite a catch for Islam.

When the Turks announced the apostasy, the Jews at first refused to believe it; but when Jewish sources confirmed it, there was no alternative. The Jews were shattered; they had believed that two thousand years of misery and slavery were about to end in spectacular triumph, and now there was this miserable anticlimax that made them a laughingstock. Christians and Muslims jeered at the Jews of Constaninople so unmercifully that most of them hid in their homes for days.

It seemed unbelievable. They had been prepared to hear of Sabbatai's triumph, or of his cruel martyrdom; but this cowardly conversion was merely unseemly and slightly comic. Lampoons began to appear in which Sabbatai and his prophet Nathan were represented as cheats and crooks, and many shamefaced believers had to agree.

When the initial disappointment had passed, the Jews of Constantinople realized that they had good reason to be relieved. Their attitude to the "infidel" before Sabbatai's conversion amounted to rebellion, and many at first expected a pogrom. (In fact, letters reveal that the Sultan was preparing a pogrom if Sabbatai had insisted on martyrdom.) The fact that Sabbatai's conversion had diverted the anger of the Turks was cause for rejoicing; in fact, it was not long before some of them were suggesting that Sabbatai had only pretended to be converted, in order to save his fellow Jews.

Further away, in places like Hamburg and Amsterdam, believers had no doubt that Sabbatai had either not converted, or that he had done so for the best of motives. Others insisted that Sabbatai had ascended into heaven, and that only his shadow remained on earth.

The great question now was how the prophet Nathan would react to the apostasy. The answer was that, after his first stunned reaction, Nathan began to search the Kabbalistic texts, and soon came up with obscure references that showed that the Messiah would have to apostatize before he fulfilled his mission. So Nathan was able to proclaim, as if nothing had happened: " . . . without any doubt, this is the year of our salvation, and our redemption is at hand."

This would come about, he explained, in the spring of the following year, 1667. But when this time came and went without signs or portents, Nathan applied his ingenuity to explaining why the Messiah had to apostatize in order to complete his mission. Faced with the possibility that his own visions and ecstasies had been self-deception, Nathan preferred to continue to believe. He seems to have regarded Sabbatai's apostasy rather as the disciples of Jesus regarded his crucifixion—as a mystical event that could only be understood if it was recognized as a total necessity.

It is unfortunate that we have no reliable account of what happened when Nathan finally met Sabbatai, sometime in mid-1667. But the old magic was clearly as powerful as ever, and Nathan departed on a mission to Rome, financed by Sabbatai. He remained a total believer for the rest of his days, as did many of Sabbatai's most vociferous supporters in Smyrna.

As to Sabbatai, who had been converted to Islam at the age of forty, he lived on for another ten years in Adrianople, continuing to have manic attacks in which he declared himself the Messiah, and behaving with his inimitable eccentricity. The faithful who settled in Turkey also converted to Islam, and frequently met with Sabbatai, who frequently received new revelations. Visitors were deeply impressed by the radiance of his face during his visions, and left with no doubt that they had seen the Messiah.

In 1671 he decided to divorce his wife Sarah, who had also become a Muslim; according to Nathan, it was because she was constantly picking quarrels with him. Then, after becoming betrothed to a girl named Esther, the daughter of a rabbi, he had another depressive phase, and took Sarah back again. Nathan, who had returned to his master, had been delighted to see Sarah rejected—he had never liked her—and he was correspondingly sorry to see her taken back.

In 1672, Sabbatai was in trouble again—this time for uttering blasphemies against Islam in one of his manic phases. He was imprisoned, and for a while, in danger of being executed. The Sultan and Grand Vizier were getting tired of their guest's bizarre conduct, and of his hordes of disciples. After one of these had paid a large bribe to have the Messiah's life spared, Sabbatai was exiled to Dulcigno on the Adriatic, in what is now the former Yugoslavia. Some disciples followed him there as Nathan preferred to travel around like St. Paul, trying to gain converts.

When Sarah died in 1674, at the age of thirty-two, Sabbatai renewed his engagement to Esther. Unfortunately, she also died before she could join him in exile, although Sabbatai declared that if he was allowed to view her body, he would resurrect her.

Then, in 1675, Sabbatai married again, this time a girl called Michal, the daughter of a Greek scholar. This new marriage again raised the hopes of thousands of faithful followers, who continued to believe that the Messiah's divine mission would be accomplished at any moment. In fact, there was yet another wave of messianic expectation in 1675.

In the following year, Sabbatai had another manic phase, when he ascended a tower—probably a mosque—and burst into song and prophecy, enraging the Turks. But they had decided to treat him as a privileged maniac. More certain than ever that he was the Messiah, Sabbatai wrote letters to believers ordering them to combine the feasts of Passover and the Tabernacle, and announcing that he was Jehovah.

A few months later on September 17, 1676, Sabbatai died at the age of fifty, leaving the believers once more in a state of confusion and bewilderment. Nathan was totally dismayed, and sank into a state of melancholia. Then, possibly reflecting that Jesus's influence became more powerful after reports of the resurrection, Nathan recovered, and announced that Sabbatai's death was not real, but merely a temporary "occultation." Nathan continued to preach his message to thousands of believers until his death in Macedonia in January 1680, at the age of thirty-six.

The most fascinating question remains. Why was Nathan so besotted with Sabbatai? There was, as we have noted, a sense in which he was better qualified to become the Messiah than his easygoing and unworldly master. Nathan was a far more forceful character than Sabbatai—brilliant, eloquent, profoundly religious, a born organizer. Yet every time he talked to Sabbatai, he seemed to fall under a spell.

The answer, I would suggest, is quite simple. Sabbatai seemed to be in the grip of some force greater than himself. When this force possessed him, he became transformed. Nathan was an intellectual, who suffered from our modern complaint: self-division, Hamlet's disease. But when Sabbatai became "possessed," he seemed to become an instrument of the power of God.

Oddly enough, the thinker who was probably best qualified to understand this was Friedrich Nietzsche, who regarded himself as an atheist. Nietzsche's first book, *The Birth of Tragedy*, written in 1872 when was a young professor at Basel, is devoted to the ecstasy induced by the Greek god Dionysus, whose followers become "possessed." Nietzsche wrote of "the blissful ecstasy that arises from the innermost depths of man, nay, of nature, at the collapse of the *principium individuationis*," that is, the principle of individuality.

Nietzsche was writing from his own experience. As a medical orderly in the Franco-Prussian war, he had been walking back to his quarters, exhausted and depressed after a day tending the wounded and dying, when he heard the sound of approaching horses, and stood back to allow them to pass. It was his old regiment, and as he watched them galloping past, on their way to battle, perhaps to death, he was seized by a tremendous exaltation, which expressed itself in the words: "The strongest and the highest will to life does not lie in the puny struggle to exist, but in the Will to war, the Will to Power."

Understandably, we dismiss the notion as dangerous and illogical. A society based on such principles would soon degenerate into fascism or anarchy. Yet most of us can also place ourselves behind Nietzsche's eyes and understand his feelings as his regiment rode past: an upsurge of vitality that seems to contradict our normal moral standards. It is as if the everyday personality, with its doubts and inhibitions, dissolved away. Nietzsche had once experienced the same thing in a thunderstorm, and wrote later: "Pure Will, without the confusions of intellect—how happy, how free."

This is what Sabbatai Sevi must have experienced when he felt "possessed." In such moments, the Jewish moral code, with its inhibitions and prohibitions, most have seemed to him absurd. Like the Brethren of the Free Spirit, he felt suddenly impelled to deny the old morality. He may well have felt that Islam suited him better than Judaism, since it had fewer laws and prohibitions.

But what is really involved here is not a matter of morality or immorality. It is a question of the individual's attitude to himself. Nathan felt weak and self-divided. He wanted a purpose that would unite him. When he first heard of Sabbatai, and his strange moods of ecstasy, he must have felt that such a person could well be the Messiah. That is why he was obsessed by Sabbatai long before he met him. And when he met him, he had no doubt. This man who seemed so gentle and good-natured, so free of self-division, could at times become the vessel of the Holy Spirit. Unlike Nathan, he had the power to speak with God.

Yet to understand the essential difference between Nathan and Sabbatai, the disciple and the master, we have to understand that it is not a matter of temperaments, but of two modes of being. We humans are essentially passive. We are born into a world of authority figures: parents and teachers and guardians of the law. Most of us would like to become successes, figures who command respect. But we cannot afford to be too different from everyone else. That would mean rejection.

In fact, there are some figures who, whether they like it or not, are forced to tread the road of rejection. They may be artists or thinkers or scientists who feel impelled to break with the old tradition, and take some new path. If they succeed in persuading others to see the world as they see it, then they become the "tradition" that influences succeeding generations.

As often as not, the struggle is painful, even self-destructive. But the people who have trodden this path see the world quite differently from their fellow men. Their actions seem to spring from a force inside themselves. Nietzsche called such people "self-rolling wheels." They do not, for example, ask, "Why has fate sent this misfortune?" or "Why has God allowed this tragedy to happen?," for they are aware of the will as a positive force, and are also aware that most people have an attitude of passivity that makes them unaware of their own strength.

Most religion is based upon the passive attitude. We are helpless puppets in the hands of fate. We are swept along by forces that are far bigger than we are. And if we happen to be religiously inclined, then we look for an organization in which we feel comfortable, surrounded by other believers. Most of us are natural followers or disciples.

In fact, the difference between the passive and the active attitudes is as thin as a sheet of paper. It is merely a change of viewpoint.

In most religions it is called "enlightenment." There is a Zen story of a monk whose attitude towards religion was too analytical and intellectual, and who was simply unable to grasp what his master meant by enlightenment. One day, as he and the master stood on a balcony overlooking a pond, the master suddenly pushed him into the water. And as he came up, spluttering and gasping, the monk shouted: "Now I understand!" His point of view had changed instantly from the passive to the active. This is also what Buckminster Fuller meant when he commented: "I seem to be a verb."

It is only when we understand this that we can grasp the basic difference between Nathan and Sabbatai, and understand that it is perhaps the most fundamentally important difference that can exist between one human being and another.

THREE

THE PSYCHOLOGY OF DISCIPLESHIP

In the mid-1970s, I began to correspond with an American professor who worked at a place called the Ukiah Institute in California. He seemed to be a pleasant and intelligent man, and one day he and his wife turned up to see us in Cornwall. It was then that I was amazed to discover that he and his "wife" (they were not actually married) had been members of the cult of the Rev. Jim Jones. In fact, they were not even sure that their two children had been fathered by the professor.

They explained that in the early days of Jones's community, there were group marriages in which several men had several wives, and vice versa. They also said that after Jones's death, many of the group left in California believed that he was still alive, and that he would come back to kill them. What struck me as strange was that they both seemed intelligent and well-educated people, and would certainly have passed anywhere for a normal middle class couple. It was hard to believe that they had been followers of a man who declared he was God, and who openly treated his female disciples as his harem.

Fortunately we have a book by an ex-disciple who goes to some lengths to explain how she and her husband became believers.

In *Six Years With God*, Jeannie Mertle describes how she and her husband, Al Mertle, were persuaded by their local minister to visit a congregation called the People's Temple, in Redwood Valley, California. It was run by the Reverend Jim Jones, a minister with a reputation as a liberal and anti-racist, who was also revered as a healer.

First impressions were good. There was a huge congregation—over five hundred—meeting in a church built to look like a barn. The choir *sounded* professional, a requirement recognized by all American evangelists from Billy Graham to Jimmy Swaggart. To listen to first-class singing gets the congregation into a good mood, and helps to undermine the sense of boredom that is associated with religious services. Then a large choir of young children, both black and white, came forward, and sang with warmth and enthusiasm. Jeannie was impressed, thinking of her own self-centered children and step-children, as she watched these radiant youngsters who were learning about social justice and love.

The next stage was less impressive. A long queue of people testified to how their pastor had healed them of various ailments, including cancer. One woman described how, during a church meeting, the Rev. Jones had suddenly cried out: "Someone needs me," and rushed to the house of a man who lay on the floor with a bullet hole in his forehead. She described how Jones had cradled the man's head in his lap, and how a bullet had fallen out of his head on the floor, and he had regained consciousness. It all sounded preposterous to Jeannie.

Worse was to come. Jim Jones, a big man with long black sideburns, and wearing dark glasses and a maroon turtle-neck sweater, began speaking about religion in a way that seemed blasphemous. In a powerful, deep voice he declared that slave owners had forced black people to accept the King James Bible, and that "any black person who still believes in the Bible is a sell-out." As he denounced the Bible for contradictions, his language became so foul that the Mertles were shocked, and expected to see him struck down by lightning. As if reading their minds, Jones looked at the sky and shouted: "If there is a God in heaven, let him strike me dead." When, after a silence, nothing happened, the congregation burst into relieved laughter.

For hour after hour Jones preached doctrines that sounded dangerously subversive to the Mertles. Jones praised the Black Panthers and attacked the Vietnam war and government corruption. Then he told the congregation that he had seen, by divine revelation, the destruction of civilization in a nuclear war; the only survivors would be his followers, whom he would lead into a cave.

This impressed the Mertles, who were worried about nuclear war. Nevertheless, Jones struck them as repellently coarse.

The preacher went on to demonstrate that he appeared to have some occult insight into the lives of people in the audience and into their personal problems, sometimes describing details of their homes which they hastened to verify. One woman was told that a pain in her stomach was cancer, but that Jones would make it pass out via her bowels; she was taken to the toilet with a nurse, and in a few minutes, the nurse returned holding a mass of smelly flesh which she claimed the woman had defecated.

After hours of this, the Mertles were exhausted and bored, but then the church provided a magnificent hot meal for everyone, during which Jones sermonized. As the congregation finally left, ushers began setting up chairs for another service. Jones's energy seemed inexhaustible.

The Mertles felt they had had enough of the People's Temple. But a flood of friendly letters arrived in their mailbox, together with candy, and they both began to have odd dreams about Jones. The day-long service haunted their imagination. Jeannie was an orthodox Christian; Al was an agnostic with a strong liberal bias. But when Jeannie looked up the Bible to check on Jones's allegations of errors and contradictions, she found he was invariably correct. Six weeks later, the Mertles went back, to be greeted by Jones with a warm smile and handshake: "We were all hoping you'd return."

The notion that five hundred people had been thinking about the Mertles was flattering. Listening this time with her critical barriers down, Jeannie found Jones's sermon inspiring. The Mertle's children also enjoyed themselves. Suddenly, they were "in," part of a warm and friendly environment in which they felt perfectly at home. It was like being back in the womb.

The Mertles soon decided to sell their home and move the 120 miles to Redwood Valley. Their new home was beautiful. When they discovered they had serious sewage problems, a large male contingent from the congregation turned up and spent a day digging new sewers, refusing to accept any payment other than a meal. Everyone was friendly and supportive. It seemed too good to be true.

A few doubts began to arise when Jeannie witnessed a session called "catharsis," in which church members were castigated for various faults; one was a woman who had simply gone for a hot dog with a new member. In the "healing service" that followed, Jeannie found herself wondering whether the "cancer" that had been defecated was really what it was supposed to be.

A few days later Jeannie's doubts suddenly vanished. Her eight-year-old son Eddie collapsed with a heart ailment, and as she drove to the hospital, Jeannie prayed that Jim Jones would heal him. When the doctor examined the child, he could find nothing wrong; the heart problem had vanished. Now Jeannie had her own "miracle" to describe in front of the congregation.

By 1971, Jones was beginning to show the first signs of the paranoia that always, sooner or later, seems to afflict rogue messiahs. The public was no longer to be freely admitted to services, because some mysterious group was trying to discredit Jones. He had to be notified well in advance of any visitor to the Temple, and he would "determine by revelation" whether that person was a "spy."

All members of the congregation had to endlessly write letters, like the ones that had brought the Mertles into the Temple. Thousands of letters were written to help defeat a political candidate of whom Jones disapproved, and he was duly defeated. But when Jeannie's boss discovered she was writing such letters on office time, she was sacked. Now she was enrolled as a full-time church worker on a monthly salary.

Jones's paranoid side became evident after another "miracle." When, one evening, there was not enough food to feed everyone, Jones announced that he was blessing the food in order to multiply it, as Jesus had done with the loaves and fishes; soon, large plates of fried chicken were carried out from the kitchen. One member joked that he had seen the chicken brought in buckets from the Kentucky Fried Chicken stand earlier that evening. Later, Jones denounced him for lying, then added: "He is paying for it—he is now vomiting." An hour later, the offender staggered out of the lavatory looking pale and exhausted. Jeannie was to learn later that Jones was capable of slipping poison into the food of those he wished to chastise.

Soon Jeannie herself was in trouble. She allowed some young student teachers, unconnected with the Temple, to give her children lessons. The Temple Planning Commission took this amiss, and the Mertles were sternly criticized for allowing their children to be taught by "morally unsuitable" outsiders, and pressured until they reversed their decision. But when ordered to sell tickets for a church event, Al Mertle got angry when told he would have to pay for them himself if he failed to sell them, and refused. Small irritations like these made them decide to quit the Temple. Jones immediately spent an evening with them, talking with all his remarkable persuasiveness, but the Mertles declined to be swayed. However, when their children refused to leave the church, the Mertles capitulated and returned, to warm embraces and assurances of affection.

One sunny afternoon, as everyone sat outdoors eating a picnic lunch, there were shots from a nearby woodland area, and Jones slumped forward over the table. After a few moments he sat up, his face twisted with pain, and declared: "I'm not ready to die yet." Then he walked slowly into the church, explaining that he had neutralized the bullets in his body. But on a later occasion, when bullets crashed in through a window of the dining hall and Jones clutched his head, it was obvious to everyone that the bullets had not gone anywhere near him; in fact, one of his henchmen was seen sneaking away holding a rifle. By that time, the Mertles had come to recognize that Jones organized his own "miracles."

Jones's fundamental lack of self-control was revealed when a black male, whose family had been looked after by the community, came out of jail. After a two-hour sermon, Jones asked him what he thought of the community.

The man replied courteously, thanking Jones for his kindness and help, but then went on to say that he disliked the hero worship Jones was trying to instill into the community, and that he and his wife therefore intended to leave. Jones lost his temper and called him an ungrateful bastard, then asked the wife if she intended to leave the community. She explained that she had to stick by her husband. At this, Jones exploded with rage, ordering his henchmen to "take that ungrateful family to the bus station. Do not give them one penny."

Everyone present was upset; it was the first time many began to suspect that their idol had feet of clay. After accompanying the family to the bus station at two in the morning, Jeannie suddenly felt a surge of hatred for Jim Jones.

In 1972, Jones began to institute an even more authoritarian regime. All church members were ordered to cut their hair short, and a squad of barbers enforced this.

When Jones heard that Father Divine (a black Messiah who claimed to be God) had died, he decided to win over his congregation in Philadelphia. Jones took his whole community, in buses, to Philadelphia, and preached a sermon praising Father Divine and declaring that he, Jim Jones, was practicing his teachings.

But when, the following day, Jones used his second sermon to invite Father Divine's followers to desert him and follow Jones to California, they ordered Jones out. A dozen of his followers returned to California, and Jones used this as an excuse to tell his own followers that from now on, they were to address him as "Father," and show him the same kind of respect that Father Divine had commanded. In fact, Father Divine's followers soon left, disgusted by Jones's attacks on their dead leader; but Jones still insisted on being called "Father."

Now Jones selected six bodyguards who accompanied him everywhere. He told his followers that in previous incarnations he had been the Buddha, the Bab (founder of the Bahai faith), Jesus, and Lenin, but hinted that in this latest incarnation, he was now God.

When he opened a church in San Francisco, he had some excuse for paranoia when the newspapers began to attack his pretensions, particularly his claim that he could raise the dead. He made his followers picket one offending newspaper for three days, until all were in a state of exhaustion. Eventually, the newspaper agreed to print, unedited, Jones's side of the story. The resulting publicity brought in many more followers from all over America, such that Jones was able to open another church in Los Angeles.

An encounter with a nine-year-old boy who was discovered to be the leader of a gang of thieves revealed the shaky foundation of Jones's authority. The boy was ordered to stand in front of the congregation, and asked if he knew stealing was a sin. "Only if you get caught," said the child. After several more unsuccessful attempts to browbeat him, Jones told him he could strike him dead. The boy folded his arms and said: "Go ahead."

Jones now whispered in the ear of one of his guards, who went out and fetched a glass of water. The boy obediently drank it. Jones made passes over him and asked him if he really wanted to die. The boy now looked ill, but remained defiant. He was given another glass of water. Suddenly, he collapsed. Jones ordered him to be carried out, then told the congregation: "Don't worry. Anthony won't remain dead."

Later, as the boy recovered consciousness, Jones ordered the lights to be turned out, then whispered to the boy that he, Jones, was the devil, and this was hell. The child fainted. For the rest of the night, church members were ordered to make noises like the damned in hell every time he woke up. The next day, terrified, the boy agreed never to steal again.

Soon after this, Jones publicly rebuked a member who had gotten drunk. The man defended himself by citing others who drank. Jones now asked them all if they thought it was fair to sit by quietly while he criticized someone else for drinking, and ordered that everyone who drank should bend over and receive three blows from a leather belt. Jeannie was astonished because the Temple had no rule against social drinking. But, along with dozens of others, she bent over and allowed herself to be beaten with a belt.

Next a teenage schoolgirl named Kathy was rebuked for getting bad grades. One of the "counselors" asked her if it was because she had sex on her mind. She looked blank and denied it. Now others began suggesting that she had a lesbian fixation on her sister. Soon the girl's own stepmother was urging her to confess, to put an end to the grilling. Kathy ended by saying what they wanted, that she wanted to suck her sister's vagina and have her sister suck hers. After this session, Jeannie was so disgusted that she stopped being a counselor.

For a long time Jones had been having sex with church members who attracted him—he seems to have been bisexual—but he now passed out a questionnaire which included the question: "Do you want to have sex with Father?" Jeannie wrote "No," but the many members who wrote "Yes" were later called by Jones's secretary and told: "If Father feels you will be helped by relating to him more closely, you will be contacted." Soon after, Jones told his followers that sex was forbidden (except with him) either in or out of marriage. Jones's wife Marceline stood in front of the congregation and stated that she had decided that, for the good of the cause, she was willing to share her husband with other women. After this, Jones bragged publicly about the number of women he had satisfied. (Oddly enough, although his following consisted largely of blacks, he only slept with white women.)

As his power mania increased, Jones's behavior became steadily more outrageous. One night, after a follower named Clifford had dozed off during a long harangue, Jones secured from his wife the admission that her husband was prudish about oral sex. Jones then turned to a shy black girl, and ordered her to remove her knickers and allow Clifford to "suck her pussy." The girl was so paralyzed with embarrassment that Jones relented. Then another black girl—she was having her period—offered to take her place, and lay down on a table with her legs apart. Clifford at first refused, but was finally bullied into performing cunnilingus on her; after this he stormed out in a rage.

By 1974, Jones was obsessed by sex, dragging it into every counseling session. "I get so tired of women begging me to fuck them. The next woman will get a fucking like she's never had before. My organ is so big she'll be sore for a week." He added: "When I fuck a woman I go on for eight or nine hours." The story about the size of his organ was disproved one day when he was relieving himself behind a blanket held by two women, and one accidentally dropped her corner, and revealed to the congregation that his member was of average size. Jones excused his lie by explaining that he had to maintain a certain image for the good of the cause.

He also "related to" male followers, announcing that every man was basically homosexual and secretly longed for a male lover. One day he accused one of the men of being so filthy that he had given him a rash. The man was ordered to lower his trousers, pull open his buttocks, and display himself to the audience. Most of the women averted their eyes. But those who peered obediently into the orifice said they could see no sign of a rash.

On another occasion, when Jones asked everyone who had had sex with him to raise their hands, one man blushed and looked away. Jones lost no time in rebuking him. "You weren't ashamed when you were squealing with delight as we were fucking the other night, were you Harry?" Harry hastened to confess that he had been fully satisfied.

Beating also became a part of the public ceremonies, and Jones had a special "beating board" constructed. On one occasion, Jeannie Mertle was forced to look on as her own sixteen-year-old daughter was publicly flogged with seventy-five lashes for hugging her boyfriend. When members began to sneak out before the "disciplines" began, Jones posted guards on the doors, and even forbade people to use the lavatory during the beatings. One woman who urgently needed to defecate was made to do it in a tin can in front of everyone.

From Jeannie's account, it is difficult to understand why the Mertles stayed in the Temple so long. They were pressured into making sacrifice after sacrifice—their home, their savings, their privacy—and suffered humiliation after humiliation, even being forced to write false confessions to all kinds of sexual misdemeanors—Al Mertle had to admit to seducing a teenager who lived with them.

But it was when Jones refused to pay Jeannie her salary, and the Mertles were threatened with starvation, that they decided they had to leave. Their seventeen-year-old daughter Linda elected to stay.

The Mertles were now subjected to all kinds of intimidation, threats and blackmail. They were told that the Black Muslims, Mafia, and Black Panthers had all been instructed to get them. Even after they had moved to Berkeley, Temple guards came and stood outside their home with folded arms. They were bombarded with anonymous hate mail. When Jeannie wrote a letter to campaigner Ralph Nader—he had been photographed shaking hands with Jones—the church found out within days, and its representative was on the telephone to the Mertles uttering more threats.

Meanwhile, Jones seemed to be winning over all the influential politicians in California, and was appointed Chairman of the Housing Commission. But it was only when the Mertles' daughter Linda defected from the Temple, and told them how much worse things had become since they left that they decided it was time to campaign actively against Jones.

At first, no one would listen because Jones was now too well connected with politicians. There were two things in their favor: first, investigative journalists are always ready to attack those who have become too successful; second, the paranoid Jones was bound to contribute to his own downfall.

This happened when he heard rumors that the magazine *New West* intended to print an article criticizing him, and ordered his followers to flood it with thousands of protest letters. The editor resented this attempt at intimidation. Then there was a break-in at the magazine and a first draft of the article was stolen. Jeannie took the opportunity to ring a reporter on the magazine and tell her story. Other defectors decided to join her. On July 17, 1977, a long article appeared telling about the beatings, the blackmail, the forced confessions. The Mertles braced themselves for more threats of violence, and possibly for these threats to be carried out. Instead, all threats suddenly ceased.

Since 1973, Jones had been building himself a haven in Guyana, in South America, which he liked to refer to as the Promised Land. He assured his followers that it was beautiful, temperate, and safe; in fact, it was a hot, steamy climate, and the jungle surrounding Jonestown (his name for the property) was full of snakes, crocodiles, and mosquitoes.

Jones made a blunder during his first public relations exercise there, ordering one of his aides to fake a stomach cancer, which he would then "cure." (The Mertles discovered that Jones used chicken livers to simulate the tumors.) The press saw through the "miracle," and Guyanan government officials declined to try and suppress the bad publicity that followed.

Jones's reaction to the newspaper attacks—the *New West* denunciation was followed by one in *Newsweek*—was to order his followers to move to Jonestown *en masse*. Within weeks, the Redwood Valley and San Francisco settlements were deserted, and Jonestown had a population of more than a thousand. There they lived in one-room shacks and in overcrowded dormitories, and discipline was stricter than ever. Jones had loudspeakers installed all over the camp, and these blared out his sermons and messages for an average of six hours a day. Jones talked endlessly about conspiracies against him, and declared that if the government tried to interfere, he and his followers would commit mass suicide. Once a week, all eleven hundred followers were gathered together, as if for a fire drill, and made to rehearse the mass suicide.

The beginning of the end came on November 14, 1978, when California congressman Leo Ryan asked the U.S. federal authorities to intervene. An ex-Temple member had described how his son had been killed under mysterious circumstances after he had left the Temple, and had asked Ryan's help in getting his granddaughters back from Guyana. Ryan had agreed, and soon other families were asking for his help in similar cases. Now Ryan agreed to go and see for himself, and to make sure that no one was being held in Jonestown against his will.

At first the Guyanan immigration authorities were obstructive, and Jones's lawyer Mark Lane equally so; it took Ryan and his entourage of journalists three days to reach Jonestown. There, in the middle of the night, they were introduced to Jones, who looked exhausted and sick—"like a man in decay," said one witness—but still wearing his trademark sun glasses.

Nevertheless, he was polite, and gave the Congressman's group a meal, then laid on a rock concert for them. A woman slipped a note into the hand of one reporter, begging his help in getting her and three others back to America; he quickly concealed it. Other people took reporters aside and told them stories of brutal punishments. Finally, twenty people asked Ryan to take them back with him.

In a long press interview, Jones played down the beatings, but admitted freely to having many mistresses and illegitimate children. Asked if it was true that married couples were ordered not to have sex he replied: "Bullshit. Thirty babies have been born here since last year." In front of TV cameras he became increasingly hysterical. "I've given my life for my people. I live for my people."

Ryan seems to have recognized the menace in the air, for in a speech at dinner, he declared, "There are many people here who believe this is the best thing that ever happened to them," and there was frenzied clapping.

On the afternoon of Saturday November 18, trucks drove Ryan's party, including defectors, to the airport. Before they left

Jonestown, one of Jones's followers had tried to cut Ryan's throat, but had been overpowered. But as the reporters prepared to board the plane, a dump truck and a tractor drew up. Jones, together with three men holding guns jumped off and began to shoot. Ryan's face was shot off; cameraman Bob Brown was killed as he continued to film, his brains spattering his camera. Two other journalists and two defectors were killed. Many more were wounded. One of the two planes had succeeded in taking off, but only after a member of Jones's entourage, who had pretended to be a defector, had forced his way on board and shot two defectors.

All that night, the survivors waited in terror, expecting Jones's men to come and finish them off. In fact, Jones had driven straight back to Jonestown and, after a long and incoherent sermon, ordered all his followers to commit suicide with cyanide. It was squirted into the mouths of the babies, then administered to the older children. Then the adults were ordered to take it, with armed guards standing by to kill anyone who refused. Over the loudspeakers, Jones's voice told his followers that they were going to meet in a better place. Within two hours, more than nine hundred people had died.

It seems likely that, up to the last minute, Jones was undecided whether he too would die because he had packed a briefcase full of money and his passport. For some reason, he changed his mind, and shot himself. His wife Marceline seems to have drunk poison. Only two or three people escaped by hiding in the jungle; these reported that guards had killed anyone who was unwilling to die. Jones's son Stephen survived, because he was away playing basketball. He said of his father: "I can almost say I hate the man. He has destroyed almost everything I have lived for."

The fear of the survivors that they would be killed seems not to have been entirely imagination; Jeannie and Al Mertle were later found dead in their home, tied up and shot to death.

The parallels with Koresh are too obvious to need underlining: the megalomania, the obsessive need to possess female followers and humiliate the males, and the steadily increasing paranoia. The parallels with Hitler and other dictators are even more relevant, for Jones actually gained some degree of political power before his own excesses began to work against him.

But the most interesting insight to emerge from Jeannie Mertle's *Six Years With God* is why normal, sensible people could come to accept a paranoid maniac as a messiah. The answer obviously lies in the sense of love and kinship that the Mertles first experienced when they joined the Temple. It seemed a haven of security, an extended family under the wise guidance of a "Father" who possessed supernatural powers.

Then why did it go so wrong? The answer obviously lies in the character of Jones himself.

Born in May 1931 into a poor farming family in Ohio, he was fascinated by preachers in local churches—he tried several denominations—and enjoyed playing the preacher with his friends, making them listen while he delivered long sermons. He was also known as a hot-tempered boy who needed to have his own way, and who became foul-mouthed when he didn't get it.

Jones married at eighteen, went to Indianapolis, and although he was unordained, succeeded in becoming pastor of a church there. His ideals of racial brotherhood and civil rights led to so many difficulties that he rented his own church, selling monkeys as a door-to-door salesman to make a living. A visit to Philadelphia to watch Father Divine in action led him to decide that he had to be more authoritarian, and he set up an "interrogation committee" that could call his followers to account and, if necessary, administer punishment. By the time he was in his early twenties, Jones was already a mesmeric preacher who demanded total loyalty.

The changing times were on his side, and by 1960 he had been appointed director of the California State Human Rights Commission, with a salary of $7,000 a year. Attacks on him—some were physical—as a "nigger lover" only increased his reputation and the size of his congregation. And as church members began to contribute money, Jones bought a fleet of buses and announced that they were moving to Redwood Valley, California, where (according to one newspaper) they would be safe from atomic radiation when the nuclear war came. This is where, in 1969, the Mertles first saw him, and were horrified and fascinated by his profanity and flamboyance.

Jones was already claiming divine revelation, and powers of faith healing. Much of this was, undoubtedly, fraudulent, but there may also have been an element of genuineness. Scientific studies of thaumaturgy suggest that most people possess healing powers. In 1882, Madame Blavatsky's colleague Colonel Henry Steel Olcott, was asked for help by the local Buddhist priest in Colombo, Ceylon; Catholics were about to set up a healing shrine, and the priest thought that a little auto-suggestion might convince his own congregation that the Catholics did not have a monopoly on miracles. The Colonel tried "suggestion" on a man with a paralyzed arm, and made mysterious passes in the air. Soon the man began to improve, and others demanded treatment.

Convinced that he was deceiving them, Olcott soon found that he was curing so many that the auto-suggestion hypothesis began to look increasingly thin. After a while, he felt that he was actually directing some miraculous force, and that it worked because he was directing it.

Olcott's experience seems to suggest that most people could develop healing powers if they had the desire and self-confidence. Whether such powers are a matter of hypnosis or auto-suggestion is irrelevant, for they work.

Jones's hypnotic personality certainly helped his own pretensions to work miracles, but in the case of the cure of Jeannie Mertle's son Eddie (when Jones was not present) it could obviously play no direct part; it seems that the explanation lies either in coincidence, or in Jeannie's own faith.

This is an important point, for it would be a mistake to assume that messiahs depend simply on their powers of deception. The influence they exert over their followers seems to create a build-up of some psychic (or psychological) force, which can cause strange things can happen.

What does seem perfectly clear, from the careers of David Koresh and Jim Jones, is that their decline into a form of insanity was inevitable. Most public men—politicians, priests, even actors—are constrained by their relation to their followers and admirers, which demands a degree of responsibility and self-control. The rogue messiah, on the other hand, sets out to convince his disciples that he knows far better than they do; he demands total belief, total subjugation to his will.

But, as we have seen, in adopting this role, he is giving free reign to the worst elements in his nature. This is why genuine religious teachers lay so much emphasis on the will of God, and on their own personal unimportance. When someone like Jones or Koresh sets out without genuine religious inspiration—instead, they have merely a desire to exercise power—they are setting into motion forces that lie beyond their control.

That the same applies even to those who possess a genuine religious impulse can be seen from the career of one whose many followers still regard him as a genuine mystic: Paul Brunton.

Born in 1898 (as Raphael Hurst), Brunton suddenly achieved fame and success in 1934 with his first book *A Search in Secret India.* "I have titled this book *Secret India* because it tells of an India which has been hidden from prying eyes for thousands of years," Brunton declared in the introduction.

The first thing the reader notes about this book is the lack of dates and place names: the writer seems to be determined to be vague. He tells how, as a youth, he was discussing metempsychosis (transmigration of the soul) with an old bookseller when an Indian who was in the shop introduced himself and invited him to dinner. This was the first of many such occasions, and the old Brahmin was soon recommending his young friend to seek out the ancient wisdom of the holy men of India.

In the next chapter, Brunton is staying in the Hotel Majestic in Bombay, working as a journalist, when he meets an Egyptian called Mahmoud Bey, who possesses magical powers. He tells Brunton to write a question on a piece of paper, then to fold it tightly. Then he tells Brunton that the question was, "Where did I live four years ago?" When Brunton unfolds the paper, he finds the answer written beneath the question. Brunton writes down another question: What journal did he edit two years ago? Again the magician tells him what he asks, and he again finds the answer written on the paper. The Egyptian then explains that he learned his magical powers from an old Jew, a student of Kaballah, whom he met by chance. The old Jew has taught him how to command spirits.

From these early chapters, the reader emerges with a suspicion that the author is a romancer in the tradition of Arthur Machen rather than a sober reporter of fact. Yet his descriptions of his visits to yogis like Sri Meher Baba, Ramana Maharshi, and Mahasaya (a disciple of Ramakrishna) carry a sense of authenticity. At the time when Aldous Huxley was discovering the "perennial philosophy," Brunton apparently knew all about it. With its mixture of exotic places and even more exotic sages, it is not surprising that *A Search in Secret India* became one of the best-sellers of the 1930s.

A Search in Secret Egypt, published in the following year, was equally successful. Again, the reader feels that Brunton is spinning romance (or embroidering fact) whenever it suits his purpose; yet again, he seems to possess genuine knowledge. For example, his assertion that the Sphinx was built thousands of years before the Great Pyramid, by survivors from Atlantis, has recently received some scientific support from a study of the weathering of the Sphinx by Dr. Robert Schoch, of Boston University. (Schoch believes it was weathered by rain, not by wind-driven sand.)

In February 1938, a young Jewish naval officer named Bernard Masson wrote to Brunton requesting spiritual advice, and they entered into correspondence. Two years later, Bernard Masson's younger brother Jack also wrote to Brunton, who was living in India as the guest of the anglophile Maharajah of Mysore. Like Bernard, he was fascinated by the stories of yogis, and was even trying to raise his four-year-old son Jeffrey in the yogic tradition. In due course, Jeffrey Masson, having achieved some fame as a psychiatrist (and opponent of psychoanalysis) told the story of his father's involvement with Brunton in a book called *My Father's Guru*.

In 1945, Jack Masson went to visit Brunton in Mysore, having been assured by his much-admired elder brother that Brunton was an avatar, an incarnation of God. Brunton proved to be a baldheaded little man with a toothbrush mustache, who looked more like a suburban bank manager than a mystic. He was, apparently, half-Jewish, but preferred not to mention this, or the fact that he had had a "nose job" to remove a Semitic curve.

Brunton assured Masson that he had been drawn to India for a special purpose, which would eventually become known to him. He also told him that "discipleship under an adept is a privilege that cannot be bought," that it could only be earned over many incarnations.

Jeffrey Masson comments: "Certainly my father wanted something no person could ever give him, and P.B. claimed to be able to give my father what no other person can give another. One wanted, the other offered, transcendence of this world, spiritual enlightenment, and wisdom."

When his brother Bernard had been sixteen, he had experienced a sense of his identity with the universe, and had been trying to repeat the experience ever since. Now Jack Masson took up the quest, and Brunton seemed to promise success and fulfillment. Which is why, in 1946, he asked Brunton to come and share his family home in a Mediterranean-style house in the Hollywood hills of California. Masson owned two large linen stores in Los Angeles, one of them five stories high, and was also a diamond broker.

From Masson's account of his childhood with Brunton, it is clear that Brunton was no confidence-man, like Koresh or Jim Jones. He ate sparingly—vegetarian food only—never touched alcohol, and meditated and fasted regularly (and induced his disciples to do the same). He sometimes spent a week subsisting only on water. He deprecated sexual activity, and Masson agrees that in this respect, there was no touch of the hypocrite about him.

Masson's mother spent three weeks fasting on water, then another week without anything at all. His father displayed equal endurance, once fasting for forty days. On the other hand, his father was not able to share Brunton's ideal of sexual purity, and while he resisted seducing a pretty *au pair* girl, he made a habit of fondling and kissing her breasts. The same *au pair* assisted young Jeffrey's sexual awakening by allowing him to hold her tight as she lay on her bed clad only in knickers. Masson remarks: "The flip side of P.B.'s 'no sex' rule was the sexually-charged atmosphere around our house." Brunton would later marry a beautiful girl who was thirty-five years his junior, but claim there were no sexual relations.

In the Algonquin Hotel in New York, Jeffrey and his sister met Aldous Huxley in the elevator, and introduced him to their parents. Huxley does not seem to have been impressed by the knowledge that Brunton was their guru.

When, at the age of thirteen, Jeffrey was sitting in meditation with Brunton, he had a brief spiritual experience. As his legs ached and his skin itched, he suppressed the discomfort, and suddenly experienced an "altered state." Brunton seemed to sense it, and when Jeffrey confirmed it, his standing with his parents rose enormously.

He began to learn Sanskrit—Brunton claimed to be familiar with it—and acted as Brunton's secretary.

Brunton claimed to be able to remember his previous incarnations, one of which was on Venus ("There are no cars on Venus."); his most recent was on the dog star Sirius, sacred to the Egyptians. He declares in *A Hermit in the Himalayas*: "The beings who people it are infinitely superior in every way to the creatures who people earth. In intelligence, in character, in creative power, and in spirituality we are slugs crawling at their feet. The Sirians possess powers and faculties which we shall have to wait a few ages yet to acquire."

Brunton said that he had personal experiences of UFOs, and added that his move to earth "was a foolish one. I was very tranquil there, but here my life is troubled." But he claimed he often traveled to other planets in his astral body at night. On this planet, Brunton preferred to remain anonymous, preferring to be introduced to acquaintances of the Massons as Mr. Opher (his first names were supposed to be Philo S.).

In many ways, Brunton was impressive. He meditated for three hours a day, and when Masson peeped into his bedroom at night, was observed to be sitting cross-legged on the floor. He ate two tomatoes for lunch and one carrot for dinner. He was always serene, and (unlike Jones and Koresh) never showed anger or looked bored. He never tried to become wealthy at the expense of his disciples, although he allowed them to pay his travel expenses to foreign countries, and over the course of years accepted around a hundred thousand dollars from Jack Masson.

Yet in spite of his spirituality, Brunton had some curiously trivial habits; Jeffrey Masson had to carefully untie parcels sent to him, and knot together the pieces of string for later use; paper towels were laid out on the balcony to dry so they could be used several times; a secretary might be sent all the way downtown to exchange a ten-cent item at a big store, spending more than a dollar in carfare.

Unfortunately, Jack Masson failed to gain the spiritual illumination that Brunton promised; his fortieth birthday—the date by which it was supposed to arrive—came and went uneventfully. Masson was fair-minded enough to blame himself for this.

There were many matters about which Brunton was mysterious. He implied that there was some evil conspiracy of the powers of darkness which he was attempting to frustrate. He told Jeffrey how he had been in Tibet, and implied that he spoke Tibetan; he also described how he had been forced to flee to escape being arrested by the Communists, leaving behind the manuscript of a book called *A Search in Secret Tibet*. (Later, Masson came to doubt that Brunton had ever been in Tibet, since he would certainly have mentioned it in one of his dozen books.)

But the real problem, it seemed, was the impending World War III, which he knew, by revelation, was to be expected sometime around 1963, give or take a year or two. (In his prediction of imminent disaster, Brunton seems to have been like all the other messiahs, including Jesus of Nazareth: it is as if the disaster scenario is essential to generating a sense of urgency and togetherness.) Brunton's disciples were advised to sell all they had and move to South America to escape the coming nuclear holocaust, and most of them did this, including Jack and Bernard Masson. Brunton promised that he would join them there, but never did.

Jeffrey Masson's disillusion came in 1961 when he went to Harvard to study Sanskrit and Indian history under scholars of world renown. It soon became apparent that Brunton's professed knowledge was a fake, and that what Masson had learned from him was a mass of errors. "The dates were wrong, the names were wrong, even the language was wrong. . . . You could not put P.B.'s books by those by Renou or Lamotte and not see the enormous gulf. . . . As a writer about Indian texts, [P.B.] was simply a charlatan." When Masson pressed Brunton about his Ph.D., Brunton claimed it was from Roosevelt University in Chicago, but became progressively vague about the details. When Masson telephoned Roosevelt University, there was no record of Brunton's degree.

Finally, Masson caught Brunton in actual fakery. At a crowded dinner table, Brunton asked Masson if he would believe in his (P.B's) genuineness if he could cause the table to rise into the air. Masson said he would. Brunton then told them all to close their eyes and rest their hands on the tabletop. Masson peeked, and saw Brunton place his own hands under the table and try to lift it. "It is beginning to move. Can you feel it?" Everyone chorused yes, except Masson, who said: "I'm not surprised, since your hands are underneath it and pushing it." Everyone was deeply embarrassed, and this was the last time Jeffrey Masson saw Brunton.

Brunton's last book, *The Spiritual Crisis of Man* (1952) was ridiculed by reviewers and sold few copies. And when World War III failed to materialize in 1963, hordes of disciples dropped away. Brunton moved to Vevey, in Switzerland, and took a tiny apartment, where he spent his last days, dying in 1981. The pretensions had vanished, and he seemed glad that the Massons treated him simply as a friend, not a guru.

In 1965, Jack Masson wrote a long letter to his brother Bernard that began "Wake up Bernard!" and listed Brunton's faults and failings. "Actually, he ruined your life and he almost ruined mine." He had told Jack Masson that he was in a "lucky cycle," and Masson had invested $25,000 in cotton which he had quickly lost. Brunton had insisted that Masson should buy him a certain house, because it was "ideally suited" to him; after Masson had paid a deposit, Brunton changed his mind. Masson sold a valuable plot of land in Los Angeles (which he had been renting to Standard Oil) and many other pieces of real estate, to go to South America to avoid World War III; financially this was a disaster that almost ruined him. After that, Brunton failed to keep his promise to go to South America. Above all, he had promised Masson spiritual enlightenment, which had failed to arrive.

By the end of *My Father's Guru*, the conclusion seems inescapable. Brunton was not an avatar or a mystic, says Masson, but a journalist with a strong romantic streak. He was fascinated by yogis and spiritual powers, but he remained a dilettante. Brunton maintained a veil of mystery to disguise the simple truth about himself, which was not particularly discreditable: that he had attended the Central Foundation School in London, then the McKinley-Roosevelt College in Chicago (not a university); that he became fascinated by psychical research and developed powers of mediumship; and that his "master" was Allan Bennett, a friend of Aleister Crowley who left England to become a monk in Ceylon.

Brunton genuinely felt he had something to teach—and after all, it was the disciples who sought him out—and he did his best, like any vicar or priest, to be a spiritual adviser. But, like many vicars and priests, his talents in this sphere were limited. He was obviously relieved, at the end of his life, to drop his pretensions and behave normally.

One friend of Brunton's later years assured me that Masson's account is flagrantly unfair, that Brunton was a true mystic, and that this is apparent to anyone who reads his journals.

What of the disciples? It cannot be claimed that they were particularly stupid or gullible. They felt, like most intelligent people, a desire to evolve as human beings, and in spite of disappointments, many did just that. There can be no doubt that the drama of messiah and discipleship occurred on a higher level than in the case of Jim Jones or David Koresh. Yet in its essentials, it remains the same: a matter of genuine aspiration mixed with self-deception. It is this matter of self-deception that deserves closer analysis.

In an essay called "The Will to Believe," William James attacks the purely scientific viewpoint, which argues that skepticism is always preferable to unproven belief. He is questioning the view of T.H. Huxley, who said that what makes people decent and honest is "not pretending to believe what they have no reason to believe, because it may be to their advantage." He is also questioning the view of the mathematician W.K. Clifford wrote that "belief is desecrated when given to unproved and unquestioned statements for the solace and private pleasure of the believer."

James argues that in matters where the intellect cannot make up its mind one way or the other—for example, whether the world was created by a benevolent God, or a malignant Devil, or that it is simply meaningless—it is better to believe what we want to believe. It is stupid, says James, to "put a stopper on our hearts, instincts and courage, and wait till doomsday" until we have enough evidence to believe make up our minds.

The simple truth, says James, is that human beings need to believe because belief leads to action, and human beings are born with a need to act. Elsewhere, he sketches a picture of what happens when human beings lack all incentive to act. He describes how the mind seems to "lose its focusing power, and be unable to rally its attention. . . . At such times we sit blankly staring and do nothing."

He goes on to say that in asylums, this state of apathy is called abulia. James knew all about it because he had experienced it himself in his youth. In a period of depression about his future prospects, he began to feel such a sense of frustration and ineffectuality that the sudden memory of a patient he had seen in a mental home—a man with a greenish complexion who stared blankly in front of him—was enough to make him feel "There but for the grace of God go I," and to bring him to the verge of a nervous breakdown.

James finally emerged from this when he suddenly decided to work on the assumption that human beings really possess free will: that when faced with a problem, they decide how much effort they will exert to solve it, and whether they will attack it with determination, or simply give up. It was this belief in the power of the mind that gradually rescued James from a sense of meaninglessness.

As soon as we look at the consequences of this "meaningless" state—staring blankly in front of us and feeling that nothing is worth the effort—we can see why we need belief so urgently. Without purpose human beings feel only half alive.

C.G. Jung even went so far as to write: "About a third of my patients are suffering from no clinically definable neurosis, but from the senselessness and emptiness of their lives." He further wrote: "Among all my patients in the second half of life . . . there has not been one whose problem in the last resort was not about finding a religious outlook."

That is to say, religion is basically purpose-hunger, and the reason that middle-aged people experience it more than young people is that so many of them are successful in life (in the financial sense) and still realize that they lack purpose and belief.

Huxley and Clifford would say it is better to have no belief at all than to believe in nonsense. But the experience of Madame Blavatsky's friend Colonel Olcott (described below) seems to contradict this. He tried inducing belief in his healing powers in other people without believing in them himself; then found, to his amazement, that he was developing healing powers. It makes no difference whether we believe that these healing powers were due to auto-suggestion; the fact remains that they worked, and that, by whatever means, Olcott really cured people.

The amazing career of Helena Petrovna Blavatsky is an instructive example of what William James meant about the power of belief.

Madame Blavatsky (born Helen Hahn in 1831) left Russia to escape an elderly husband, and spent twenty years wandering around the world. She was forty-two when she landed in America, and found everyone talking about the new craze called Spiritualism, in which spirits of the dead were contacted through mediums. Madame Blavatsky had always had the power to make strange things happen: when she was around, flowers fell out of the air and rapping noises resounded.

Colonel Olcott, a middle-aged lawyer, was interested in spiritualist phenomena and wrote about them in a newspaper. He and Madame Blavatsky met at a seance in 1874 and immediately took to each other. She told him that she had met certain "spiritual Mahatmas" in Tibet, mysterious god-like beings who lived in the Himalayas, and who did their best to guide the evolution of humanity. They called themselves the Brotherhood of the Great White Lodge.

Notes addressed to the Colonel often fell out of the air, which Madame assured him, were from the Mahatmas; they usually contained instructions about Madame Blavatsky's needs. The Mahatmas even suggested that he should desert his wife (with whom he was on bad terms) and move in with Madame Blavatsky, which he was glad to do. Their relationship was totally non-sexual.

As the fashion for spiritualism began to fade, HPB (as she was known to her admirers) and the Colonel decided to found a society for the study of ancient wisdom; they called it the Theosophical Society, and launched it in September 1875. Even before that—in the summer of that same year—she had handed the Colonel a few pages that she had written at the "order" of the Brotherhood of the Great White Lodge. It was the beginning of a book entitled *Isis Unveiled*, which would achieved unexpected success when published two years later.

Isis Unveiled was an attempt to create a scripture for the Theosophical Society; HPB claimed she wrote it under spirit-dictation. It begins by attacking both modern science and Christianity—one for its narrow materialism, the other for its narrow dogmatism.

There is, she declared, a far more ancient wisdom, a legacy of the sunken continent of Atlantis. What followed was a remarkable digest of world religions and philosophies. At the very least, *Isis Unveiled* is an amazing compendium of mysticism, Eastern religion, and occult lore.

But although the Theosophical Society and *Isis Unveiled* achieved immediate success, the fickle American public soon turned its attention elsewhere, whereupon Madame Blavatsky and Colonel Olcott decided to move to India, where their success was immediate and widespread. The Indians were flattered that a European should think their culture preferable to that of the West. Within five years, the Theosophical Society had branches all over India and Ceylon.

Then disaster struck. A discontented housekeeper denounced HPB to a Christian newspaper as a fraud, claiming, for example, that she had made a model of the chief Mahatma, Koot Hoomi, and walked around the house with it on her shoulders on moonlit nights. An investigation by the Society for Psychical Research was highly skeptical of HPB's claims. In March 1885, accused of forgery and fraud and threatened with legal proceedings, Madame Blavatsky was forced to flee back to Europe.

All was not lost. Two years earlier, a disciple named A.P. Sinnett had written a simplified version of Theosophical doctrines in a book called *Esoteric Buddhism*, and this became an unexpected best-seller. It declared on the first page that the author had obtained his information from "secret Masters" from Tibet. Since Sinnett was the editor of India's most influential newspaper *The Pioneer*, he could not be lightly dismissed as a crank.

Sinnett explained how the book had come to be written. Sinnett had apparently handed Madame Blavatksy letters addressed to Koot Hoomi, and lengthy answers had appeared on his desk. The result was a brief and clear compilation about Atlantis and Lemuria, the early history of the earth, reincarnation, *kama loca* (the realm of spirits) and the secret teachings of the Buddha; his book went through numerous editions.

So when Madame Blavatsky returned to London, she found hordes of faithful disciples who were uninfluenced by the newspaper scandals. Unfortunately, she was dying of Bright's disease. She presided over her adoring disciples for six more years, and died at the age of fifty-nine, in 1891. Annie Besant, a famous socialist and feminist, took over the leadership, and the Theosophical Society has continued to flourish to this day.

The question of how far HPB was a fraud must be left open; there are too many independent accounts of her "occult powers" to doubt that she was a genuine medium. One disciple, Charles Johnston, watched her tapping her fingertips on the table, then saw her raise the hand well above the table, while the tapping noises continued. Seeing his astonishment, she sent "astral taps" onto the back of his hand, which he could both feel and hear. He said it felt like tiny electric shocks.

Colonel Olcott and others claimed to have seen Koot Hoomi when Madame Blavatsky could not have been playing tricks. The logical conclusion is that she was part genuine, part fraud. But unlike most rogue messiahs, she never became paranoid, and always retained her sense of humor. After rebuking a female follower who had two lovers, telling them that absolute chastity was necessary to achieve initiation, she ended: "I cannot allow you more than one."

This story was told by W.B. Yeats, who was twenty-nine when Madame Blavatsky came to London, and who lost no time in visiting her. He found her fascinating—"a sort of female Dr. Johnson"—and saw immediately that it was absurd to ask whether she was genuine or a fraud. She told one follower that the earth was shaped like a dumb-bell, with another globe stuck on at the north pole, and the follower repeated this to Yeats, apparently unaware that Madame Blavatsky was pulling his leg.

What emerges very clearly from Yeats's account is that HPB was so much more intelligent and so much more vital than most of her disciples that the question of telling them the exact truth did not arise; most of them would probably not have understood if she had tried.

Yeats is of central importance in this study of messiahs and disciples, for he enables us to understand the basic motivation of the disciple. Yeats was a typical romantic, who, like Wordsworth, felt that the "world was too much with us," and loathed with a raging passion the boredom and vulgarity of everyday reality. He was in total agreement with the child in Blake's poem, who asks:

Father, O Father! what do we here
In this Land of unbelief and fear?
The Land of Dreams is better far,
Above the light of the Morning Star.

Yeats's early poetry is a determined attempt to turn his back on this dreary everyday world and to inhabit the land of dreams. His father, a painter, was a skeptic and an atheist, but Yeats found his rationalist faith unsatisfying. He longed for evidence of "other realities," and was strongly influenced by the world of the Pre-Raphaelites, with its visions of pale, beautiful women, and medieval knights.

As a child Yeats had been fascinated by stories of fairies and the supernatural, and this interest was renewed in his teens by a psychic female cousin, who claimed that she often saw people who were "not of this world." One evening, as they walked by a river, they saw a light moving over the water at a place where there were dangerous currents. Yeats's cousin said she saw a man walking in the water, although Yeats could see nothing. Then they noticed a similar light moving up the slope of the mountain Knocknarea, and when it reached the top in five minutes—Yeats timed it—he knew that no human being could climb it in that time.

After that, Yeats began frequenting "fairy hills" and questioning old women about them. Yet his interest in fairies remained in the realm of wishful thinking; he found it impossible to believe in their actual existence.

In London, he made a habit of wandering around with Shelley's *Prometheus Unbound* in his pocket, repeating poetry under his breath. "In London I saw nothing good and constantly remembered that Ruskin had said to some friend of my father's, 'As I go to my work at the British Museum I see the faces of the people become daily more corrupt.'"

This is what Yeats wanted to believe, that this civilization of bricks and concrete is somehow a lie, and that the truth lies in some other reality. He wrote poems about his longings—for "pearl-pale high-born ladies" with "passion-dimmed eyes and long, heavy hair"—and admitted that he indulged in auto-eroticism until he looked pale and exhausted. He liked to write about people who found their way to fairyland, or who set out on a long journey looking for some ultimate beauty:

> *What the world's million lips are*
> *searching for*
> *Must be substantial somewhere. . . .*

What he was trying to do, of course, was to focus an intellectual vision, the vision that he found in the work of great poets, but the physical world kept distracting him.

In his autobiography, Yeats speaks of his fascination with a passage in Shelley's lyrical drama *Hellas*, which Shelley wrote in 1821 to express his sympathy with the Greeks in their War of Independence against Turkey. Yeats writes of his obsession with "Shelley's dream of a young man, his hair blanched with sorrow, studying philosophy in some lonely tower, or of his old man, master of all human knowledge, hidden from sight in some shell-strewn cavern on the Mediterranean shore."

In *Hellas*, the Turkish Sultan Mahmud II expresses his desire to speak with this old Jew, who is called Ahasuerus, and is believed to be the Wandering Jew of legend. His adviser Hassan explains how those who would speak with him must "sail alone at sunset" to the island of Erebinthus, and cry aloud "Ahasuerus!" If his request is granted, a meteor will arise and light him "through the soft twilight to the Bosphorus."

> *Thence, at the hour and place and*
> *circumstance*
> *Fit for the matter of their conference,*
> *The Jew appears. Few dare, and few*
> *who dare*
> *Win the desired communion . . .*

Yeats admits that he had been attracted to Theosophy "because they had affirmed the real existence of the Jew, or of his like, and . . . I saw nothing against his reality." In other words, Madame Blavatsky offered Yeats the hope that the substance of his dreams was real.

Before leaving Dublin for London, Yeats had attended a seance in which he found himself making spontaneous movements that he would not control; one was so violent that it broke the table. Yet he found himself suspecting the impulse was simply an unknown part of his own mind. What he saw in Madame Blavatsky's house convinced him that the spirits were real.

On his first visit, a cuckoo in a non-functional cuckoo clock came out and hooted at him. When he told Madame Blavatsky, she said casually: "It often hoots at strangers." On another occasion, the room filled with a strong smell of incense, although someone who came into the room could smell nothing. One evening, Yeats saw a red light shining on a picture of one of the Tibetan Masters in a dimly lit room; as Yeats approached, the light faded and vanished. When he told Madame Blavatsky what had happened she said: "I was afraid it was mediumship, but it was only clairvoyance," and added: "If it had been mediumship, it would have stayed on in spite of you. Beware of mediumship; it is a kind of madness; I know, for I have been through it."

Significantly, Yeats was finally thrown out of the Theosophical Society because he found their teachings too abstract; what he craved was the certainty that these "other worlds" of Theosophy were real. This led him to begin a series of unsuccessful experiments to try to raise the ghost of a flower, and induce dreams with a pure form of indigo. The Theosophists felt that he was trying to drag Theosophy down to the material level, failing to see that what he was really doing was trying to lift everyday reality up to the immaterial level; they asked him to leave.

After this, Yeats made the acquaintance of a student of Kaballah named MacGregor Mathers who, together with a student of occultism named Glenway Wescott, created a society called the Golden Dawn, devoted to the practice of magic.

The founders claimed that the society had originated in the discovery of a cipher manuscript in a secondhand bookstall, and that the decipherment of this manuscript had led to a correspondence with a Fraulein Sprengel, a member of a German magical order, who gave permission for them to found an English branch. Fraulein Sprengel was almost certainly an invention of Mathers and Wescott, and it was later proved that her letters were forged.

Yet there was a sense in which Golden Dawn magic seemed to work. Mathers told the actress Florence Farr to place a symbol written on cardboard against her forehead and close her eyes; when she did so, she saw a cliff top above the sea. Mathers had shown her a water symbol from the Kaballah.

Yeats was given a symbol written on cardboard, and saw a black Titan pushing himself up from ancient ruins; Mathers had given him a symbol of salamanders, or fire spirits. Mathers explained that it was not necessary to use a cardboard symbol; it would have been sufficient if he had imagined it. And he proved his point when walking in a field of sheep with Florence Farr; after Yeats told her that he was going to imagine that he was a ram, all the sheep ran after him. This view of symbols and the unconscious would later be developed in the psychology of Jung.

So for Yeats, Madame Blavatsky and Mathers served the essential function of messiahs; they enabled the poet, who had so far assumed that his imaginings were a form of escapism, to feel that there was a "way of knowledge" that could actually achieve results.

In 1897, Yeats went to stay with his friend Lady Gregory at Coole Park in Galway, Ireland, and accompanied her on expeditions to collect fairy stories from the local peasantry. For the first time, Yeats began to take seriously the notion that fairies—or some kind of "nature spirits"—might actually exist; the stories told by country people sounded too factual to be lies or self-deception. This led him once more to an interest in Spiritualism, and he began to attend seances. Yet by this time, the romanticism of his youth—he was now thirty-two—began to give way to realism; he no longer found it necessary to believe in Shelley's old Jew. His poetry gradually ceased to be romantic and mystical, and took on a new down-to-earth tone.

The need for self-dramatization—as a young poet with his hair blanched with sorrow—now lay behind him, along with the need to believe in fairies who carry children off to the land of heart's desire. But we can see clearly that when this need had existed, it was not an insane delusion, but a strategy for dealing with problems that he found exhausting and oppressive: a method of attacking the world.

All human beings have the same need to develop and mature. In order to do this, they require certain experiences, as children require certain vitamins if they are to grow up healthy. We all want to do interesting things, to meet interesting people, to encounter interesting challenges. We all want to act, to do, rather than merely be acted upon. People who are too timid, too unsure of themselves, remain undeveloped and frustrated. And, as William James points out, in order to act we must have a belief to act upon. A man who lacked all belief would be like a becalmed ship, or like James' patient who suffered from abulia.

To understand the messiah phenomenon, we must understand that "believers," whether they are the followers of the Rev. Jim Jones, or Paul Brunton, or Madame Blavatsky, should not be seen simply as dupes, but as hungry people who are looking for "food." They want to believe because they want to act, and they want to act because they want to evolve. The alternative is misery and stagnation.

What, admittedly, is far more puzzling is the compulsion that drives the messiahs themselves to behave in a way that seems to guarantee their own destruction. . . .

FOUR

THE MESSIAH AS KILLER

The philosopher Auguste Comte never actually became a "messiah." In fact, as a thinker who regarded himself as a strict rationalist, the idea would have horrified him. In spite of which, he came so close to it that his story is one of the great "might-have-beens" of history.

In the mid 1820s, Comte began the most heroic attempt ever made to solve all the problems of humanity. He called this magnificent intellectual edifice his "positive philosophy," but these words convey only a dim idea of its sheer grandeur.

Comte's burning conviction was that the basic problem of humanity is false belief—superstition. Get rid of this, he said, and rely instead on science and common sense, and earth would turn into heaven.

The troubles of humanity, Comte contended, started with religion. Man was afraid of natural forces, like thunder and lightning, so he turned them into gods and worshipped them. This, he admits, was not entirely a bad thing, for it gave us a set of unified beliefs, and transformed man from a self-centered animal into a social being. Comte calls this the theological stage of development.

It is after that that things go into serious decline. Man begins to use his reason to question authority, and society degenerates into a kind of free-for-all, with everybody grabbing what they can. This, says Comte, has destroyed all the great civilizations of the past. But although our civilization has arrived at this dangerous stage (which he calls the metaphysical stage), we are the first to have an excellent chance of survival. We have developed science, and it has given us new certainties that cannot be overthrown by reason; on the contrary, reason supports them. There will be no more illusions or superstitions, only the calm, cool light of knowledge. As man applies this knowledge to society itself, we shall slowly create a heaven on earth, without poverty, without war, without misery.

Comte called this "the positive stage." The book in which he expressed these ideas, the *Course of Positive Philosophy* (written between 1830 and 1842), had an immense influence, and many came to regard Comte as the greatest philosopher of his time.

Bearing in mind the disasters set in motion by Shoko Asahara, Jim Jones and David Koresh, we may well feel that an updated version of Comte's philosophy is exactly what is needed to guide humanity through the next millennium. It would have to begin from the recognition that although the world's major religions are great humanitarian ideals, they are not divinely inspired, and that the world's sacred books are the products of the mind of man, not of God. Then humanity would be ready to embark on the age of positive philosophy, and religious, as well as political, messiahs would become a memory of the distant past.

Unfortunately, the problem is more complicated than it seems. To begin with, Comte himself is hardly an advertisement for his religion of reason. A disastrous marriage led him to a mental breakdown and a period in an insane asylum. After separating from his wife, Comte fell in love with a young married woman whose husband had deserted her; when she refused to yield to his entreaties, he tried emotional blackmail, which undoubtedly contributed to the illness that killed her. Comte then attempted suicide by throwing himself in the river. After her death he maintained a kind of religious devotion to her image, not unlike Dante's idealization of Beatrice.

The crisis made him aware that man has deep emotional needs that cannot be satisfied by the worship of mere reason, or even of art. Man has a craving to open his soul to the universe, to be flooded by a feeling of awe and wonder, to lose his individuality in the contemplation of something greater than himself.

To his credit, Comte had the courage to confront this problem. In his last great work, *A System of Positive Politics* (written between 1851 and 1854), he boldly invents a new religion, complete with holy days, saints, prayers and rituals. The object of devotion of this new religion will be humanity itself, which he calls the "Great Being." Comte does not deny God, but he feels that God is an unproven hypothesis, and therefore irrelevant to his religion of humanity. Man must learn to recognize that the highest good he knows is the Brotherhood of Man. When man grasps that the old religion is only a superstition, he will recognize that he himself is capable of becoming a kind of god, and that every time he serves his fellow man, he becomes a little more godlike.

Comte's "Church of Humanity" is based on a thirteen month calendar, in which each month is named after some great man: Moses, Homer, Aristotle, Archimedes, Caesar, St. Paul, Charlemagne, Dante, Gutenberg, Shakespeare, Descartes, Frederick the Great and Bichat (the French anatomist). As this list shows, he had no animus towards religious figures; every day of the year is a feast day for some "saint" of humanity, including Buddha, Mahomet and St. Augustine.

Astonishingly, Comte's new religion gained many followers, and there were still remnants of his Church of Humanity around as late as 1960. It is an amusing thought that, if he had not died at the age of fifty-nine—a mere three years after he published his scheme for the Church of Humanity—he himself would have been venerated as a kind of messiah, and probably forced to accustom himself to the mantle of a prophet.

If his Church had run true to form, he would undoubtedly have found himself forced to control hordes of devoted followers, and to distinguish between the competing claims of jealous disciples. In other words, he would have learned that the real problem of humanity is not superstition, but a strange mixture of the will to power and the will to believe, which seems to make us incapable of distinguishing truth from falsehood.

Comte was probably correct: the science of sociology (a word he invented) may one day enable us to understand the chemical composition of fanaticism, perhaps even to defuse it. But if so, it will have to confront the problem that is the subject of this book: what makes human beings such easy prey for messiahs?

Why tell Comte's story here? Because before going on, it is necessary to underline the point that the study of messiahs is not a branch of psychopathology. They cannot be understood as if they were madmen who think they are Napoleon or Julius Caesar. They are as logical as you or I or Auguste Comte (if that can be called logical).

That is to say, most of them are normal human beings whose aim is to satisfy the same desires that the rest of us have, particularly the craving for self-esteem. But for some odd reason, this desire tends to explode out of control, like the cells in a cancer. It is at this stage that they become capable of violence, even of murder.

What follows is a typical case of a messiah whose approach was as logical as Auguste Comte's.

Jeffrey Don Lundgren, the son of Mormon parents, was born on May 3, 1950, in Independence, Missouri. He claims to have had a difficult childhood, with a father who treated him harshly and a mother who was more concerned with keeping her home spotless than giving affection to her children. In 1970, he married Alice Keehler, whom he met at Central Missouri State University; Alice was pregnant when they married.

Lundgren found that providing for a family was less easy than he expected, and after six months, he joined the navy, leaving his wife at home. His superiors noted that he would at first seem to be hard-working and efficient, then would lose interest in the tasks assigned to him.

By the time he left the navy two years later, two sons had been born, and he still felt no better equipped to support a family. He returned to the university, but left without a degree because, it was rumored, of irregularities in funds entrusted to his charge. In the many jobs he held over the next five years, he showed the same tendency to impress at first with his vigor and efficiency, then to allow himself to run out of steam and drift. He was fired from most of his jobs. He was also arrested for passing bad checks. By the time his wife had given birth to two more children, he was physically mistreating her, and having affairs with other women.

In 1980, two television sets and some other electrical equipment vanished from the Missouri hospital where Lundgren was working as a maintenance man. They were found in Lundgren's home, and he explained that he had taken them home to work on them. The hospital disbelieved him, but agreed not to press charges; instead, he was asked to resign.

Both Lundgren and his wife had been closely involved with a breakaway sect of the Mormon church, called the Reorganized Church of Latter Day Saints (which, in fact, regarded itself as the original Church). But although Lundgren had done his best to draw "gentiles" (non-Mormons) into the Church, he had failed to progress in the hierarchy; this, like his repeated failures to find regular employment, rankled him. By now, he was getting desperate.

Then, in 1981, he told Alice that he had realized that the Church was a political organization, and that he had finally figured out how to manipulate it; he predicted that within six months he would be invited to join the Melchizadek Priesthood.

The steps he took to fulfill this prediction are not clear, but presumably they entailed gaining the approval of the local church elders by displaying enthusiasm and proficiency in the Mormon scriptures. Within less than six months he had become a Melchizadek Priest.

Lundgren's biographers seem to believe it was at this point that he also discovered a talent for scriptural interpretation, and the fact that this brought him the kind of admiration that he craved. He began to run a small study group in which he taught his own interpretation of the Book of Mormon, teachings that differed fundamentally from those of the Reorganized Church. Lundgren also discovered that religion can be made to pay. A local businessman began to support him with several hundred dollars a month, and he seems to have received donations from other members of his group. By the mid-1980s, Lundgren had acquired enough followers to feel that it was time to start his own breakaway sect in some distant place. He chose Kirtland, Ohio, because of a Mormon text that declared: "Come to Ohio, for there ye shall receive power."

The Mormon religion was founded by Joseph Smith, the son of a farmer, who was born in Vermont in 1805. According to Smith, an angel called Moroni appeared to him on the night of September 21, 1823, and told him where he might find a set of gold plates, bearing the history of the former inhabitants of America; they were buried in a hill about four miles from Palmyra, New York.

Smith finally uncovered the plates in 1827. On leisure time provided by fifty dollars contributed by his first disciple, a farmer called Martin Harris, Smith translated them with the aid of a pair of silver spectacles called "Urim and Thummim," and published The Book of Mormon in 1830. (The plates were returned to the angel Moroni, so no one but Smith ever saw them, although Smith copied some of them on a piece of paper and allowed Harris to show it to a New York professor named Anthon, who pronounced the characters genuine.)

Part of The Book of Mormon, the Book of Lehi, was thrown on the fire by the wife of the Prophet's disciple Martin Harris, who declared it the work of the devil.

The Book of Mormon, written in "reformed Egyptian," professes to give the history of America from the time of its settlement by the people of Jared, who came from the Tower of Babel, more than two thousand years before Christ; they eventually destroyed themselves through warfare.

About 600 B.C., a number of Israelites, fleeing from Jerusalem, built a boat and sailed to Chile. These included four brothers. From one of the brothers, who was fair, descended a white race, the Nephites; from the other three, who were dark (because they were rebellious and ungodly) descended the Indians, or Lamanites.

After his death on the cross, Jesus Christ appeared in America and preached the gospel. In A.D. 385, when the Nephites were almost wiped out by the Lamanites near the Hill Cumorah, their prophet Mormon wrote their history, which was buried in the hill.

From its publication, The Book of Mormon was received with derision and skepticism, its opponents insisting that it began as a romance written by a clerical gentleman called the Rev. Solomon Spalding. No one had any doubt that Smith was a confidence trickster who had invented the whole story. In his book *A Gathering of Saints*, Robert Lindsey writes: "In a caustically anti-Mormon book published in 1834, *Mormonism Unveiled*, E.D. Howe, an investigative journalist of the day, published a collection of affidavits from friends and neighbors of Smith who described him as a lackadaisical and lying religious con man who claimed supernatural powers that enabled him to find buried treasures in ancient Indian burial mounds with stones and divining rods." Lindsey describes how, when a forged letter from Joseph Smith appeared in 1983, describing digging for money, it was sold to a top Mormon official, who suppressed it and housed it in a secret vault.

As long ago as the mid-1920s, the official historian of the Mormon Church, Brigham H. Roberts, appealed to church leaders to "help him resolve problems" about The Book of Mormon. One problem was that it contained so many similarities to a book called *A View of the Hebrews*, written in 1823 by the Rev. Ethan Smith. Another problem was that The Book of Mormon refers to the ancient Hebrews using steel, and to domestic animals that were unknown in remote times. Referring to many similar examples of discrepancies, Roberts concluded that, "The evidence, I sorrowfully submit, points to Joseph Smith as their creator."

Ignoring the rising skepticism, Smith himself continued to receive revelations from God, which were relayed to his small band of disciples. The indignation created by the book aroused curiosity, and Smith soon began to accumulate dozens of followers. But the general hostility against the Church of Latter Day Saints, and another revelation from God finally led him to decide to move elsewhere.

It was in Kirtland, Ohio, that Smith's Mormon followers first established themselves, and built a temple that cost $70,000 from funds mostly contributed by well-to-do members. The citizens of Kirtland were as hostile as the New Yorkers towards a group they perceived as hopelessly deluded cranks. The Saints established their own bank and printed their own currency, but when both collapsed, they were forced to move on.

Five of the twelve "apostles" appointed by Smith denounced him for ruining their lives and left. Smith went on to found a new headquarters in Nauvoo, Illinois. He seems to have taken a number of wives from among his flock; he eventually had twenty seven—the full count may be as many as forty eight—but when he announced, in 1843, that he had received a divine message approving polygamy, he and his brother Hyrum were arrested by the state governor. That night—June 27, 1844—a mob stormed Carthage jail and shot Smith and Hyrum dead.

His successor, Brigham Young, led the Mormons to Utah, where they founded Salt Lake City three years after Smith's death.

With incredible energy they irrigated the desert and arranged the transportation of thousands of converts from Europe. When Young announced the doctrine of polygamy in 1852, he was deprived of the governorship of the territory. Nevertheless, when he died in 1877, he left behind him seventeen wives and fifty-six children. It was 1890 before the Church disowned the doctrine of plural marriage, although in practice it continued to be permitted.

It was in August 1984 that the new self-proclaimed Mormon prophet, Jeffrey Lundgren, moved with his family to Kirtland, and established himself as one of the guides to the Temple that had been built by Smith. The disciples had provided enough money for the move, and Lundgren began to supplement his income by helping himself to "contributions" to the Temple provided by visitors, and profits from the bookstore. Church authorities would later estimate that he had pocketed about $21,000.

One by one, followers began to move to Kirtland to join the new prophet. Lundgren soon announced that he had, through revelation, located a spot where the plates of The Book of Mormon were buried, and followed this up with a story about meeting an angel in the Temple. His powers as an interpreter of The Book of Mormon seemed to increase, and so did his study group.

One of the new disciples, an overweight young woman called Sharon Bluntschly, was electrified one night when Alice Lundgren confided to her that her husband was a prophet who had actually met Joseph Smith (who was alive and well) and who had had a vision of himself as Christ on Calvary. At that moment, Lundgren walked in, seemed to sense that something was going on, then rebuked his wife sternly for telling secrets, all of which convinced Sharon that it must be true. She raised no objection when Lundgren told her that her paycheck—she was a supermarket clerk—should be turned over to him.

Lundgren soon developed doctrines about the Apocalypse. When this comes about, Christ would return to earth—to Kirtland—and after an earthquake, the Temple would be raised to the top of a mountain. Until that time, Lundgren and his small band of the elect must defend the Temple from the forces of evil. According to him, these included all existing churches. One follower who had been giving Lundgren his paycheck left the group, feeling that Lundgren was becoming paranoid.

From September 1986, Lundgren began purchasing firearms (rifles, semi-automatic weapons, and handguns) to defend the Temple against assault. He taught that anyone who was not a member of their small group was an enemy, and that shooting and killing might become necessary.

In April 1987, two more disciples moved from Independence to Kirtland. These were Dennis and Cheryl Avery, and their three daughters: Trina, thirteen; Rebecca, eleven; and Karen, five. Lundgren was not entirely happy about the move. To begin with, he felt that Cheryl Avery dominated her husband, and Lundgren, like most prophets, taught that woman was intended to be subservient to man.

Besides, her husband, seven years her senior, seemed to entertain some doubts about Lundgren's vocation, and would often ask awkward questions in Bible class. The Lundgrens also thought that the two eldest Avery daughters were rebellious and rude. The family had only one thing to recommend them: $10,000 left over from the sale of their house in Independence. It took Lundgren just three months to persuade them to hand this over to him, promising that he would pay their rent. In fact, he seldom did so. The Avery's finally had to flee under cover of darkness to avoid paying the backlog of rent.

By October 1987, the officials of the Church had decided to remove Lundgren from the guide service. They had noticed the sharp fall in donations and bookstore profits since Lundgren had been in charge, and had reached the logical conclusion. What they heard about his teachings sounded thoroughly heretical.

The dismissal meant that Lundgren would have to vacate his house, which was provided by the Church. He rented a nearby farmhouse, and told his followers, now numbering a dozen or so, that they could also move in, so that they could all be part of a family. In effect, this meant Lundgren could become a kind of dictator. He alone was allowed to use the telephone and collect mail from the mailbox.

The arrangement also had the advantage of swelling his income, since the followers had to hand him their paychecks. According to his wife, his sexual demands were also becoming more peculiar, and included eating excrement and smearing it on the body of his sexual partner. One of the followers found a large dildo and a glossy homosexual magazine in the prophet's truck.

Much of their time was spent in attending Bible classes, and even more of it in military training. Lundgren conformed to the basic tradition of messianism in announcing that the end of the world was imminent. He explained that on April 30, 1988, they would have to take over the Temple by force, and that when this happened, there would be a great earthquake in which the unbelievers would be destroyed. By now, the Avery family was counted among the infidels, for they had begun to pester Lundgren about his failure to keep his promise of paying their rent.

As April 30 approached, the police began to take an interest in Lundgren and his followers. One dissident member had left the group, alarmed at Lundgren's increasingly violent fantasies, and informed the police about the projected take-over of the Temple. Lundgren thereupon changed his mind, and told his followers that the take-over had been postponed because God was displeased with the amount of sin in the group. When one girl decided to defect, Lundgren and his wife took her to the barn and lectured and screamed at her for hours. She walked out nevertheless.

In October 1988, a violent thunderstorm was followed by a double rainbow. Lundgren announced that this was the beginning of the end. The thunderstorm was the breaking of the first of the Seven Seals in Revelation; the breaking of the Second Seal would signal the killing of ten followers who had shown themselves unworthy. At the top of this list was the Avery family.

From this point on, Lundgren began bringing a Colt .45 to his Bible classes. By February 1989, he was actively planning the murder of the Averys. After that, he announced, the faithful would leave town and venture into the "wilderness." He ordered his group to begin digging a pit in the barn to serve as a grave.

On April 17, the Averys were brought to the farm, believing that they were about to accompany the rest of the group on a camping holiday. They were given dinner, after which Alice Lundgren and her three younger children departed in the truck, leaving only the eldest, Damon, behind. Then Dennis Avery was asked by one of the followers to go to the barn to help sort out the camping equipment. There he found five men waiting for him, and one of them—it was Ronald Luff, Lundgren's second in command—placed a stun-gun to his head and pulled the trigger. It failed to work, and Avery only cried aloud in pain. The five men then threw him to the floor and bound his hands, feet and mouth with tape. After that he was thrown into the pit dug in the floor, and Jeffrey Lundgren shot him in the heart. Meanwhile, someone ran a chainsaw to drown the noise of the shots.

Cheryl Avery was the next to be invited to the barn. There, Ronald Luff tried to shoot her, but the gun jammed. He told her: "Just give up—it will be easier that way," and she sank to the ground and was tied up. Then she was lowered into the pit, and shot in the back of the head by Lundgren.

Trina, the eldest, was told that her mother wanted her in the barn. She was also tied up with tape and shot in the head. So, over the next quarter of an hour, were Becky and Karen. When all the Averys were dead, their bodies were covered with lime, held down with rocks, then buried under earth. Piles of rubbish were moved to conceal the spot.

The next day, by pure chance, two policemen came to the farm to question the Lundgrens about the plan to storm the Temple. After two hours, they left, having learned nothing. Later that day, when the police returned, the farm was abandoned. No one noticed anything unusual about the barn.

Five days later, the group set up camp on a site in the Canaan Valley, near Davis, in West Virginia. There, the prophet told his disciples, they would purify themselves and see God. In mid-May, they moved to a still more remote site.

It was there that Lundgren began to display the sexual rapacity which seems typical of rogue messiahs. For a long time he had had a hankering for an attractive disciple named Tonya Patrick, whose husband Dennis was regarded by Lundgren as a potential enemy. At the new campsite, Dennis was told that Tonya's obedience could not atone for his own rebelliousness, and that Tonya and her daughter Molly would have to move in to the Lundgren's tent; Lundgren backed up the demand by thrusting his revolver into Dennis's face and telling him that if he had any objections, he should state them immediately. Dennis decided to hold his peace.

A few nights later, while Alice slept deeply, Lundgren crept into Tonya's bed and had sex with her. She made no protest, explaining later that she was afraid for the lives of her husband and daughter. Lundgren soon grew tired of secrecy, and announced that Tonya would be his second wife. Either she could be pierced with a sword and die to atone for her sins or "pierced" with his penis and live. Alice Lundgren and Tonya's husband Dennis decided that it would be better if Tonya lived.

Soon after this, Lundgren announced to his followers that his status was now higher than that of Moroni or Jesus: he was the "god of the earth."

In July 1989, Lundgren invented a new ceremony called Intercession. The women must intercede with God for their husbands. In this ceremony, the woman had to enter Lundgren's tent, fully clothed, then do a striptease to music. Her knickers were the last item to be removed and these were then handed to Lundgren, who was seated on the bed, naked but covered with a sheet from the waist down. Lundgren then wrapped them around his penis, and Alice would masturbate him. The woman was also expected to masturbate as she danced.

When he had achieved orgasm (the shedding of his semen, he explained, was analogous to Christ's shedding of his blood) he would stand up and ask, "Are you stripped of pride, my daughter?" and the naked woman would have to go and embrace him. Then she was permitted to dress again—it had to be slowly and seductively—and put on her semen-stained knickers, which she had to wear for the rest of the day.

In the afternoon, the ceremony was repeated with another female disciple whose husband, meanwhile, had to sit in his tent and read the Bible. When his wife returned, he had to kneel before Lundgren and pledge allegiance to the new "god of the earth."

Lundgren continued to hate Tonya's husband, and when another male follower, Keith Johnson, seemed to take his side, he flew into a rage, after which he calmed down and declared that Keith's wife Kathy would now have to intercede to save her husband. Since she had also been guilty of uttering untruths, her mouth would also have to receive his "sword."

On August 25, Kathy Johnson successfully interceded for her husband. Since Alice was not present, Lundgren made her his mistress. In fact, this had been his intention ever since she had danced in front of him, then bent over and showed her vagina. Lundgren claimed that this was a vagina God had showed him in a vision, and ordered him to find. When Kathy left his tent that day, Lundgren had found the vagina of his dreams, and Kathy was a woman in love.

With this new demand upon his sexual energies, Lundgren decided to return Tonya to her husband Dennis. Lundgren was not, in fact, pleased with Tonya, because she complained about his sexual prowess.

The wet and cold winter of 1989 was Lundgren's undoing. Kathy was now pregnant; so was Sharon Bluntschly. The group was also broke. Two members, Richard Brand and Greg Winship, decided that they wanted to leave to sort out their thoughts; Lundgren threatened them with death if they dared to breathe a word about the murders.

The rest of the group now moved to the farm of Ronald Luff's brother Rick in Missouri. But Rick Luff was outraged by Lundgren's multiple marriages, and ordered them either to behave themselves or get off his property. The group left, and now began to scatter. Kathy Johnson joined the Lundgrens in San Diego, hoping that Alice would reconcile herself to a plural marriage. Alice showed herself unyieldingly hostile to the idea.

Meanwhile, the much-cuckolded Keith Johnson, still in love with his pregnant wife Kathy, decided to tell all. He contacted a friend in the Bureau of Alcohol, Tobacco, and Firearms—the downfall of David Koresh—and told the story of the murders. In fact, the Federal authorities were disinclined to take him seriously; nevertheless, they passed on the information to the Kirtland police.

They in turn, tried to contact Dennis and Cheryl Avery, and learned they were nowhere to be found. They searched the barn mentioned by Keith Johnson but could see no obvious sign of any disturbance of the floor. But on January 3, 1990, they finally discovered an eight foot square area of the dirt floor that looked as if it had been dug up. A few hours later, they discovered the body of Dennis Avery. The next day, the other four bodies were located. On January 7, 1990, Jeffrey Lundgren was arrested in a motel in San Diego; so were Alice and Damon Lundgren.

In July 1990, thirteen cult members went on trial in the Lake County Courthouse: five of the men—Lundgren and his son Damon, Ronald Luff, Richard Brand, and Daniel Kraft—were charged with murder; the other eight with conspiracy to commit murder. Lundgren was found guilty and sentenced to death; his wife and son to life imprisonment. Ronald Luff also received life. Three of the women were given from seven to twenty five years, having entered into plea bargaining. Greg Winship received from twenty years to life, Richard Brand fifteen years to life. Kathy Johnson—now the mother of Lundgren's child—received one year. As of 1991, she continued to believe that Lundgren was a god, and that he would walk out of prison to join her when he felt so inclined.

There is a sense in which the story of Jeffrey Lundgren throws more light on the psychology of rogue messiahs than any we have considered so far.

To begin with, there can be no possible doubt that he started out as a con man. We know that he passed dud checks, was fired for stealing television sets, and stole money from the Temple in Kirtland. He is one of the few messiahs who began his career as the kind of crook who could have landed in jail. Paul Brunton was a kind of religious mystic. Jim Jones began life as a fighter for human rights. Even David Koresh seems to have believed that he possessed some God-given insight into the scriptures. Lundgren became a messiah simply because he was tired of being a failure. His claim to know where the golden plates were buried, to have seen an angel in the Temple, and to have talked to Joseph Smith, are all obvious examples of the wiles of the religious con man.

Yet that view still leaves us with a major question. What possessed him to ruin everything by murdering the Avery family?

The clue lies in the ceremony he called Intercession, in which the female disciple had to do a strip tease, then remove her knickers and hand them over, while Lundgren was masturbated by his wife. Lundgren turned into reality a fantasy that most males can appreciate—being a kind of Haroun Al Raschid, whose harem is expected to satisfy his every whim.

The problem, as Freud recognized, is that society provides its members with security at the expense of frustration. Most healthy males would enjoy having a harem. Most women would probably enjoy a wider sexual experience, if it could be obtained without endangering their domestic security, in, let us say, a society in which no stigma was attached to having lovers. We all want as wide an experience as we are capable of absorbing, because it enables us to mature, to realize our potentialities as a human being. But we also recognize that to give free reign to these impulses would cause endless problems.

As a young man, Lundgren had accepted these limitations, although, like most undisciplined people, he tried to escape them with a little dishonesty. His moment of revelation seems to have come when he recognized that the Church was a political organization, and when he worked out how to manipulate it.

Experience proved him correct. Suddenly, he was faced with the exciting prospect of more freedom than he had thought possible. It simply depended on using his charisma and his talents as a teacher. When Lundgren broke with the Church—or the Church broke with him—he realized that he could live very comfortably on the contributions of disciples. Suddenly, life was pleasanter than he had ever dared to hope.

Then the Averys introduced a note of discord, particularly Dennis, who was less susceptible to Lundgren's charisma than his wife. The sensible response would have been to order them to leave. Unfortunately, Lundgren owed them $10,000. As far as he could see, the only way out of this intolerable situation was to kill them, then move further into the wilderness, where his dreams of power would not be contradicted by jarring realities.

The killing of the Averys must have been another moment of revelation. Lundgren had struck them down like an avenging angel. In doing so, he had also bound the males closer to the group. They could not betray him without betraying themselves. It was time for the next step in self-fulfillment: to realize his sexual daydreams. So he devised Intercession, which was in many ways more satisfying than crude seduction. The man who merely possesses a woman always has a sneaking suspicion that nature is manipulating him like a puppet. But Intercession combined the detachment of voyeurism with the symbolic surrender of the female. Lundgren was the master.

Like the serial killers discussed in the introduction, Lundgren was seeking the ultimate sexual experience, the orgasm that would turn him into a god. But by the time that happened, reality had caught up with him, and it was time to settle the bill.

What this curious case demonstrates is that the messiah syndrome has the power to turn an ordinary crook into a kind of madman.

Now it should be clear why I have brought together in this chapter two characters as utterly different as Comte and Lundgren. For they only *seem* to be polar opposites: one a rationalist, one an emotionalist; one a scientist, one a messiah. Yet look a little more closely and the difference begins to blur. Comte was every bit an emotionalist as was Lundgren, and in pursuing his own aims (power, sex, money), Lundgren was every bit as rational and logical as Comte. Both Comte and Lundgren tried to found a new religion. Comte had come to recognize what Lundgren—and William James—knew all along: that religion is not intended to appeal to the intellect, but to the emotions.

A few years ago, in a country where I was lecturing, my wife and I were placed in the care of a young American teacher who was a Mormon convert. He was charming and intelligent, but when he begged us to look into Mormonism, I did not tell him that I had looked already, and had been unconvinced. When, at the end of our stay, he presented us with a copy of The Book of Mormon, I had not the heart to tell him that I already had a copy, as well as half a dozen other works on Mormonism. Instead I promised to take it away and read it.

I would not have dreamed of arguing with him. Our relationship was based upon a perfectly solid foundation of mutual liking and respect. Why should I have hurt his feelings by expressing skepticism? I felt that he was better off believing in Mormonism than believing in nothing.

Reason actually plays a fairly small part in human relations. There would be no point whatever in attacking Lundgren or Koresh or Jim Jones because what they taught was contrary to reason. We are surrounded by people who, by that strict standard, ought to be in a madhouse. Our conviction of our own sanity may be no more than a prejudice. In the case of most religions, it certainly is.

So let us, where the argument of this book is concerned, merely take note that the perfectly normal insanity of most human beings is going too far when it ends in murder.

FIVE

A TASTE FOR POWER

The LeBaron story is longer and more complex than any presented so far in this book, and the insights it offers are proportionately greater. If the Lundgren case demonstrates that the messiah syndrome can turn an opportunist into a homicidal maniac, the incredible series of murders committed by Ervil LeBaron and his family demonstrate that messianism can be as contagious as measles.

Dayer LeBaron was the grandson of Benjamin Johnson, one of Joseph Smith's first disciples; Smith had converted him when he was only fifteen. Johnson was also one of the first saints to hear of God's latest "decree" about multiple marriage. After telling him about it, Smith married two of Johnson's sisters.

After Smith's murder, Johnson became one of Brigham Young's closest supporters; he took seven wives, and in 1883 was declared a Patriarch of the faith.

Understandably, young Dayer (born in 1886) worshipped his grandfather, for this man was nothing less than a walking fragment of history; he had seen and taken part in all the great events that Dayer had studied in school. It must have felt a bit like being the grandson of William the Conqueror.

And one day, when Dayer was a teenager, Benjamin Johnson changed his whole life by placing his hand on his grandson's head and declaring: "When I die, my mantle will fall upon you, as the mantle of Elijah fell upon Elisha." From then on, Dayer was possessed by the conviction that, whatever happened, his life would be quite unlike that of ordinary men.

In 1905, five years after the death of his grandfather, Dayer discovered a box containing one of the Patriarch's manuscripts. This document excited him because it referred to a "prediction by the Prophet (Joseph Smith) relating to a testimony I should bear when I had become hoary with age." Surely there could be only one testimony his grandfather could mean: that he himself, and not Brigham Young, was Joseph Smith's true heir? This, in turn, would explain Johnson's mysterious words about his "mantle" falling on his grandson. It would mean Dayer LeBaron was the true heir to Joseph Smith, the "One Mighty and Strong Prophet" of God.

Dayer was ready for this revelation. Life over the past few years had been anticlimactic; now it suddenly became more interesting. Yet he was still not sure what he was supposed to do.

There was only one clue. His grandfather had advised him that the future of Mormonism lay in Mexico; Johnson himself had once fled there when he was in trouble with the state authorities for polygamy. After much prayer and inner searching, Dayer decided that he was being called to Mexico. He and his young wife, Maud, moved there in 1911.

What followed was again anticlimactic, as they landed in the middle of the Mexican Revolution. In 1912 Dayer and his family hastened back to the United States. God still seemed reluctant to explain what he had in mind. Praying for guidance, Dayer seemed to hear an inner voice that advised him to return to Mexico. So once more he sold his home and moved, but when nothing happened yet again, his inner voice prompted him to return to Arizona. In thirteen years he moved back and forth nine times between Mexico and the U.S. He was a sorely puzzled and troubled man.

Then, in 1923, Dayer was shaken awake in the middle of the night by his grandfather, who was wearing white robes and a crown of gold. Andrew Johnson told him that his mission was about to begin, and that the first step was to take an attractive teenager named Onie Jones as his wife. Since this was now against the law in Utah, Dayer persuaded his wife Maud to divorce him, then married Onie. Maud continued to live with him as if nothing had happened. The family moved back to Colonia Juarez in Mexico, where the number of LeBaron children swelled to nineteen, but only ten would live to adulthood.

Life in Mexico was difficult, for things had changed since the Revolution, and bigamy was frowned upon. The LeBaron children encountered a great deal of mockery and hostility at school. One of them, Lucinda, had a mental breakdown that would last, on and off, for the rest of her life. Dayer decided to move his family to a new site across the mountains, which he christened Colonia LeBaron.

In 1934, Dayer's eldest son, Ben, had a psychotic episode. After a period in an insane asylum, he suddenly decided that he was the true heir of Joseph Smith, the "One Mighty and Strong Prophet," and therefore the legitimate leader of the Mormon Church. Ben's brother Alma soon became a convert. When Dayer was on his deathbed, Ben succeeded in persuading him to transfer the "descent" to himself. Unfortunately, after another period in a mental home, Ben threw himself into a river and drowned.

Another of the elder brothers, Wesley, also announced that he was the Prophet, and he began building a fleet of flying saucers to take himself and his followers to heaven. He seems to have been discouraged by his inability to make them fly, but never wholly abandoned his claim to being the true heir of Joseph Smith.

Ervil LeBaron, one of the younger brothers, had at first been convinced that Ben was the Prophet; but the common sense of his next-eldest brother, Joel, led him to change his mind. It looked as if the LeBaron family was moving back towards sanity and normality. Then came the bombshell. Brother Joel suddenly announced that the Prophet's mantle had fallen on him. According to Joel, he had climbed a mountain and talked to an angel, who had confirmed it.

Oddly, Ervil was once again convinced. He became Joel's most faithful disciple, and Joel in turn appointed Ervil to the second highest position in their newly formed Church of the Firstborn. Ervil was a tall, powerfully built man, and a good speaker. Joel could also deliver a powerful sermon, but he was personally a quiet and modest man. His brother was altogether more dominant and eloquent. When Joel moved away to found another colony in the mountains, he left Ervil behind in charge of the church at Colonia LeBaron.

It was a fatal mistake. Without his brother, Ervil began to realize how pleasant it felt to have power. He began to dress in tailored clothes and drive new cars. He also took charge of the mating of his flock, and frequently had a revelation from God that some attractive teenager had been selected to be his wife. In due course he acquired thirteen of them, some American, some Mexican. He even took away the wife of one of the church members and married her while her lawful husband was away in the United States. The youngest of his wives was only thirteen.

Unlike Joel, Ervil was the kind of person who enjoyed giving orders and making new rules, which he preferred to call laws. In due course, Joel heard murmurs of protest, and returned to Colonia LeBaron. He lost no time in doing away with some of Ervil's more repressive laws and soothed the protesters. Ervil meekly accepted the Prophet's authority.

Amazingly, Joel then repeated his mistake; he went away to found another colony called Los Molinos, and again left Ervil in charge. Once again, the intoxication of power turned Ervil into a dictator. His sermons, always rambling and bewildering, became even longer; one lasted ten hours. Convinced that enemies wanted to kill him, he began carrying a gun. The only person he seemed to trust was a disciple named Dan Jordan, who often had to listen to Ervil's diatribes about the Prophet Joel.

In due course, Joel returned, and was once more overwhelmed with protests about his younger brother. This time he took decisive action, and relieved Ervil of his position. Strangely, Ervil took his dismissal well, saying: "You don't know what a relief this is to me."

But disagreements between the two brothers continued to multiply. Joel had entrusted Ervil with the buying of some land around Los Molinos, on the Baja peninsula; now he found that Ervil had made out the deeds to more than eight thousand acres in his own name instead of in that of the church. There were legal wrangles, and Joel announced the excommunication of his brother and Dan Jordan, to take effect at the church's next conference.

Ervil retaliated by declaring that he was the true heir to the mantle of Joseph Smith, and issuing a privately printed book in which he declared that his enemies and detractors would suffer the "Blood Atonement."

One week before the church conference, Joel drove from Los Molinos to Colonia LeBaron. There a young church member who happened to be a follower of Ervil began talking to him about some abstruse theological point. Since the sun was hot, the young man invited Joel into the empty house before which they were standing; the unsuspecting Joel followed him inside. Not long after, Joel's teenage son saw Dan Jordan drive up, and enter the house. Suddenly there were sounds of a struggle and two shots. Dan Jordan and the young man hastily left the house and walked away. When Joel's son ran in to see what had happened, he found his father lying dead on the floor in an empty room. He had been shot twice in the mouth while someone had held him down on the floor.

With a warrant out for his arrest, Ervil vanished to the United States. Four months later, tired of being on the run, he walked into a Mexican police station and gave himself up. The trial dragged on throughout most of 1973; on December 13, Ervil LeBaron was sentenced to twelve years in prison for being the "intellectual author" of his brother's murder. The LeBaron saga had been playing on for almost forty years.

The rejoicing of Joel's followers was short-lived. The next day, the verdict was overturned by a higher court for technical irregularities, and Ervil LeBaron was set free.

Now the undisputed leader of the Church of the Firstborn, Ervil had no doubt he would be recognized by Joel's followers in Colonia LeBaron and Los Molinos. It was an unrealistic expectation; they regarded him as a butcher. Besides, they already had a replacement for Joel—his younger brother Verlan, whom Joel had appointed Patriarch after excommunicating Ervil.

Throughout 1974, Ervil became increasingly restive and indignant; it seemed that he had murdered his brother for nothing. If he wanted to be the undisputed Prophet, it seemed there was only one way: to murder Verlan.

Soon after dark on December 26, 1974, a wooden house in Los Molinos suddenly burst into flames. Firefighters with buckets of water eventually overcame the blaze. It was at that point that the shooting began. Men emerged out of hiding and began firing at random into the crowd. Others tossed Molotov cocktails into houses. People screamed and ran; yet, oddly, no one fired back. The inhabitants of Los Molinos had been told that God would protect them. When the raiders left, less than an hour later, eleven men and four women lay wounded, and more than two dozen homes fire bombed. Two of the victims would die later. The main objective—brother Verlan—was unharmed since he was away on a trip.

A few weeks later, there would be another murder: that of Neomi Chynoweth, one of the wives of Ervil's follower Bud Chynoweth. She was taken out into the bush and then shot to death by Vonda White, Ervil's tenth wife. No one has ever established exactly why she was killed, or why Ervil ordered the murder.

Ervil, meanwhile, was back in the United States, trying to spread his ministry among the Mormons, and doing his best to persuade them that they owed him ten per cent of their earnings. One of the men he targeted was a farmer named Bob Simons, who also believed that he was a "Prophet of God."

Bob had arrived at this conclusion after a mental breakdown and electric shock treatment. When he received a pamphlet about a new prophet called Ervil LeBaron, Simons was curious and wrote to him. By now, Simons was running a successful farm and attempting to carry his religious message to the Indians. LeBaron and Dan Jordan called on him and tried hard to convert him, but it seemed pointless to Simons to reduce his own status by accepting another man as his prophet.

After many long theological wrangles, Simons became aware that Ervil was hoping to seduce one of his younger and prettier wives—that, in fact, he had made her an offer to take her into his own family. That was too much. Simons wrote Ervil LeBaron an angry letter denying his authority. Ervil decided that Simons had to die.

The man he chose to carry out the execution was a Mormon whom Simons trusted, Lloyd Sullivan, who had confided to Simons that he now also had his doubts about the Prophet. On April 23, 1975, Lloyd Sullivan arrived at the Simons ranch to take him to meet some Indians who were searching for a white prophet. Eventually, they arrived at the spot, in the remote countryside west of Salt Lake City. Simons climbed out of the car and peered into the distance, looking for his potential converts. Two young men— Eddie Marston and Mark Chynoweth—stepped quietly out of the bushes. Marston pointed a shotgun at Simons' head and pulled the trigger, blowing off the back of his skull. After that, the three men buried Simons in a grave that had been dug hours before he was killed.

Once Ervil had accepted murder as a solution to his problems—and, moreover, had once gotten away with it—he could see no reason to stop. Killing Bob Simons was pointless; it solved nothing. But it soothed his wounded vanity—one more victim was buried in an unmarked grave. LeBaron at least felt confirmed in his sense that he was a man to be reckoned with. Like Jeffrey Lundgren, he justified murder by regarding it as the Blood Atonement sanctioned by the Lord.

The next murder took place in June 1975; the victim was another rebellious cult member, Dean Vest. Trouble had started when Vest asked permission to take a sixteen-year-old girl named Rena Chynoweth as his second wife; his first wife had left him and moved to Seattle. Ervil was reluctant, for he had been sexually molesting Rena since she was twelve. Now he married Rena himself, and gave Vest another woman named Linda.

The problem was that Linda preferred Ervil, and soon left her husband's bed for that of the Prophet. After that, Ervil sensed that Vest was disillusioned with the cult and was preparing to leave. He had his own reasons for wanting to prevent this; Vest owned a barge worth $10,000, and Ervil wanted that money. He told his wife Vonda—the one who had killed Neomi—that he had chosen her to murder Vest.

It happened sooner than planned. Vest heard that his first wife and daughter had been involved in a traffic accident, and prepared to fly to Seattle. It was his bad luck that Vonda happened to be baby-sitting in his home that day. When he told her that he was flying to Seattle to see his wife, she was convinced that he had no intention of returning. So while Vest did his packing, Vonda found a loaded revolver. Then, wearing rubber gloves, she approached Vest from behind and shot him twice. Blood gushed from his mouth and he collapsed. Vonda then shot him carefully in the head.

She ran upstairs and cleaned the gun, and washed her hands to get rid of gunpowder marks. After that, she rang the police and told them that someone had entered the house while she was upstairs with the children, and had shot Dean Vest. The police disbelieved her—there were blood spots on her shoes—and in spite of her indignant denials, she was taken into custody.

A few months later, Ervil got himself arrested again. He made the mistake of returning to Mexico, and was recognized by a member of brother Verlan's congregation. He was arrested, and he and his lieutenant Andres Zarate went on trial for the attack on Los Molinos. Incredibly, he was once again acquitted. One writer on the case hints at the corruptibility of Mexican officials; whatever the reason, Ervil LeBaron was again a free man by December 1976.

The next murder was Ervil's own daughter, Rebecca. Ervil had married her to a rich follower, Victor Chynoweth, who lived in Denver, although Chynoweth already had a wife called Nancy. Rebecca hated the marriage; Nancy treated her as an interloper, and when she had a baby, Nancy took it over and treated Rebecca as a hired nurse. Rebecca became increasingly angry and bitter.

Early in 1977, she was sent off to Dallas, Texas, where her father had set up a repair business for domestic appliances. There she was just as miserable. What she wanted was to be reunited with her baby, and allowed to return to Mexico. Rebecca even hinted that she might go to the authorities and talk about her father's activities.

In April 1977, Ervil told her that she would be allowed to collect her baby in Denver, then fly to Mexico. Eddie Marston—he had killed Bob Simons—and another "soldier" called Duane Chynoweth, collected her for the drive to the airport. Instead, they took her to a lonely road and strangled her with a rope. Rebecca's grave has never been located.

It was at about this time that Ervil began to plan his most ambitious crime so far. The victim was to be his brother Verlan. But in order to lure Verlan to Utah, Ervil planned another murder—that of Mormon cult leader Rulon Allred, who ran a fundamentalist group with three thousand followers. In the early days, Allred had been a friend, but he had been alienated by the apostolic claims of the LeBaron brothers. The plan was to murder him, then murder Verlan when he attended the funeral.

Two women were selected to kill Allred: Ervil's thirteenth wife, Rena Chynoweth, and Ramona, wife of Dan Jordan. On May 10,

1977, the two women checked into a motel in Murray, south of Salt Lake City, where Allred ran a naturopathic clinic. As they sat in the waiting room, Allred looked in, then returned to his laboratory. Rena followed him, drew the revolver and shot him seven times. With one of Allred's eleven wives standing there, she even tried to deliver the *coup de grâce* with a final bullet in the head, and missed.

The two women then hurried out of the clinic, removed their wigs and bulky outer clothing, worn as a disguise, and were picked up by Eddie Marston, who had been baby-sitting Ramona's child in the car; they drove back towards Denver. Left behind in Murray were three more "soldiers" whose job was to kill Verlan when he came to the funeral.

Ervil's planning had been correct; Verlan LeBaron did fly up to Utah four days later for the funeral. But when the assassins arrived there, they realized that their task would be impossible; there were not only thousands of mourners, but also fifty policemen to ensure that Allred's killers did not strike again. With their quarry only a hundred yards away, the killers decided they had to abort the mission.

In fact, the police had already discovered the vital clue that would bring Ervil LeBaron to justice. Two men scavenging in a waste bin had found a plastic bag containing bullets, an empty box that had held a newly purchased gun (complete with the gun's serial number), and crudely drawn maps showing the way to Allred's clinic. Fingerprints were found on empty soda cans, and a reversible jacket matching the description of one that the killer had worn was also found.

A check on the gun's serial number revealed that it had been purchased in Denver, and that the buyer was Nancy Chynoweth, the wife of LeBaron's wealthy follower Victor. Although Nancy insisted that the gun had been stolen from her, she was extradited to Salt Lake City on a murder charge.

One of LeBaron's daughters, Alicia, was interviewed by police. She had married outside the sect, and was no longer involved in it. Asked which of Ervil's followers would commit murder if he gave the order, Alicia replied: practically all of them. The LeBaron children and members of the cult were all schooled in total obedience.

But Alicia was able to offer a useful suggestion. Her mother Delfina (the Prophet's first wife) was deeply unhappy and anxious to escape. A phone call from her six months before had revealed that she believed her life was in danger. Now the police began looking for Delfina, and they were aided by coincidence: just as Delfina's mother was being interviewed by a policeman, Delfina rang up to say that she had just escaped from a cult house in Dallas, and was about to take a bus to El Paso. A policeman spoke to her, and when Delfina stepped off the bus, the police were ready to escort her to safety.

The story she had to tell made it clear that she was lucky to still be alive. When her daughter Rebecca had left to collect her baby in Denver, Delfina was suspicious; she was sure Rebecca's life was in danger. She tried hard to find out her present whereabouts, hoping to warn her. Eventually, she learned from her other daughter Lillian that Rebecca was dead. Her misery made Ervil realize that she was becoming a danger; he ordered Lillian's husband, Mark Chynoweth, to kill her. Delfina realized in time that she was destined to be the next Blood Atonement, and succeeded in escaping to the bus station.

Delfina now begged the police to bring her two teenage sons from Dallas; two days later, the police walked into a repair shop and placed fourteen-year-old Isaac and nine-year-old Pablo in protective custody. Isaac, who had listened to most of the cult's murder plans, would eventually testify in court against his father.

A false entry in a motel register—it was the motel where the assassins had stayed—provided a car registration number; the car proved to belong to Rena Chynoweth's father. And the handwriting in the register was identified as that of Rena herself. The police now had the name of Allred's killer.

It was at this point that Delfina's son Isaac began to talk, telling what he knew of the group's murderous activities. By the time he had finished, the police also knew the names of those who had taken part in the Los Molinos raid, and the murders of Bob Simons and Dean Vest.

On September 23, 1977, hundreds of police took part in an ambitious operation to place Ervil LeBaron and his "soldiers" under arrest. It was not wholly successful; Ervil and his son Arturo escaped; so did Eddie Marston and Rena Chynoweth. But Victor and Mark Chynoweth, and Lloyd Sullivan and Ramona Marston, were captured. After a preliminary hearing, at which Isaac LeBaron gave evidence against them, they were bound over to appear on trial.

The prosecution now learned they had another ally. Lloyd Sullivan (who had lured Simons to his death) had turned against Ervil. To begin with, LeBaron had prophesied in 1974 that all other Mormon sects would collapse by May 3, 1977, and would accept Ervil's leadership. Sullivan had been shaken when this prophecy proved false, and even more shaken when LeBaron tried to explain it by declaring that the Lord often gave false dates to test the faithful. He had also been disillusioned to find that, on his return from the mission to kill Verlan at Allred's funeral, the Prophet had fled to Mexico.

Now free as he awaited trial, Sullivan contacted Verlan LeBaron, and told him of the plans to kill him. After that, he agreed to testify against the cult in exchange for immunity. To the prosecutors, it seemed that nothing could now prevent the conviction of the other three accused.

They were mistaken. Not long before the trial, Lloyd Sullivan died of a heart attack. His death left the prosecution with a fatal lack of evidence. The result was that when Vonda LeBaron was tried for the murder of Dean Vest, the judge declared a mistrial. Vonda was held in custody pending a retrial, but it was a bad blow, for the evidence against her was overwhelming.

In November 1978, Mexican police swooped on a remote ranch and caught Ervil LeBaron, Rena Chynoweth, and Dan Jordan, LeBaron's most faithful lieutenant. By an absurd mix-up, Jordan was mistaken for LeBaron, and LeBaron was allowed to go free, but the other two were handed over to the American police. Eddie Marston, the killer of Bob Simons, was also caught and handed over. But the result of Lloyd Sullivan's death was that Eddie Marston's trial for murder ended in a not guilty verdict. In March 1979, Victor Chynoweth, Mark Chynoweth, Rena Chynoweth and Eddie Marston were also acquitted on the Allred murder charge. Ervil LeBaron's incredible luck was continuing to hold.

It was about to run out. At her second trial, Vonda was found guilty of the murder of Dean Vest, and sentenced to life imprisonment. On June 1, 1979, Ervil LeBaron was finally captured in the mountains near Mexico City, and handed over to the American police. He went on trial the following May. His brother Verlan testified against him; so did his son Isaac. The defense was that LeBaron was not the cult leader: that the true leader was the dead Lloyd Sullivan, aided by his son Don. But by now the evidence against Ervil LeBaron was overwhelming. The jury took only three hours to find him guilty. The judge sentenced him to life imprisonment.

Two years later, on the afternoon of Sunday August 16, 1981, a guard looked into Ervil LeBaron's cell and saw him doing push-ups, a method he had once used to convince disciples that he was the mighty and strong Prophet. Three hours later, LeBaron was found lying on the floor of his cell; he had died of a heart attack. His brother Verlan was driving to Mexico City that same day when an oncoming car went out of control and struck his car head on; Verlan was killed outright.

The death of Ervil LeBaron must have caused many people to heave sighs of relief. For the Mormon Church, he had been a monstrous embarrassment ever since the press had begun to refer to him as "the Mormon Manson." Church spokesmen protested that he had been excommunicated more than thirty years earlier; but the fact remained that LeBaron considered himself the true heir of Joseph Smith, and in the eyes of the general public, he was a Mormon.

Utah lawmen who had spent so many years putting him behind bars had also had their misgivings; Ervil seemed to have a habit of finding legal loopholes. Then there were some of those ex-disciples whom Ervil had regarded as traitors; these included Mark and Duane Chynoweth and Eddie Marston. In the Point of the Mountains State Prison, Ervil had declared that his son Arturo was to be his heir as the Prophet of God, and Marston and the Chynoweths had refused to accept the appointment, with the result that Ervil had denounced them in a work he called *The Book of New Covenants*. That meant that they were now prime candidates for Blood Atonement.

Incredibly, there would be twenty more murders before the LeBaron saga finally came to an end.

The immediate effect of Ervil's death was to cause a three-way split in the Church: Arturo LeBaron, Dan Jordan, and Mark Chynoweth each proclaimed himself Ervil's successor. But with his father's backing, Arturo's claim was clearly the strongest.

Arturo, together with a large contingent of brothers and sisters, moved to Phoenix, Arizona, where he ran a thriving business stealing and reselling pickup trucks. His chief lieutenant was a man called Leo Evoniuk, who had met Ervil in prison and had become a convert. The thin, tense Arturo and the relaxed, overweight Evoniuk seemed to make ideal partners in both religion and crime.

Within weeks of Ervil's death, the Chynoweths, who were in Texas, were receiving threats from Arturo and Evoniuk, urging them to rejoin the fold or face Blood Atonement. Then Arturo decided to move his auto-theft operation to a ranch at La Joya, in Mexico, and the threats stopped.

This was not because Arturo had ceased to regard the Chynoweths as traitors, but because in the Mexican wilderness, Arturo and Evoniuk had begun to quarrel. Evoniuk moved out, then decided that he had made a mistake, and that it was Arturo who should have moved. Evoniuk returned with a contingent of gunmen and besieged the ranch; after hours of fighting Evoniuk's men were driven off.

The episode made Arturo aware of the importance of his "soldiers." And when Lorna Chynoweth, one of Ervil's wives, proposed returning to the United States with two of her sons—Andrew and Aaron—Arturo decided that it was time for her to die. Lorna was given permission to leave, but within a few miles of the ranch, she was strangled and buried.

Arturo was the next to die. He returned from a trip to Dallas to find Leo Evoniuk waiting for him, and while he was running to take cover, Evoniuk shot him five times in the back.

Isaac LeBaron, the youth who had given evidence against his father, became increasingly convinced that he was next on the death list, and begged the police for protection. When they turned him down, he went to stay with Mark Chynoweth and his sister in Houston, Texas. It was a strange decision, in view of the fact the

Chynoweths regarded him as a traitor, and indicative of the youth's weariness and desperation. The next day he was also dead, a shotgun wound in the head and the shotgun lying between his feet. No one asked why there were two more bullet holes in the wall of the room.

Arturo's place had been taken by his brother Heber, who struck everyone as an altogether more pleasant and relaxed character, although perhaps excessively fond of sex. Cult members describe him lying in the back of a cab, having sex with several of his half-sisters lying in a row. What no one realized was that Heber was a psychopath.

Soon after becoming the Prophet, Heber started exacting revenge for his brother's death. The first on the list was Gamaliel Rios, suspected of plotting Arturo's murder with Evoniuk. He was driven into the countryside, and murdered by one of his closest friends, Andres Zarate, with blows from a tire iron.

Gamaliel's brother Raul died a few days later, shot from ambush. Their sister Yolanda—she was one of Ervil's wives—was taken to Dallas and murdered soon after; she was also accused of complicity in Arturo's murder.

Andrew Chynoweth, whose mother Arturo had murdered to prevent her taking him back to America, now also began to show signs of wanting to return to Dallas, to rejoin a wife who had deserted him; Heber suspected him of intending to abandon the cult, and as Andrew was about the climb into his car, he was shot down, then buried while he was still alive.

By killing off so many of his best workers, Heber was destroying his own financial base. At this point, he made the curious decision to embark on a career of bank robbery. This brought to a head the smoldering dissatisfaction that his half-brothers and sisters were beginning to feel about his homicidal tendencies. His strong-minded wife Tarsa, sister of the murdered Andrew, decided that he had to go. Heber was invited to a family conference where, to his astonishment, he found that the subject under discussion was his own leadership.

But in spite of his psychopathic tendencies, Heber had the common sense to know the alternative to a peaceful abdication was immediate death; he agreed to be deposed, and Tarsa's unaggressive brother Aaron was appointed in his place. Tarsa further under-mined her husband by having one of his most faithful "soldiers" killed; Alex Zarate was shot in his sleep by his half-sister Patricia LeBaron, with whom he had been having a clandestine affair.

In spite of his demotion, Heber was still determined to prove his worth by going ahead with a career of bank robbery. His first attempt—it was in a town called Richardson, near Dallas, on November 5, 1986—was so incompetent that he was caught and thrown in jail. The cult quickly raised the $50,000 bail, and Heber escaped back to Mexico.

Leo Evoniuk had moved to Carmel, in California, where he ran an irrigation business. He had also launched a Millennial Church of Jesus Christ, devoted to spreading Ervil's teachings. On May 21, 1987, Evoniuk received a call asking him to give an esti-mate for digging a drainage ditch. After leaving for the appoint-ment, he was never seen again.

Back in Mexico, a new outburst of killing exploded when Ervil's old lieutenant, Andres Zarate, was suspected of wanting to return home. It was Aaron, the new Prophet, who shot Zarate in the head. Soon after that, Mary LeBaron, Arturo's wife, and Sandra LeBaron, daughter of the murdered Yolada Rios, were also killed. Sandra was only thirteen years old.

Murdered with them was Jorge LeBaron, Ervil's son by his sec-ond wife Maria; he was regarded as lazy, and unwilling to take part in murders. While conducting this purge, Aaron and Tarsa also decided that Heber's eighteen-month-old baby had better be dis-posed of; the child was sickly and inclined to vomit his food. Heber was given the task of murdering his own son, and did it by placing his hand over the child's face and suffocating him.

Dan Jordan, Ervil's faithful lieutenant, was living quietly in the town of Bennett, in Colorado, together with three wives and a horde of children. In August 1987, he was astonished to find a large crowd of teenage LeBarons knocking at his door. Led by Aaron, they begged Jordan to give them shelter, explaining that the group in Mexico was being led by a power-mad Heber and an equally psy-chopathic Andrew LeBaron.

Jordan had no way of knowing that Andrew was dead and that Heber had been deposed, and was still less inclined to suspect that the mild Aaron was the new Prophet. Besides, they were a source of cheap labor. He welcomed them in and set them to work on his farm.

In October they all went off for the hunting season to the Manti-La Sal National Forest in Utah. On October 16, 1987, Dan Jordan made his way towards the communal toilet on the campsite. He failed to recognize the man standing outside as Heber until it was too late; he was killed by a bullet to the chest. The police who were called in confronted a bewildered group of teenagers who claimed to be baffled by the murder, and let them go.

Back at Jordan's ranch, Aaron proceeded to expound his gospel to Jordan's wives and family. He did it so effectively, waving a gun, that they were prepared to hand over the title deeds (which had been Aaron's long-term goal since he knocked on the door). But one of the wives succeeded in telephoning the police, who arrived in time to abort the transaction. Aaron was taken into police custody, and the other LeBarons sent on their way.

Back at the La Joya ranch, Aaron decided that it was now time to call the other traitors to account. These were Mark and Duane Chynoweth and Eddie Marston, all of whom had become successful businessmen—they were still working in household appliances—in Houston. It was this decision that would finally bring Ervil LeBaron's children within the reach of the law.

The Chynoweths and Eddie Marston knew they were on the death list, and maintained a constant vigilance; their suburban neighbors found them pleasant but oddly uncommunicative. On June 27, 1988, Duane Chynoweth—he had taken part in the slaughter at Los Molinos—was asked to pick up a washing machine; he took his nine-year-old daughter Jennie along for the ride. As Duane walked towards the front door, a man with a blond beard climbed out of a parked car and walked down the path, pointed a gun at Duane Chynoweth, and pulled the trigger. Then, as Chynoweth collapsed on to the ground, he fired two more shots into his head.

The gunman was walking away when he heard screams coming from Chynoweth's station wagon, and saw the horrified face of the small girl looking at him. He leaned through the window and shot her in the mouth, then hurried away. It was four o'clock in the afternoon.

Mark Chynoweth was sitting in the office of Reliance Appliances when a bearded man walked in, pulled out a gun, and began shooting. When he left a few moments later, Mark Chynoweth was dead. Outside, a car was waiting to pick up the killer.

Eddie Marston had also been called out to collect a washing machine, and had just climbed out of his pickup truck when a car stopped by the end of the driveway. The bearded man who climbed out of it pointed a gun at Marston's chest and fired; then he bent over the body and sent another shot into the head. Like the other murders, this one had taken place within seconds of four o'clock.

The "four o'clock murders" caused a nationwide sensation. It was not long before the Houston police discovered that the victims had been lieutenants of Ervil LeBaron. But here the trail came to an end. It seemed that Ervil's successor had been his son Arturo, but Arturo had been murdered two years later. As far as anyone knew, the sect no longer had a Prophet.

Four days later, on July 1, two police officers were carrying out a routine check on the cars parked behind the King's Inn Hotel in Phoenix, Arizona. They radioed the license number of a black Chevrolet Silverado, and received word from headquarters that it had been stolen in Fort Worth, Texas. Inside the motel, they learned that the car belonged to a woman who had registered as Christina Adams, and taken three rooms. Apparently there were six people (three women and three men) with her. After keeping the place under observation for several hours, the police arrested all seven.

In the rooms, the police found items that suggested they had arrested members of a car-theft racket. There were several ignition switches, and notebooks listing license numbers. They also found a gun, street maps of Houston, and a false beard and mustache.

The suspects refused to answer questions, and the next morning three of the women were released. They returned with enough money to bail out two of the men; one man and woman remained in custody.

The Phoenix police were soon proved correct in their suspicions about car theft; a check on license numbers found in the notebook revealed that many were of stolen cars. They decided to re-arrest the five suspects they had allowed to go free.

Meanwhile, back in Texas, the Houston police were having no success in solving the four o'clock murders. But they had learned that the LeBaron family frequently changed aliases. One of these aliases they learned, was Mary June Whitt, used by Linda LeBaron, Ervil's fifth wife. A routine telephone call to Phoenix to find if Mary June Whitt was known there revealed that she had been involved in a car-theft case in the previous year, and had skipped bail. With her at the time had been a younger woman called Patricia Newman. The Phoenix police had learned by chance that Patricia Newman was also one of the women arrested at the King's Inn Hotel, although she had called herself Valerie Davies. Suddenly, the Phoenix police realized that the seven car thieves they were holding were also the four o'clock murderers of Houston. At least some of their names had to be LeBaron.

Checks on the LeBaron family supplied the probable identity of the three men in custody: Heber LeBaron; his step-brother Doug Barlow; and his half-brother Richard LeBaron, who was only seventeen. These were almost certainly the three men who had killed Eddie Marston and the Chynoweths in Houston.

But the police had a serious problem. They were not sure which of the men had committed which murder—all three had worn blond beards and mustaches, almost certainly fakes. If the police took the case to court without being certain, their chances of success were minimal. For the time being, they had to be content with the car-theft charges. In August 1989, Heber LeBaron, Doug Barlow, Richard LeBaron, Cynthia LeBaron, and Tarsa LeBaron were all found guilty of car theft. Heber and Barlow received ten years each, the two women five years, and Richard LeBaron three and a half.

It was a disappointing result, but it was better than nothing. Natasha LeBaron, another of the women arrested in Phoenix, was sent to prison on an unrelated charge of selling stolen washing machines.

It was Natasha LeBaron who would finally be responsible for bringing the four o'clock murderers to justice, not by betraying them, but by becoming the victim of yet another LeBaron murder. Out of prison in 1991, Natasha had rejoined her brother Aaron in Monterey, Mexico's third largest city. In this cosmopolitan atmosphere, she began to rebel against the cult's discipline, which was most effective in the claustrophobic atmosphere of small communities. When she began a romance with a local man, she was warned that she would be regarded as an apostate, but ignored the threat.

On October 31, her fifteen-year-old brother Thomas came to her apartment, and told her that he needed help digging graves. The victims, he said, would be Cynthia LeBaron, the sister of Richard, and Arturo's widow Delfi; both were becoming rebellious and disobedient.

Natasha had just finished helping dig the first grave when her brother slipped a steel wire round her throat and pulled it tight. Then he threw her into the grave and covered her with earth. Other group members were told she had tired of Monterey and taken a job at a beach resort.

But Natasha's boyfriend found this story unbelievable; he knew that she would not go "walkabout" without saying goodbye. Finally, he persuaded Cynthia LeBaron to go and check Natasha's apartment. When Cynthia found that all Natasha's clothes and belongings were still there, she knew that her half-sister was dead.

Now Cynthia recalled how she had made an unexpected visit to Aaron and Tarsa a few weeks earlier, and how Aaron had asked casually whether anyone else knew she was there. She had thought fast, and claimed that her boyfriend was waiting on the corner. Now she was fairly sure that, if she had admitted she was alone, Aaron would have killed her.

It was at this point that Cynthia decided to go to the police and tell them all she knew about the cult, including the four o'clock murders. On May 1, 1992, she was in the Houston police headquarters, together with Natasha's younger sister Jessica.

Now, at last, the police learned how Aaron had planned the four o'clock murders, and how his family had carried them out with the precision of a military operation, using stolen cars, walky-talky radios and disguises that made the killers look alike. Cynthia described how Doug Barlow had killed Eddie Marston, how Heber had killed Mark Chynoweth, and how her own seventeen-year-old brother Richard had killed Duane Chynoweth and his nine-year-old daughter Jennie. Cynthia also gave details of the murders of Leo Evoniuk and Dan Jordan, also committed by Heber. She was able to lead them to the body of Leo Evoniuk, buried by a roadside outside Carmel.

On January 11, 1993, the four o'clock murder trial opened in Houston. The defendants were Heber LeBaron, Doug Barlow, and Patricia LeBaron. Patricia, disguised as a man, had driven a getaway car. Richard LeBaron, who had killed Sandra LeBaron and Jennie Chynoweth, was dropped from the indictment for giving evidence for the prosecution. On May 26, 1993, all three defendants were sentenced to life imprisonment without parole.

SIX

HOW TO TRANSFORM REALITY

On July 1, 1959, Dr. Milton Rokeach began one of the most memorable experiments in the history of psychiatry.

He brought together in the same mental ward three men who were all firmly convinced that they were Jesus Christ. He wanted to see whether, confronted with other delusional systems, the patients would suddenly recognize that they were "mad." The English philosopher James Mill (a disciple of Comte) had believed that it ought to be possible to reason madmen out of their delusions; in effect, Rokeach was asking whether madmen can reason one another out of their madness.

He acknowledged his debt to another psychiatrist, Robert Lindner, whose book, *The Fifty Minute Hour*, had appeared five years earlier. Since Lindner's case of Kirk Allen is of some importance to what follows, it is necessary to look at it in some detail.

Kirk Allen—it is the pseudonym Lindner chose for his patient—was a physicist who, from the hints Lindner drops, was involved in the making of the atom bomb. His superiors became worried about him because his work was becoming casual and slipshod. Questioned about this by his division chief, Allen finally let slip the comment: "I'll try to spend more time on earth from now on." Although he seemed sane, the chief decided he needed psychiatric treatment, and sent him to Lindner in Baltimore.

Allen certainly looked normal. But the story he had to tell revealed that he was suffering from a peculiar form of delusional insanity. He thought that his true identity was as a ruler on Mars.

(In fact, Lindner does not specify the planet, but as we shall see, its identity seems reasonably certain.)

Allen's account of his early life revealed how the fantasy had developed. His father had been a distinguished diplomat, and Allen had spent his childhood in Hawaii. He had not even learned to speak English until he was six years old. His mother, thirty-five years her husband's junior, left the child completely in the charge of his Polynesian nurse. It was not until someone made a critical remark about the child's inability to speak English that the nurse was removed to other duties and Kirk began to pick up his own language.

This sudden disappearance of a mother figure—which is what the nurse had been—was a severe shock to Kirk, who became intensely lonely. A subsequent governess who was obsessed with cleanliness, and scrubbed him with scalding water twice a day, made things worse.

Finally, when he was about twelve and beginning to show the first signs of adolescence, a young and sex-starved governess made a habit of stripping in front of the mirror in his bedroom, until one day, as he lay naked on the bed, she saw that he was aroused, whereupon she lost no time in seducing him; from then on, he was expected to satisfy her three times a night, and sometimes during the day. This governess eloped with a married man, leaving Kirk with a sense of guilt. Sex among Hawaiian children—and adults— was open and casual, but the governess had made him see it as something furtive and forbidden. Kirk now felt lonelier than ever.

In childhood he had fantasized that he was one of the characters in the *Wizard of Oz* books. Now he threw himself back into reading with a new passion. An odd coincidence increased his tendency to fantasize. He read a novel by a favorite English author in which the name of the chief character was the same as his own; this so fascinated him that he read it straight through three times. A few days later he encountered another character with his own name in a volume by an American writer.

Finally, Kirk came upon a series of books in which the hero bore his own name. These were set on another planet, and Lindner's description makes it clear that they were Edgar Rice Burroughs' Mars books, in which the hero, Captain John Carter, has a series of remarkable adventures on Mars, finally achieving the position of ruler. (Lindner never identifies the books, presumably since this would indicate the real name of his patient.)

After the two earlier experiences of a hero bearing his own name, Kirk was not surprised by yet another coincidence; in fact, he said, "I think I expected it somehow, and when it happened, it was as if I had known it all the time, and was finding something that had been lost." He felt that these stories were literally about himself—that they were his own biography, differing from a normal biography only in the fact that this one took place in the future. "Nothing in these books was unfamiliar to me: I recognized everything—the scenes, the people, the furnishings of rooms, the events, even the words that were spoken." This may be because he read them over and over again until he knew them by heart. Kirk became so obsessed that he began constructing maps, genealogical tables, charts, and diagrams. Then he began constructing the subsequent life of "Kirk Allen" where the author had left off. He lived in two worlds, one as an ordinary schoolboy, the other as the ruler of Mars.

Then came another shock. His father died, and his mother moved to America, enrolled Kirk in a prep school, then vanished to live her own life. Suddenly, he was more lonely than ever before. He went on to university, was a brilliantly successful student, then was recruited to work on the atom bomb at Los Alamos, New Mexico. (Here Lindner's hints become so clear as to be unmistakable.) After the war Kirk became a section chief in a scientific establishment (which again sounds like Los Alamos), where his work continued to be satisfactory, although all his spare time was devoted to his fantasy.

Another trauma turned Kirk's fantasy into an alarming kind of reality. After the nymphomaniac governess, he had been guilt-ridden and nervous about sex. Now he formed a friendship with an attractive divorcee, a geologist who worked at the same establishment. He enjoyed her companionship, but she wanted more. Her hints about sex filled Kirk with anxiety, but when he tried to break off the relationship she refused to let him.

One day after dinner in her apartment she made such a determined attempt at seduction that Kirk fled back to his own room. There he flung himself with redoubled passion into the "records" of his life on Mars, and in a problem that had lately been occupying his thoughts. He had been working on a map of a planet in another galaxy, but was unable to recall certain details. He had a "memory" of flying over the planet and taking aerial photographs, and he seemed to recall that he had stored these photographs in his filing cabinet in his palace on Mars.

Now, galvanized by the negative emotional energy produced by revulsion, Kirk found himself feeling even more deeply frustrated by his inability to gain access to the aerial photographs. As he thought this, "My whole being seemed to respond with a resounding 'Why not?'—and in that same moment I was there." He found himself sitting at his desk on Mars, dressed in the robes of his high office, then making his way to the secret room and consulting the photographs in the filing cabinet. After studying these for a while, and committing them to memory, he was suddenly back on earth, prepared to continue with his map.

From then on, Kirk Allen could transport himself to Mars whenever he felt like it, and experience it in all its physical reality. He asked Lindner: "Have I discovered the secret of teleportation? Do I have some special psychic equipment? Some unique organ, or what Charles Fort called a 'wild talent'? Damned if I know!"

This is why things had suddenly begun to go wrong with his work, and why he was sent to Lindner for treatment.

Lindner did not look upon Kirk as a madman who needs to be cured. He realized that Kirk Allen believed that, in some sense, he spent half his time on Mars. But then, there was a sense in which Allen was right. His trips to Mars had a reality that the human imagination seldom achieves: it was literally as if he was there. Living his "normal" life among ordinary people, Kirk felt himself in the position of one of those heroes of a fantasy or horror story who tells the reader: "I know that the experiences I am about to relate will never be believed, yet they are true nevertheless." Kirk Allen knew they were true. Reading Lindner's account, we have to admit that it is just conceivable that there was something more than fantasy involved, and that he had developed some peculiar faculty that may be latent in all human beings.

How could such a patient be "cured"? Lindner decided that the answer lay in what has sometimes been called participation therapy, and which was developed by a number of existential psychologists as early as the 1930s. Here the psychiatrist ceases to think of himself as a doctor, and tries to share the patient's fantasy or neurosis.

In Lindner's case, the results were startling and unexpected. Lindner admits that he had always been a fan of old fashioned science fiction—not the sophisticated post-war variety of Van Vogt and Ray Bradbury, but that of H.G. Wells, Doc Smith, A.A. Merritt, and Stanley G. Weinbaum. So he found it easy to enter into Kirk's fantasy; it was a pleasure as well as a professional duty. He began studying Kirk's "records" and charts, looking for inaccuracies that he might bring to Kirk's attention.

He describes a typical incident. He was studying one of Kirk's star maps when his patient arrived, and when Kirk, concerned at his baffled expression, asked if there was something wrong, Lindner growled, in the best tradition of *Star Trek*: "Plenty. These distances are all fouled up. Either your astronomical projection from Srom Norbra X is wrong or the maps are way off." Together they pored over the map, and made various suggestions about how the error came about, while Kirk did calculations on the back of an envelope. When Lindner suggested that it was not, after all, so serious, Kirk exploded: "Not serious! Why, man, these maps are used by my pilots. No wonder I've lost so many!"

At this point, Lindner suggested that the error may have arisen because these charts dated back to the age before interstellar flight, and that if Kirk could check on the date he made the maps, it might explain the discrepancy. Kirk brightened up and agreed to make a trip to Mars to find out. The next day he declared that Lindner had been right; a trip to the institute where the maps were kept revealed that these pre-dated the age of interstellar flight. Both men heaved a sigh of relief.

In fact, Lindner recognized that he was becoming obsessively involved in Kirk's fantasies. As a child and adolescent, Lindner admits, he had been a Walter Mitty, conjuring up situations in which he was the hero. Now what had begun as a game developed into a disturbing reality. When some discrepancy appeared in Kirk's accounts, Lindner experienced acute anxiety. He began to enter into Kirk's fantasy world with a devotion comparable to

Kirk's own. It began to invade his thoughts and behavior; fragments of the Martian language would drift into his head, and refuse to go away. The real world began to lose its appeal. "With Kirk's puzzled assistance I was taking part in cosmic adventures, sharing the exhilaration of the sweeping extravaganza he had plotted." Gradually, fantasy turned to psychic distress as Lindner became aware that he was being sucked into the whirlpool that had engulfed Kirk.

The end, when it came, had a touch of bathos. One day, while Lindner was thumbing through the notebook that contained Kirk's latest observations about some crucial question of Martian geography, and ignoring his patient, Kirk stood up and went to the window. He looked troubled, and finally admitted: "It's a lie, all of it." For weeks, he said, he had not been making the trips to Mars, but merely inventing the material that Lindner wanted. As Lindner had begun to share his delusion, so Kirk had become increasingly aware that it was a delusion, and that he had dragged his psychiatrist into it. "I realized I was crazy. I realized I've been deluding myself for years." Yet even after the fantasy had become hollow, Kirk had felt obliged to continue, to supply Lindner with the information he craved.

In fact, without fully intending to, Lindner had "cured" his patient. The patient had also cured Lindner.

This story throws an interesting light on the problem of messiahs and their disciples, showing, for example, how easy it is to enter a shared world of illusion. But by far the most interesting part of the story is how Kirk actually found himself "transported" to Mars. What had been merely a rich fantasy had suddenly turned into reality.

Up to that point, Kirk had been inclined to believe that the Mars stories were his own biography, but it had still been part of a kind of novel he was writing in his head. Now the crisis of the attractive colleague reinforced the fantasy with a flood of psychic energy that made it into a reality.

This is the most difficult part to grasp. Most of us are fantasists, but our fantasies never become as real as the world around us. We find it hard to believe that Kirk really found himself sitting at his desk on Mars, then went to the secret archive, where he was able to study the aerial photographs. Yet we know that something of the sort can easily be achieved under hypnosis; the hypnotized subject can hold a conversation with someone whose existence the hypnotist has suggested. And in *The Story of Ruth*, psychiatrist Morton Schatzman describes how a girl whose father had tried to rape her as a child began to hallucinate her father with such realism that she saw him as a real person, standing there in the room.

What seems to happen is that the enormous powers of the unconscious mind respond to a crisis by creating an alternative reality. This is the strategy by which the unconscious defends a personality whose existence is threatened by deep anxiety, and prevents it from disintegrating.

In the case of Kirk Allen, the basic energy involved was clearly sexual. His problems began with the nymphomaniac governess. Most of us may feel that a twelve-year-old boy would enjoy being seduced and introduced to sex with an attractive young woman. But we are forgetting that a boy's sexual fantasies involve situations in which he takes the lead, or in which the woman of his dreams mysteriously yields and gives herself willingly.

The key words here are "yields" and "gives." The essence of male sexuality lies in the fact that it is active, not passive. By using Kirk as a sex toy, the governess had turned this basic situation upside down. Now instead of lusting after pretty teenagers and wondering how they can be persuaded to remove their clothes, Kirk cannot get out of his head the vague fear that they might turn and pursue him. Any hint of a sexual demand is enough to make him flee. His attitude is exactly like that of a girl who has been raped and is now terrified of sex.

His Martian fantasies are essentially a substitute for sex. He is a benevolent despot on Mars, and his fantasies provide a substitute for the self-esteem that is induced in most males by sexual conquest.

The attempt of the female colleague to seduce him revived all the old tensions, and he fled back to his room and took refuge as usual in his Martian alter-ego. Now, more than ever before, Kirk needed his fantasies. In this personal crisis, the unconscious mind rises to the occasion, sending a kind of waking dream, and suddenly he finds himself on Mars.

Why did this ability disappear when the psychiatrist entered his fantasy? Lindner's explanation is that "it is impossible for two objects to occupy the same place at the same time. It is as if a delusion such as Kirk's has room in it only for one person at a time. . . . When, as in this case, another person invades the delusion, the original occupant finds himself forced to give way." Lindner cites a case in which two women who suffered from the delusion that they were the Virgin Mary were introduced on the lawn of a mental sanatorium. The reaction of the older patient was "Why, you can't be, my dear—I am the Mother of God." The other replied firmly: "I'm afraid you are mixed up—I am Mary." After a brief but polite argument, the elder turned to the psychiatrist and asked: "What is the name of our Blessed Mary's mother?" He replied, "I think it was Anne." The older patient then informed the other: "If you are Mary, I must be Anne, your mother," and the two women embraced.

It was in an attempt to apply Lindner's theory that only one person can occupy the same delusion that Dr. Milton Rokeach decided to introduce three patients who each believed he was Jesus Christ.

The eldest of the three, Clyde Benson, had been a farmer who had drifted into alcoholism as a result of personal problems, and had been hospitalized for seventeen years. Joseph Cassel was a French Canadian who had once had ambitions about becoming a writer, but developed paranoid delusions over ten years, during which time he had worked as a clerk in a job he hated. Leon Gabor was the son of East Europeans who had emigrated to America, and his mother was a religious fanatic who exercised total domination. His committal was preceded by long periods of absenteeism from work and increasing inadequacy in confronting everyday problems. In fact, all three were basically inadequate personalities who found it hard to cope with life.

Rokeach was hoping that being brought together in the same ward might force them to recognize that they were suffering from delusions, and cause them to recover their sanity. In fact, the first result was that the three quarreled for weeks, and each decided that the other two were mad. It obviously disturbed them deeply that their belief systems were being attacked. At one point Clyde struck Leon; then he decided that the other two were corpses animated by machines.

Leon's response to the challenge was to change his name to Dr. R.I. Dung. The R.I. stood for "Right Idealed." Rokeach quickly recognized that Leon had not wavered in his belief that he was Christ; he had merely adopted a Christ-like strategy of pretending to be the lowest thing he could think of—dung. This was meant to disarm criticism and divert attacks. Under the surface, Leon remained as convinced as ever that he was Christ.

The situation was obviously deadlocked, and again Rokeach decided to try to break it by applying Lindner's theory. He was encouraged by a comment made by Eugen Bleuler, the great psychiatrist who had influenced C.G. Jung. Bleuler believed that schizophrenics use a "double entry bookkeeping system," in which they claim to be one thing, but secretly know that they are another. Rokeach was inclined to think that this was true of Leon: below the surface, he knew perfectly well that he was not Jesus Christ or Dr. Dung. The problem, as Rokeach saw it, was to get Leon to admit it.

Leon had never been married—he had been too dominated by his mother—but he nevertheless declared that he had a wife called Madame Yeti (who was also God), and that he was expecting to hear from her. Rokeach decided to try the effect of turning this fictitious woman into reality. Accordingly, he wrote Leon a letter beginning: "My dear husband" and signed "Madame R.I. Dung," in which she announced that she would be coming to visit him on Thursday afternoon.

Leon's first response was disbelief. He told an aide that he did not believe the letter was from his wife, and that he felt someone was trying to impose on him. On the afternoon his wife was due to visit, he went outdoors, and remained there until visiting time was over.

Leon's "wife" then telephoned him; again, Leon was suspicious, sure that she was an impostor. A few days later, he received another letter, this time signed "Madame Yeti Woman," which declared that she was glad she had spoken to him on the telephone, and enclosed a present—a cigarette holder. Leon threw this into the wastepaper basket, then retrieved it, apparently signaling that he was not, after all, quite sure that Madame Yeti was not his wife. Yet there was obviously some sense in which he knew that his wife did not exist. Would he finally acknowledge this to himself, and be cured of this particular delusion?

The next episode revealed that this was unlikely. When Madame Yeti wrote to him asking him to meet her in the store, Leon took a shower, then went to the store. When he found no one who resembled his wife, he asked an aide where he could find the employee's cafeteria, and when told, exclaimed that he had gone to the wrong place. Obviously, he did believe that he had a wife. This seemed to dispose of the "double bookkeeping" hypothesis.

More letters from Madame Yeti seemed to convince Leon of her existence. But eventually, he began to reject the letters, particularly after she had suggested that he should give up calling himself Dung. Rokeach decided to see if he could retrieve the situation by pretending to be another of Leon's delusions, an uncle called George Bernard Brown. Leon received a phone call from George Bernard Brown which assured him that Madame Dung had his best interests at heart, and that he should not reject her. Leon interrupted: "Your voice doesn't sound like my uncle," and hung up.

A female research assistant named Miss Anderson now came to work in the hospital. It was soon clear that Leon had made Miss Anderson a part of his delusions; he decided she was God. Since Madame Yeti had also been God, this seemed to imply that he believed Miss Anderson was his wife. He began having long interviews with her after group sessions, in which he rambled at length about his delusions, and obviously became increasingly attached to her.

For a while it looked as though Miss Anderson was going to bring him back to sanity. Then his basic mistrust took over. Leon felt that the weekends she spent away from the hospital represented an abandonment, and he sulked when she came back. When she returned from a vacation, he refused to speak to her privately after the group sessions. Clearly, he had decided that having a wife was too much of an emotional strain, and that he was better off with his delusions.

Rokeach met the same kind of failure when he tried to lure Joseph Cassel out of his world of private fantasy. In many ways,

Joseph seemed a better candidate for a cure than either of the other two. Rokeach had observed the effect of showing the three Christs press cuttings about a lecture in which Rokeach had actually described his experiment. Joseph was the only one who acknowledged that the cuttings were about himself; the other two seemed to see no connection between the lecture and their own case.

Because Joseph sometimes referred to Dr. Yoder, the superintendent of the Ypsilanti State Hospital, as his Dad, Rokeach now began writing letters to Joseph signed "Dr. Yoder," in which Yoder accepted the role of Joseph's father, and offered him good advice. At first Joseph began to improve, and to show signs of increasing acceptance of reality. He wrote letters to his wife and his father, with whom he had abandoned contact long ago.

When Dr. Yoder suggested that Joseph should go to church, he began going to church. Dr. Yoder's letters continued to be encouraging, and by Christmas, Joseph was writing to all his relatives. When Dr. Yoder gave him permission to stop working in the vegetable room, which Joseph hated, he was overjoyed. Joseph thanked him in a letter which began "My Dear Dad."

When Joseph complained about his health, Dr. Yoder promised him a "new miracle drug." In fact, the drug was a placebo, but Joseph's symptoms (stomach pains) quickly improved. In one of his letters, he boasted that if he could get out of the hospital, he would write books and become a great writer. Dr. Yoder immediately encouraged him, suggesting that he might write a short story, or an article, or even an autobiography. But Joseph now began to make excuses; he obviously lacked the application to make good his promise. And as Dr. Yoder pressed him to write, he addressed a long letter to President Kennedy, asking for a job in Washington. "The situation had apparently aroused Joseph's long-dormant, deep-seated inferiorities," said Dr. Yoder.

But since Joseph continued to address Dr. Yoder as "Dear Dad," there still seemed a good chance that his loyalty to the doctor might lead him to abandon some of his delusions. Dr. Yoder prescribed another drug, which would restore Joseph's sense of values, and Joseph was soon declaring that he felt much better. But when Dr. Yoder began attacking another of his delusions (that the hospital was some kind of English fortified stronghold) Joseph resisted. He was willing to do many things for Dr. Yoder, but not relinquish any of his delusions. He had gone as far as he was willing to go.

After two years, Rokeach finally abandoned the experiment. The three Christs were as fixed in their delusional systems as ever. Yet his attempt had not been entirely a failure. At least he had disproved Bleuler's "double bookkeeping" hypothesis—insane people are not taken in by their own delusions—as well as Lindner's belief that a delusional system would break down if reality began to invade it. The delusional systems of the three Christs had resisted all attempts at invasion, the only minor success being Leon's change of name to Dr. Dung.

Looking back at the case, it becomes clear that Rokeach's original hypothesis was mistaken. Like James Mill, he was still partly convinced that mad people could be reasoned out of their madness.

What Rokeach had failed to take into account was that all three Christs were inadequate personalities, whose delusions were a psychological defense against a sense of vulnerability. Before his incarceration, Clyde had responded to a series of personal problems with heavy drinking, Joseph by drifting and turning his back on his responsibilities, Leon by increasing inefficiency at work. Each had retreated hopelessly into a distrust of life. At a certain point, as had been the case for Kirk Allen, their unconscious minds had come to the rescue by cutting them off from reality with a delusional system that allowed them some degree of self-esteem and mental freedom.

Rokeach's attempts to make them face up to reality were firmly resisted. Reality frightened them. It was like trying to persuade a naked man to go out in a snowstorm.

By contrast, W.B. Yeats, whom we met in chapter 3, represents a successful attempt to meet the challenge. As with Kirk Allen or the three Christs, his first line of defense was to reject the world he hated, and to declare his belief in an alternative world: fairies, Atlantean myths, spirits. He knew that this world cannot compete, in sheer concreteness, with the solid world he lived in. Yet after all, this is always true of the world of ideas. It does not seem true that the earth goes around the sun, yet it is. Science may be more abstract than everyday reality, but it is truer. So Yeats could feel that there was a perfectly real sense in which his alternative world was the real one.

Yeats's increasing success as a poet and dramatist gradually reduced this need for defenses, and his poetry reveals an increasing capacity for self-assessment. It could be argued that this later realistic work goes too far, in accepting that the mythological world of his early poetry was merely a kind of ladder that enabled him to clamber up out of the dullness of everyday reality, the "foul rag-and-bone shop of the heart." But his last poems certainly reveal a man who is completely adjusted to reality, and who recognizes that his own sense of purpose is somehow connected to human evolution, and the "profane perfection of mankind." Clearly, insisting that fiction is some form of higher reality can serve a valid and useful purpose.

It is worth describing how Clyde Benson came to be in the Ypsilanti State Hospital in the first place.

The son of a dominant father and a deeply religious mother, Clyde was nevertheless "overprotected from the day of his birth." Throughout his life he "maintained a childlike dependence on his parents." This, then, was not the kind of person who was ready to go out and face the battle of life.

At twenty-four, Clyde married a girl whose character was stronger than his own; she babied him, as his own mother had done. For the first ten years of marriage they lived with his parents. Then, with his father-in-law's help, Clyde bought his own farm. He was forty-two when his wife died following an abortion, and he was left in charge of three daughters. Then, struck by a series of misfortunes, including the death of his father, mother, and father-in-law, he began to drink heavily. Clyde married a second time, but drank so heavily that within a few years he was penniless. At that point he deserted his second wife and new family and took a cheap room; soon after, his wife divorced him.

One night Clyde was arrested for drunkenness. In jail, he became violent, ripped up his bedding, stripped himself naked, and tried to break the windows. Then he began to rant, declaring that he was Christ, that he had heard his first wife's voice from an airplane. This was the point at which he was committed to the mental hospital. (Incidentally, the other two "Christs" had similar histories. They were men unable to face life, who turned their backs on their responsibilities.)

It could be said that Clyde's illness began in his overprotected childhood. He was always moody, and had an uncontrollable temper, but his first wife treated him like a difficult child who has to be humored. Her death, and the death of his other three main protectors—his father, mother, and father-in-law—left him feeling vulnerable and terrified. His eldest daughter refused to stay home and keep house for him; instead, she married and moved away. This is when Clyde began to drink. After that, life was one long retreat from reality. When he was finally alone and abandoned, living in a cheap room, his unconscious mind solved the problem for him by sending him delusions. You might say that it was a sound and sensible solution of his problems; it made sure that he was once again protected and looked after.

So what advantage would there have been in allowing Rokeach to cure him? Clyde would have been back in the situation that terrified him before—trying to face reality with inadequate resources. The same was true of the other two Christs. Rokeach's attempt at a cure was a total failure because he did not understand the situation. What we can see here is that the unconscious mind creates delusions, to prevent a collapse into total inadequacy and life-failure.

The same is obviously true of Kirk Allen. But this case is even more interesting because Kirk continued to live a normal life without obvious signs of mental instability. His mental voyages to Mars had always provided him with an alternative to the everyday world; now his unconscious responded to the new threat by turning these fantasies into reality, a remarkable indication of the miraculous powers of the unconscious mind.

If we apply this insight to David Koresh, we can see that his problems started when he felt weak and inadequate as a child. His triumph in school sports reversed this attitude, so that he felt it worthwhile to take a more aggressive stance towards the world. Yet success eluded him, and sexual humiliation underlined the sense of defeat.

Now David Koresh had always taken refuge in the scriptures in much the same way that Kirk Allen took refuge in Edgar Rice Burroughs. When his attempts to become a rock star failed, Koresh concentrated on his other lifeline, the scriptures. Unlike Kirk Allen or the three Christs, Koresh had once tasted the sensation of triumph, so he applied all his will and sense of purpose to success in this direction.

We can see that to ask, "Did he really believe he was the son of God?" is as irrelevant as asking if Clyde Benson believed he was Jesus Christ. It was Koresh's way of adjusting to a hostile world, of becoming what all of us wish to be: a "Somebody."

The vitally important insight here is that the same thing applies to disciples. They are also in the same position of facing a hostile world. Like Clyde Benson, they long for a protector. We have seen how Jeannie Mertle was drawn into Jim Jones's People's Temple because at first it gave her a sense of womb-like security.

We can also see that when Jim Jones demanded to be addressed as Father, it was not simply an expression of his will-to-power; it was also a recognition that his disciples wanted a father figure. When he faked miracles, he knew that his disciples wanted to believe that he was a miracle worker. He was responding to their need as much as to his own. If he had been able to take his disciples on a mental voyage to Mars, their faith would have been even stronger; they wanted to escape from the oppressive, boring, difficult everyday world.

To dismiss all this as a delusional system is to overlook the most important thing about it: it is also a tranformational system, a method of transforming reality. The aim of Yeats's early poems was to transform his everyday reality into something else, to present himself with a reality he preferred to the world of late nineteenth-century London. The aim of Kirk Allen's fantasies was to transform his reality, and in this aim, he was even more successful than Yeats. Why? Because his fantasy was backed by the immense emotional force of sex: the fantasy was a kind of substitute for sexual potency.

This raises a point of fundamental importance in this study of rogue messiahs and their disciples: sex is one of the most powerful of the transformational systems. The difference between Kirk

Allen's fantasies before and after the secret filing cabinet episode is that they took on a new degree of reality: in fact, they ceased to be mere fantasies. But this is also true of the sexual fantasies of an adolescent boy. Lying in bed, he can fantasize the presence of the girl next door to the point of intense physical excitement, and even of orgasm.

We are inclined to dismiss this as mere imagination, yet in its way, this transformational activity is as remarkable as Kirk's transportation to Mars. Imagination can suddenly influence the body, as if a fantasy of flying could actually lift us into the air. Sexual fantasy imposes its own truth in the intractable world of physical reality. This is even more apparent in the case of fetishism, where sexual arousal is caused by an object, such as an item of underwear, a shoe, even an umbrella. It seems incomprehensible that someone could masturbate with an inanimate object until we understand that the object is *transformed* by sexual desire into something else, such as a living woman.

Even romantic sexual attraction—the kind that might be experienced by an innocent virgin—depends upon this transforming function. The women in the early Yeats poems, with "cloud-pale eyelids, dream-dimmed eyes," are pure idealizations.

> *It had become a glimmering girl*
> *With apple blossom in her hair*
> *Who called me by my name and ran*
> *And faded through the brightening air.*

Real women are not like this, as Yeats must have known, since he had sisters. Yet when he fell in love, he immediately imposed this idealistic, pre-Raphaelitic image on his "beloved." In this, Yeats was like all other romantic young males, and even those who regard themselves as totally unromantic. The desire to possess is so great that it transforms the object of desire into an idealization.

Everyone must have noticed how, the first time we experience a vague attraction to a member of the opposite sex, we also notice his or her less attractive features. Then, as the acquaintance progresses, these are edited out, until they cease to exist, or no longer matter. The will to fall in love is itself a transformational system.

The same transformational system can be seen in Jeannie Mertle's description of her initial revulsion towards Jim Jones, and how it changed over the course of a few weeks into devotion. The devotion of disciples is a kind of chemical reaction between the charisma of the rogue messiah and the transformational system of the disciples, like an Alka Seltzer dropped into water.

It is tempting to say that transformational systems are methods of deceiving ourselves, but this would not be entirely accurate. When a male is in a state of intense sexual excitement, he sees the cause of this excitement as a kind of archetypal female, as Yeats recognized:

> *When my arms wrap you round I press*
> *My heart upon the loveliness*
> *That has long faded from the world.*

In such moments, everything about women and womanhood seems to be grasped all at once, in a kind of bird's-eye view. And the bird's-eye view is, by definition, far more inclusive than the worm's-eye view we take when not roused to a high level of perception by sexual energy.

This also explains why most messiahs are so unashamedly promiscuous. The messiah and disciple exist in a heightened transformational system, like Kirk Allen on Mars. Jones's assumption that most of the women in his congregation wanted sex with him was probably accurate. Under these circumstances, sex is no longer seen as promiscuity; the transformational system has raised it to the level of a ritual or sacrament, like holy communion.

To understand this is to understand why the rogue messiah phenomenon cannot be understood in terms of logic and rationality. It takes place on a far more intense level. Milton Rokeach expresses this clearly when he compares the experience of schizophrenia to the experience of psychedelic drugs. Speaking about Leon's attitude to Madame Yeti, Rokeach says:

> Our data do not suggest that he only pretended she existed. . . .
> My own personal experience with LSD . . . makes the halluci-
> natory experience somewhat more understandable psychologi-
> cally. At one point during the time I was under the influence
> of this drug, the phonograph was on. A woman soloist was

singing a hauntingly beautiful melody. I saw the voice lift itself
out of the record player; it looked ghostlike and ribbony. I saw
it travel across the room toward me; then I felt it pushing its
way into my right ear (not my left). And then I heard her
singing the rest of the song inside my head. While this was
happening, I knew it was a hallucination. But still, I experienced it. . . . I am therefore now inclined to believe that the hallucinations or delusions of psychosis are more than simply matters of pretense or of hyperimagination which a little persuasive
logic will prove cannot be so.

Neither would it be entirely accurate to say that the drug was
here the transformative agent; it was Rokeach's own imagination,
somehow amplified by the drug. If we can grasp that sex and discipleship operate through a similar transformational system, we shall
begin to understand why both lie beyond the reach of James Mill's
naive logic.

SEVEN

THE PSYCHIATRIST AS MESSIAH

The view of sex described in the last chapter is, of course, closely related to Freud's notion of the libido. Freud regarded sex as the ultimate transformative system, which can produce effects similar to hallucinations. In fact, under certain conditions, it can produce hallucinations.

Freud arrived at this insight as a result of a case treated by his colleague Josef Breuer. The patient was a young girl called Bertha Pappenheim (Freud calls her Anna O) who had become a dual personality. She would break off a sentence, and suddenly throw a cushion at the person she was speaking to, or even climb a tree; moments later, she would become herself again, and resume the sentence, with no memory of what had happened since she broke off. This second self spoke only English (Bertha spoke German) and suffered from various hallucinations. Bertha also suffered from a paralyzed right arm.

One day, as Bertha was lying in an absent state, muttering to herself, someone in the room repeated one of her phrases. She then began to speak, and went on to tell a kind of fairy story, gradually becoming more fluent as she went on. The story began with an account of a girl sitting by a sick bed. When this was over, she woke up feeling calm and relaxed.

Questioning Bertha in her somnolent state, Breuer learned that one of her symptoms, her inability to drink a glass of water, originated when she saw a dog drinking out of a glass that had been left on the floor. When she woke up from hypnosis, she was able to drink normally.

Breuer learned that the paralysis of Bertha's arm had dated from a time when she was sitting by the sick bed of her adored father, who subsequently died. She had fallen asleep with her arm over the back of a chair, so that it "went to sleep." She had a waking dream in which she saw a black snake writhing towards her father, and woke up. The next day, the sight of a branch in the garden reminded her of the snake, and her arm became paralyzed. After telling Breuer about the snake dream, she woke up cured. Freud was fascinated by the fact that she had cured herself by talking, and this became the basis of the "talking cure," one of the most original features of psychoanalysis.

Breuer's wife became increasingly irritated by her husband's obsession with his patient, and when Breuer finally noticed this, he decided to break off the treatment. Bertha had in any case greatly improved. That same evening she had another "attack," and Breuer found her lying on the bed moving her hips as if in childbirth—or sexual intercourse. So far she had been a prim woman who had never once alluded to sex. Breuer calmed her with hypnosis, then fled in a panic and left Vienna on an unplanned holiday.

Freud, like Breuer, concluded that Bertha was sexually infatuated with the therapist, a phenomenon he came to call transference. The thought of Bertha's repressed sexuality planted a seed in his mind which gradually grew into the fully-fledged sexual theory, in which the tremendous force of repressed sexuality festers in the unconscious mind.

When female patients began to report that they had been sexually abused by their fathers, Freud initially concluded that the majority of adult neuroses are caused by sexual abuse in childhood. But he eventually came to reject this view, and decided that the patients were relating fantasies which they perceived as reality. This only reinforced his sexual theory, for it seemed to prove that daughters had a secret wish to be seduced by their fathers, and that conversely, sons had a desire to possess their mothers. This is the famous Oedipus complex, whose corollary was that the sons unconsciously wanted to murder their fathers. It seemed all the more plausible to Freud because his own mother was a pretty and attractive woman who was many years her husband's junior.

The tremendous opposition aroused by his theory convinced Freud that he had touched a sensitive nerve, and that the sexual theory must be true: all neurosis, without exception, is due to some sexual problem.

We can see that the examples Rokeach's three Christs, and even Lindner's Kirk Allen, suggest that this is an oversimplification. The origin of mental illness is a feeling of inadequacy in the face of the difficulties of living. Most people fight back, and go on fighting back. Clyde, Joseph, Leon—each surrendered to discouragement, retreating from their problems and slipping into a state of increasing inefficiency. Under similar circumstances, many people have nervous breakdowns, or even commit suicide. The three Christs were rescued by their unconscious minds, which provided hallucinations that enabled them to function more or less normally. The fact that the hallucinations were related to religion seems to support the view expressed by Jung, that man has a religious function, rather than Freud's sexual theory.

It is true that Kirk Allen's Martian fantasies were basically the result of his seduction by the nymphomaniac governess. But this was because she had damaged his "transformational system" and made him afraid of sex. He poured his sexual energy into fantasy, and eventually turned the fantasy into reality.

In Freud's subsequent development we can see all the characteristics of the messiah—the increasing authoritarianism and paranoia, the deep resentment towards anyone who challenged his views. When Ernest Jones suggested that they create a committee of six loyal members, who would form a kind of Praetorian guard, Freud was delighted, and presented each of the six with an engraved Greek jewel. Oddly, he insisted that this committee—eventually it became the Psychoanalytic Association—should be kept secret, aware of the implications of a committee of "disciples," even though there were only six rather than twelve.

His friend (and disciple) Jung became increasingly dissatisfied with the rigidity of the sexual theory, particularly when Freud said to him one day: "My dear Jung, promise me you will never abandon the sexual theory." It seemed strange that a scientist should be asking him to cling to a theory rather than to be prepared to modify it according to the facts. (But since we know that there is no great gulf between science and religion, this need hardly surprise us.)

Total disillusionment came when Freud was relating one of his own dreams to Jung. When Jung asked for some personal details that might throw light on it, Freud gave him an odd look and answered: "But I cannot risk my authority." "At that moment," said Jung, "he lost it altogether." He had perceived that the relation Freud wanted between them was that of messiah and disciple rather than of equal colleagues.

In short, Freud had turned the sexual theory into a closed system, a walled city, a religion based on dogma. Any challenge to the closed system aroused all the violent resentment of the Right Man, the messiah.

Even so, Jung admits that Freud "still meant to me a superior personality, upon whom I projected the father. . . . His friendship meant a great deal to me." In fact, Freud used his charm and charisma to draw disciples into a personal relation so deep that they were like flies trussed up in spider-silk; if they even tried to break away, the results were traumatic.

When his brilliant and witty disciple Viktor Tausk dared to defend the satirist Karl Kraus—he had attacked psychoanalysis, saying, "Psychoanalysis is the disease for which it claims to be the cure"—Freud set out to undermine his self-esteem, which was so successful that Tausk shot himself. Another disciple, Herbert Silberer, made the mistake of approving some of Jung's mythological theories; like Tausk, he was excommunicated in the most brutal way, and hanged himself. Both Jung and Wilhelm Reich (another Freudian) had nervous breakdowns after being excommunicated. All had come to regard Freud as a father figure, such that the total withdrawal of his approval plunged them into depression. The relationship between Freud and his disciples enables us to understand why the followers of Jim Jones and David Koresh were willing to commit suicide for him.

Jung's break with Freud came as a result of his increasing conviction that Freud was ignoring the importance of the religious impulse. For Freud, religion was an illusion, while Jung was the son of a clergyman. He had experienced a religious crisis in his teens, and was obsessed by the mystery of human suffering, old age, and death. His attempts to find the answers in his father's theology books convinced him that these ideas were drivel.

Although he had lost his Christian faith, Jung continued to seek the answers in works like Goethe's *Faust* and Schopenhauer's

World as Will and Idea. He began to devour philosophy. Like Kirk Allen, Jung began to see himself as a dual personality; the part visible to the world was a schoolboy, but the reality was a wise old man. On top of a mountain, "where ever-new abysses and panoramas opened out before my gaze," Jung felt that he was at last looking at the *real* world, and experienced a deep sense of awe.

Jung had also had personal experience of the negative powers of the unconscious mind. As a boy of eleven, he hated school. One day, another boy knocked him down and he struck his head on the ground. Jung recalls thinking: "Oh good, now I shan't have to go to school any more." He began having fainting spells, and had to stay at home; doctors thought he might be epileptic.

One day, hiding behind a shrub in the garden, he heard his father telling a friend: "I've lost what little I had. What will become of the boy if he can't earn his own living?" Suddenly full of guilt, Jung hurried to his father's study and began working. He had a fainting fit, but pressed on; he also ignored a second and third fainting fit. Then, quite suddenly, the fainting fits went away. Jung had succeeded in disconnecting the unconscious mechanism that was making him ill. He comments: "I had learned what neurosis is." He had come close to self-induced chronic invalidism.

Soon after this Jung had what he regarded as a mystical experience. Walking along a road from school, he suddenly felt as if he had emerged from a cloud, and had a feeling: "Now I am myself." Before that, he had not yet had an "I." "But at that moment I came upon myself. Previously I had existed too, but everything had merely happened to me. . . . Now I knew: I am myself now, I exist."

This experience is of basic importance, for it is obviously what happens to men who become convinced they are messiahs: Now I exist. They pass from the passive to the active attitude. Every time Koresh seduced an under-age girl, he must have felt: Now I exist.

Jung became fascinated by the occult. After discovering a book on Spiritualism in a friend's home, he began to read everything he could find, and became convinced of the reality of psychical phenomena. Soon after, a walnut table in the dining room split with a loud report, and a bread knife in a drawer shattered into several pieces; Jung believed these were poltergeist phenomena. Jung's cousin, named Helly Preiswerk, developed mediumistic powers; in trance, her everyday self was replaced by a series of remarkable personalities, some of whom spoke languages unknown to the girl.

So when Freud assured Jung that religion was an illusion based on repressed sexuality, and that psychical phenomena were a kind of wishful thinking, he had no doubt that his mentor was revealing severe intellectual limitations. But Jung had no desire to confront Freud. Instead, he began to play a double game, writing a book about mythological symbols and the unconscious mind in which, although he made full acknowledgement of the importance of sex, he concluded that man's deepest needs are for meaning and purpose. In other words, man is, by nature, a religious being.

In a chapter called "The Sacrifice" Jung came out into the open and stated that Freud's view of sex "is incorrect if we take it literally." This was the beginning of the end of their relationship. Soon after *Symbols of Transformation* (the book in question) was published, Freud began a letter "Dear Dr. Jung" instead of "Dear Jung." A semi-reconciliation was effected, but when Freud wrote Jung a patronizing letter, Jung exploded, and told Freud that he was sick of his habit of treating his pupils like patients, or like naughty children. "Meanwhile you remain on top as a father, sitting pretty. For sheer obsequiousness, no one dares to pluck the prophet by the beard."

In calling Freud a prophet, Jung was putting his finger on Freud's basic fault: his messianic pretensions, his craving to be an absolute authority figure. Freud responded with a soft answer, admitting that his anger had been caused by "a bit of neurosis." But Jung was in no mood for drawing back, and advised Freud that it was time to get rid of the "bit of neurosis."

Jung begged Freud to "take these statements as an effort to be honest," and not to "apply the deprecatory Viennese criterion of egoistic striving for power or heaven knows what other insinuations from the world of the father complex." Jung was reacting violently to the psychoanalytic trick of always being in the right, and accusing those who disagree of being in the grip of neuroses that make them incapable of facing the truth. In 1913, Jung resigned the editorship of the *Psychoanalytic Yearbook*, and in the following year, resigned as president of the Psychoanalytic Association.

But the battle had undermined Jung's self-belief; Freud's accusations of power-seeking had struck home. (The irony of the situation, as we can see when we view Jung's life in retrospect, is that his messianic pretensions were as great as Freud's.)

In 1913, Jung came close to a nervous breakdown, struggling with dreams of disaster. The curious result is that he began to experience the same kind of hallucinatory consciousness as Kirk Allen. Seated at his desk in December 1913, struggling with a sense of terror, Jung allowed himself to relax and "drop." "Suddenly it was as if the ground literally gave way beneath my feet, and I plunged into dark depths." Like Alice in Wonderland, Jung landed on a soft mass, and found himself in the entrance to a cave, guarded by a dwarf with leathery skin. He waded through icy water towards a glowing red crystal; when he raised it, he saw the corpse of a blonde-haired youth floating by, followed by a black scarab, and by a red sun rising out of the water. Blood poured out of the opening underneath the crystal.

From then on, Jung found that his fantasies had taken on a reality comparable to the ordinary world, and images in these fantasies—an old man called Philemon, a girl called Salome—seemed to be real people. In effect, he was experiencing a psychotic state like that of the three Christs of Ypsilanti. And although his own fascination with the unconscious brought him through the crisis—it took him until 1918—Jung would always retain a capacity for visions and waking dreams, which he called active imagination.

He describes one of these in his autobiography: "One night I awoke and saw, bathed in bright light at the foot of my bed, the figure of Christ on the Cross. It was not quite life-size, but extremely distinct; and I saw that his body was made of greenish gold. The vision was marvelously beautiful, and yet I was profoundly shaken by it. A vision as such is nothing unusual for me, for I frequently see extremely vivid hypnagogic images."

The main conviction that emerged from these years was the certainty that man has a "transcendent function," a craving to evolve, to transcend himself, and that it is the blocking of this function that leads to mental sickness, Jung wrote.

Freud, of course, regarded this as so much gibberish and self-delusion; he would never cease to regard Jung as a renegade who had achieved fame by embracing psychoanalysis, then making his own bid to usurp the throne. To the end of his life, Freud never deviated from his belief in the sexual theory.

Jeffrey Masson, whose account of Paul Brunton has already been discussed, later became a Freudian psychiatrist, choosing the European psychoanalyst Kurt Eissler as a kind of father figure. Masson's book *Final Analysis* describes his increasing disillusion with psychoanalysis, and his eventual "excommunication" when he dared to question one of Freud's theories. From the opening pages of Masson's *Final Analysis*, we are aware of how far psychoanalysis depends upon the same basic techniques as those used by messiahs to convince their disciples.

Masson went to see his first psychoanalyst (whom he calls Dr. Bergman) because he could not understand why he often felt sad for no reason, and why he was unable to fall in love. He told Bergman: "My problem is that I'm not able to fall in love, though I sleep with many women." The analyst's reply was, "I should have such a problem." Masson found this deeply off-putting, because it meant that the analyst was revealing his own secret desires, and therefore failing at the very beginning in the role of "guru and father figure" that Masson wanted so urgently.

When Masson decided to become a psychoanalyst, he was told that he would first have to undergo psychoanalysis. His account of his four years of analysis under Dr. Irvine Schiffer is both amusing and disturbing. Schiffer declined to be the father figure. When he asked Masson what he was thinking, Masson said: "That I would probably never know if you were married and had children." "Wrong. I am married, and have four children." Again, Masson felt upset; he didn't want to see Schiffer as a potential friend—and therefore an equal—but as a father figure who could be trusted to solve all Masson's problems.

Here we see the basic mechanism that binds the disciple to his master. The messiah does not unbend and disappoint; he knows that his disciples want an authority figure, and he does his best to live up to it. In due course he becomes rigidly fixed in this role, until the slightest challenge to his authority arouses paranoia.

In that case, is it not better to have a guru like Schiffer who rejects this role? Masson's account suggests that it is not. According to Masson, Schiffer wanted to be an authority and a non-authority at the same time. When Masson admitted that he was puzzled by the "tacky furniture" in the consulting room, Schiffer said: "Fuck you, my mother died recently and those were her things, and I'm proud to have them here." When Masson criticized him for being constantly late, he flew into a rage and shouted. When Masson voiced other criticisms, they were dismissed as "adolescent rebellion." This was a confrontational relationship, like one between squabbling schoolboys, not the master-disciple relationship Masson longed for. "I desperately needed for him to be the man he claimed he was, the man I wanted him to be." Every disciple since time began would echo that sentiment.

This craving for an authority figure finally influenced Masson's attitude in spite of Schiffer's refusal to play the role. When Schiffer wrote a book, Masson enthused about it for weeks; his wife thought it poorly written and badly argued, and when Masson himself read it later, he agreed, admitting, "Such is the strength of transference." It seems that Schiffer knew that, in spite of the confrontational relationship, he would eventually inspire the transference phenomenon. Such is the nature of discipleship.

It is nevertheless hard to understand the strategy of analysts like Bergman and Schiffer, and many others Masson described in his book. Were they declining the role of guru? This seems unlikely, since a psychotherapist is, by definition, a kind of guru. The impression that emerges is that their attitude arose from the basic practice of psychoanalysis: the assumption that the patient has a "splinter" lodged somewhere in the unconscious, and that it is festering. The analyst's business is to probe until the patient winces; the analysis depends upon the "talking cure," letting the patient free-associate until the "splinter" comes out.

This fails to take account of the fact that Bertha Pappenheim, who first inspired the talking cure, was in a state of serious neurosis that involved a split-personality. Her problems had arisen as a result of the profound depression she experienced as she watched the slow and painful death of her beloved father. When the mind is in a state of low pressure, every molehill becomes a mountain; the thought of drinking water tainted with a dog's saliva produces deep revulsion that is likely to occur again every time the patient raises a glass to her lips. To talk about such a problem helps to get it out of the system.

By comparison, Masson's psychological problems were insignificant. Since falling in love seems to involve a kind of chemical affinity, inability to fall in love merely suggests the absence of that affinity between two persons. Feeling sad about nothing in particular is a typical romantic malaise, a craving for a stronger sense of purpose. A dozen works of nineteenth century romanticism supporting this view could be mentioned here. Neither of these problems are likely to be solved by the talking cure; the first can only be solved by meeting the right person, the second by somehow generating a strong sense of purpose. Masson's instinct was to look for a guru, since the business of a guru is to give the disciple a sense of purpose.

Masson was eventually excommunicated from psychoanalysis because he questioned Freud's abandonment of the sexual abuse theory. Modern research into multiple personality has shown that incest and childhood sexual abuse are more common than is usually assumed. That is why Masson therefore suggested that Freud was wrong to abandon the sexual abuse theory.

Masson seemed unaware that, in doing so, he was undermining Freud's sexual theory itself, which was based on the assumption that patients were creating false memories of incest, and that this in turn indicated that women had a secret wish to be seduced by their fathers. He was startled by the fury that erupted when an article about his talk was published in *The New York Times*, and deeply upset when his guru, Kurt Eissler, turned against him. In retrospect, the controversy that led to Masson's expulsion from his post as archivist of the Freud papers, and from the International Psychoanalytic Association, seems inevitable; and Masson's astonishment, naive.

One result of his expulsion was an iconoclastic book called *Against Therapy: Emotional Tyranny and the Myth of Psychological Healing*, in which Masson argues that psychoanalysis, and psychotherapy in general, amounts to a multi-million dollar confidence trick.

Masson's view is relevant here because it could also be regarded as an attack on the notion of messiahs. He explains: "The structure of psychotherapy is such that, no matter how kindly a person is, when that person becomes a therapist, he or she is engaged in acts that are bound to diminish the dignity, autonomy, and freedom of the person who comes for help."

The main thrust of Masson's book is that ever since psychiatrists came into existence in the nineteenth century (when they were called alienists), they have imposed their own ideas on their patients. Masson cites the case of a boy who told his doctor: "You are a pig and crazy. You are the same person who did those immoral things in my room, and you are doing to me precisely what the people at home did to me too." Instead of trying to find out if the boy had been sexually abused at home, the doctor had him locked up because he suffered from "sexual hallucinations."

Yet when Masson comes to discuss Freud, there is not the all-out attack that might have been expected. Instead, he devotes a long chapter to one single case, that of the patient called Dora, in which Freud showed himself particularly insensitive. Dora (Ida Bauer) was the daughter of a wealthy industrialist, and she had become depressed, suicidal, and difficult to live with. She was particularly rebellious with a close friend of the family Freud calls Herr K.

Freud naturally began by assuming that the problem was sexual, and that it was due to some "original psychic trauma." Dora explained that when she was fourteen, Herr K. had seized her in his arms and kissed her. Although she disliked it, she had kept silent; but when, two years later, Herr K. propositioned her while she was on holiday, Dora slapped his face and insisted on returning home.

She told her father what had happened, but Herr K. denied it, saying that it was all her imagination, due to reading books on sex. Her father believed him, and this probably upset Dora more than Herr K.'s advances. They were telling her that she was suffering from delusions, which must have caused deep anger and mental conflict. Dora was also convinced—correctly—that her father was having an affair with Herr K.'s wife, and that her father wanted Freud to talk her out of this conviction.

In fact, Freud believed her, both about Herr K.'s behavior to her, and her father's affair with Herr K.'s wife. Freud was also inclined to agree with Dora that her father had tacitly agreed to hand her over to Herr K. in exchange for Herr K.'s wife. This being so, the natural resolution of the situation was for the doctor to form an alliance with the patient, assure her that he knew she was not imagining things, and persuade her that her father's adultery and Herr K.'s advances were not such terrible things after all. Here was a case where the talking cure would probably have worked and reconciled a patient to her situation.

Instead, Freud arrived at the astonishing conclusion that Herr K.'s kiss had caused sexual arousal, and that Dora wanted to marry him. However, she happened to know that he had also tried to seduce a governess. The governess had told Dora about this, and Dora had been outraged to hear that Herr K. had used precisely the same words in his attempt to seduce her. This, according to Freud, was why she regarded his proposition as an insult; he believed that she had then decided to tell her father in order to get revenge.

When Freud told her this, Dora thanked him warmly and left—and came back no more. We can see why. It was a double insult. Dora's father had implied that she was mad, and now this "stupid" doctor was assuring her that she had been sexually aroused by Herr K.'s kiss and that she really wanted to marry him. Since she knew this was untrue, what point was there in remaining the patient of such an idiot?

Perhaps the most disturbing thing is that Freud wrote up this case as one of his triumphs, telling his friend Wilhelm Fliess—like Breuer, he finally broke with Freud because he felt that Freud was too obsessed by sex—"It has been a lively time, and has brought a new patient, an eighteen-year-old girl, a case that has opened smoothly to the existing collection of picklocks."

Masson might have cited many other cases to demonstrate the way that Freud imposed his own sexual interpretation on his patients. For example, there was the case of Hans, who developed a phobia about going outdoors because he overheard a friend's father say: "Don't put your finger near that horse; it could bite." Freud concluded that Hans wanted to seduce his mother and kill his father, horses being a symbol of masculinity.

Then there was the case of a Russian whom Freud called "the Wolf Man" because he had once dreamed of wolves. The Wolf Man suffered from low vitality and a sense of meaninglessness. After several years of analysis—the Wolf Man was, fortunately, rich—Freud concluded that, as a child, he had seen his parents making love "in the animal position," hence the obsession with wolves. In the famous paper he wrote on the case, Freud admits that the love-making scene was only an assumption, but in the rest of the paper goes on to refer to it as fact. Although the paper is regarded as a classic of psychoanalysis, the Wolf Man was never fully cured.

But it is not Masson's intent to make an all-out attack on Freud as being little better than a witch doctor, although everything he says clearly points to this conclusion. The reason for this is not clear. It may be because Masson continues to regard Freud, on whose writings he has expended so many years, as a kind of father figure, or it may be because he is not willing to put himself completely beyond the pale of the psychoanalytic establishment. In fact, Masson attempts to draw no general conclusions from the Dora case, and passes on to Freud's disciple Ferenczi, then to Jung, whom he attacks as a Nazi, then to more recent therapists, like John Rosen and Fritz Perls, who make easy targets. The book ends with a general air of inconclusiveness.

Perhaps this might have been deduced from Masson's preface, with its dubious argument that psychotherapists are "bound to diminish the dignity, autonomy, and freedom of the person who comes for help." The truth is that a person goes to a psychotherapist for the same reason that he might call in a plumber or roofing specialist: because he wants to put the problem into more competent hands than his own. The real argument against most psychotherapists is not that they diminish the dignity of the patient, but that they are not competent to offer the help that is needed. All the same, there are obviously occasions when psychotherapists succeed, as Lindner did with Kirk Allen. Masson's overall dismissal does not inspire confidence in his judgement.

What is certainly interesting about psychoanalysis—particularly about cases of delusional psychosis—is the light it throws on the problem of messiahs and disciples. People become disciples for the same reason that they go to psychoanalysts. Are the messiahs as bogus as the psychotherapists Masson criticizes? Are deception and fraud already inherent in the relationship? Or are we, as Jung would contend, dealing with something that is altogether deeper and more problematic?

EIGHT

STRANGE POWERS

When Madame Blavatsky died in 1891, a young Austrian named Rudolf Steiner had just completed his university thesis, and started a job at the Goethe Archives in Weimar, Germany.

Thirty years younger than Madame Blavatsky, Steiner was an exceptionally slow developer, who had discovered Theosophy only in the previous year. He would spend seven years at the Goethe Archives, building up a reputation as a scholar, but remaining otherwise unknown. His works, such as *The Philosophy of Freedom* (1894), an attack on the current materialism, failed to make an impact. Back in Berlin, he became an unsuccessful editor. Things began to improve in 1899, when he was asked to give a series of popular lectures for working men at a fee so low that few others would have accepted it.

This modest scholar was an immense success with working men, and his lectures were crowded. Soon he was lecturing at many workers' colleges, and at the Giordano Bruno Union (a rationalist, anti-religious organization) on the history of philosophy.

In August 1900, when he was thirty-nine, Steiner was asked to lecture on Nietzsche to the Berlin Theosophical Society. His lecture was received enthusiastically, and subsequent talks on mysticism were equally successful, although one member of the audience told him that his ideas were not in accordance with those of Annie Besant, the leader of the London Theosophical Society.

One evening, an attractive young woman called Marie Von Sievers asked Steiner whether it was not time for a new spiritual movement in Europe, and Steiner agreed enthusiastically that indeed it was. His lectures on "Christianity as a Mystical Fact" and on Plato and Platonism brought him an increasing number of admirers. In 1902, he traveled to a Theosophical congress in London, and was appointed to form a German branch of the Society.

The rise of Anthroposophy, which is what Steiner called his version of Theosophy, is one of the most amazing success stories of the twentieth century. From 1902 onward, Steiner's personal following increased at a rapid rate. He lectured tirelessly and published book after book, with titles like *Knowledge of Higher Worlds* and *Occult Science–An Outline.*

He was to lecture, on average, once a day for twenty-five years— around six thousand lectures in all. At a Theosophy congress in Paris in 1906, his lectures had a larger attendance than the official Theosophic events. His mail was so enormous that it had to be carried to the post office in laundry baskets. He lectured in most of the countries in Europe, and most major cities in Germany had an Anthroposophic group.

In 1913 a follower presented him with a large plot of land near Dornach in Switzerland, and on this he began to build a headquarters, which he called the Goetheanum. By the beginning of the First World War, Steiner was one of the most successful "messiahs" that Europe had seen since Sabbatai Zevi.

The essence of Steiner's doctrine was that the physical, everyday world is a mere veil that covers a spiritual reality. He had grown up within sight of the Alps, in a small town surrounded by beautiful woods, and he claims that he was continually aware of the presence of invisible beings. One day a strange woman had entered the station waiting room—his father was a train station master—and asked him to help her; then she walked into the stove and vanished. Later, Steiner heard that a female relative had committed suicide at the moment he saw her.

Steiner's most striking teaching is that spiritual reality exists inside man. In order to grasp it, he must learn the art of descending inside himself like a man in a diving bell exploring the depths of the ocean. In this way, we can even communicate with the dead.

In an age that was becoming disillusioned with materialism, this doctrine, combined with Steiner's teachings about Christ (to whom he attached supreme importance), Atlantis, and the active forces of darkness (which he called Ahriman and Lucifer), aroused intense enthusiasm, and by 1912, Steiner's followers could be numbered in hundreds of thousands.

His downfall began with the war. The German general von Moltke could not make up his mind whether to hurl all his forces at the French in one terrific blow and smash them, or to be cautious and divide his forces. He asked Steiner to come and see him and asked his advice. In fact Steiner arrived too late, and the decision to divide the forces, which was to cost Germany the war, had already been made. Moltke's decision turned the war into a stalemate that would cost millions of lives, and he was dismissed. When it became known that Steiner had been to visit him, Steiner was blamed for the disastrous decision.

In the misery that followed the war, Steiner's doctrine of invisible worlds seemed suddenly irrelevant. In a time of galloping inflation, who cared? What the Germans wanted was some kind of practical solution to their problems, and this was offered by the Communists. Within a year or two, these solutions were being opposed by the National Socialists under an ex-corporal named Adolf Hitler. Undoubtedly, history had played a very nasty trick on the founder of Anthroposophy.

To make things worse, Steiner's political suggestions seem hopelessly unrealistic. His main contribution was an idea he called the Threefold Commonwealth—in effect, a society in which thinkers and artists would make the decisions, while the politicians and businessmen would ensure the smooth running of the state. It sounded like—and is—complete moonshine. While Steiner was preaching against patriotism, Hitler was preaching the need for a new German nationalism. Both Nazis and Communists began to heckle Steiner at his meetings, and in Munich he was physically attacked, and had to escape from his hotel by the back door.

On New Year's Eve, 1922, after Steiner had delivered a lecture on the "Spiritual Communion of Mankind," the Goetheanum was burnt down. Whether it was arson or an electrical fault has never been established. It was rebuilt, but just over three years later, in March 1925, Steiner was dead, worn out with lecturing and with the enormous demands of his disciples and admirers.

In retrospect, the most interesting question is why Anthroposophy achieved such success. The answer, as with all messiahs, lies in the character of the man himself. In *God is My Adventure*—one of the great best-sellers of the 1930s—Rom Landau describes his reaction to seeing Steiner lecture. "To be quite candid, I was slightly terrified. There was something frightening in his deepset eyes, in the ascetic face, bleak as a landscape in the moon, in the strands of jet-black hair falling over the pale forehead. I do not remember ever having seen a man in whose presence I had such an eerie feeling."

But, Landau admits, this soon gave way to a perception of "how human and simple he was." It was this simplicity that had such an effect on Steiner's audiences. This man was outlining the spiritual history of the human race, and he spoke quietly of spiritual realities as one who lived with them every day. He claimed that much of his knowledge came from the Akashic Records. These are the invisible impression that events are supposed to make on a kind of "psychic ether," and which can be "read" by those who are in tune with it. Steiner claimed to be able to converse with the dead, and to be able to see the past incarnations of the people he spoke to. Yet all these claims were made diffidently and sincerely by a man whose manner seemed as down-to-earth as a professor of civil engineering.

What is Steiner doing in the present book, since there is obviously no sense in which he qualifies as a rogue messiah? It is because he makes us aware that the messiah is also a social phenomenon, someone who is called forth by the needs of his time. In 1900, the world was ready for someone who talked about spiritual reality with the quiet authority of an expert on bridge building. To put it crudely, Steiner was in a seller's market. There was an immense hunger for ideas about mysticism, the spiritual history of mankind, the great religious teachers, and Steiner rode this wave like a surfer.

The year 1914 ended that world like a thunderclap. Suddenly the future belonged to another "prophet," Adolf Hitler, with his ideas about how to end unemployment and restore the Germans to their ancient Saxon heritage. Steiner's epoch came to an end, as abruptly and as brutally as the prosperity of the 1920s ended in the Wall Street crash.

Steiner's problem was that he had been too prominent, too successful, to be allowed to depart peacefully from the stage of history. In this respect he was less fortunate than another Theosophical guru, Jiddu Krishnamurti, who happened also to be the cause of Steiner's break with the Theosophists.

In 1909, the Rev. Charles Leadbeater, the librarian of the Theosophical Society, had seen a beautiful thirteen-year-old boy on the beach near Adyar in India; the child proved to be one of the eight sons of an Indian civil servant, who was also an officer of the Theosophical Society in Madras. The boy's father agreed to allow Leadbeater to adopt Jiddu and his younger brother Nitya.

Leadbeater, like Steiner, claimed to be able to read people's past incarnations, and he was immediately convinced that the boy was the latest incarnation of Maitreya, the World Teacher, (whose last incarnation had been Jesus Christ), destined to save mankind in the twentieth century. Annie Besant was equally impressed, and Krishnamurti was made financially secure by an endowment, given a home in France, and educated (at the Sorbonne) with a view to taking his place as the savior of mankind.

The German Theosophical Society, under Steiner, was outraged by this attempt to foist the new messiah on them, and in 1913, broke with the London lodge; from then on, Anthroposophy went it alone.

For the next seventeen years, an enormous organization was built up around Krishnamurti—it was called the Star of the East—and a large stadium was built for him in Sydney, Australia, from which he could proclaim his message to the world.

Other sites were purchased in the Ojai Valley, in southern California, and in the Rishi Valley in India, while a Dutch follower gave Krishnamurti the use of a castle in Holland. It is a sobering example of how easily a messiah can be promoted, and then foisted on a passive and expectant public.

Then, to the shock and dismay of his mentors, Krishnamurti announced in 1929 that he was not the messiah, and that from now on he would live as a man among men. In his renunciation speech he declared: "I maintain that truth is a pathless land and you cannot approach it by any path whatsoever, by any religion, by any sect. . . . I do not want followers." He advised them to put away religious practices and to look inside themselves for enlightenment.

Another version of this history is told by Rom Landau, which he claims to have heard from the philosopher, P.D. Ouspensky. Ouspensky claimed that Leadbeater and Annie Besant believed that any gifted young man brought up as the messiah, would actually develop into one, and that Krishnamurti was chosen because he seemed a suitable candidate.

But Landau, who joined a gathering of Theosophists at Castle Eerde, in Holland, found Krishnamurti a disappointing experience. "Krishnamurti's lectures were too vague to give me clear answers to any of my questions. Everyone should find truth for himself; should listen to no one but himself; should consider unification with happiness as his true goal. But when I asked how this could be achieved, I received no clear answers. . . . You asked him about your personal troubles, your religious beliefs . . . and he would talk to you about mountain peaks and streams running through fields."

In spite of his renunciation, or perhaps because of it, Krishnamurti remained as popular as ever, and continued to lecture to large audiences until his death, at the age of ninety, in 1986. He also published many books, and those who have written about him bear witness to his personal charm and charisma.

Now it could certainly be argued that Krishnamurti was the prototype of the genuine guru, as contrasted with Steiner's messianic pretensions. Krishnamurti makes no claims to revelation; he approaches his audience as a man who speaks directly from his own experience, and he advises his listeners to look inside themselves for truth, and have nothing to do with religions.

All this might be more convincing if Krishnamurti's message was clearer. Unfortunately, Rom Landau's complaint that his teaching was too vague to be useful continued to apply throughout his life. The essence of Krishnamurti's teaching remains frustratingly difficult to define. Its main emphasis is on the fact that people live in a private world inside their own heads rather than in the real world. We need to relax into the real world of the present moment.

This teaching seems close to Taoism—to abandon strenuous effort and live naturally—and also to Zen. It is also possible to understand what Krishnamurti meant if we think of our sensations as being on a holiday, with the wide-awake receptiveness to impressions, scenery and people, the sense that everything is interesting. Yet, as Landau complained, Krishnamurti seems unable to make any suggestions as to how this can be achieved. He is even on record as saying: "I have nothing to offer you."

Steiner and Krishnamurti are an interesting contrast. Although he was a modest man, Steiner accepted the messianic role thrust upon him, and died of overwork. Krishnamurti foresaw the dangers of becoming a "world teacher," and made a determined effort to escape. Yet, like Steiner, he died in harness. It is not so easy for the guru to escape the demands of his disciples. A university professor can relax outside the classroom and live his own life, but a guru has renounced the right to live his own life.

This problem becomes even clearer in the case of one of Steiner's most extraordinary contemporaries: George Ivanovich Gurdjieff, one of the most remarkable gurus of the twentieth century.

Unlike Steiner, Gurdjieff was unwilling to accept the public role of messiah; in fact, one condition of joining his groups was to observe the strictest secrecy. In spite of which, as we shall see, he was unable to escape the penalties that seem an inescapable part of the messiah's life.

Born in Alexandropol, in Southern Russia, in 1877, Gurdjieff was fascinated from an early age by tales of the occult. He saw a paralyzed man walk away cured from the tomb of a saint, and watched a table leg tap out answers to questions during a seance. His disposition was deeply religious, and he visited many shrines.

He was also intrigued by the question of hidden knowledge, and was still only a teenager when, in ruins of an ancient city, he found a monk's cell, and a number of decaying parchments which, when deciphered, proved to contain references to an esoteric "Sarmoung Brotherhood." Gurdjieff and a friend went off in search of this brotherhood, although they seem to have had no immediate success. Yet eventually, many years later, Gurdjieff located a Sarmoung monastery in the Himalayas, and absorbed some of the traditional knowledge of the monks. He also learned hypnotism, and often earned money by hiring a hall and putting on a show.

In 1909, Gurdjieff came to St. Petersburg, and found it full of disciples of Madame Blavatsky and Rudolf Steiner, as well as guru-figures like Rasputin. There and in Moscow he became well-known in Theosphical circles. He also became a successful businessman. It was at this time that Gurdjieff began to form his first groups, to which he could impart what he had learned in the past twenty years.

Gurdjieff's basic ideas are easy to summarize. Men believe that they possess self-consciousness and free will. In fact, nearly all our reactions are mechanical; we are little better than machines or robots.

As to consciousness, the truth is that man is basically asleep. He walks around in a kind of dream. Occasionally, some crisis or moment of intense happiness causes him to "wake up." When this happens, he realizes that consciousness could be completely different, infinitely richer, and more interesting.

The aim of Gurdjieff's teaching, sometimes referred to as "the System," was to devise means by which people could wake up. He acknowledged that this demands immense effort and constant vigilance. Rigorously practiced, this develops in human beings a certain resistance to "mechanicalness," which Gurdjieff calls "essence." He also devised various exercises: for example, he taught extremely complex dances requiring immense concentration that could enable his pupils to achieve this higher state of wakefulness.

In 1915, Gurdjieff met his most important follower, Peter Demianovich Ouspensky, a science journalist who had written a book about the fourth dimension.

P.D. Ouspensky had also been obsessed from an early age with the conviction that man is capable of a far wider and deeper form of consciousness, and he had traveled in the East looking for masters who might be able to teach him how to achieve it. The search had ended in disappointment. Then he met Gurdjieff, who spoke of the battle against "sleep," and described the mental disciplines that could be used to overcome "the machine." Ouspensky became a leading member of Gurdjieff's group.

The 1917 revolution caused them all to flee from Russia, and they found themselves, after many wanderings, in Constantinople. It was there that Ouspensky learned that one of his earlier books, *Tertium Organum*, had been translated into English and had been a considerable success. He received enough royalties from this to move to London. There he held meetings in which he taught the doctrines of the "war against sleep" through self-observation, and the attempt to "understand the machine." His success was tremendous, and soon his followers had raised the money to buy a house at Virginia Water.

Meanwhile, Gurdjieff, who had been denied a visa to settle in London—the foreign office suspected he was a Russian spy—had formed an Institute for the Harmonious Development of Man at Fontainebleau, near Paris. His success was considerable, and many eminent people became his disciples. He traveled to America, where his pupils gave exhibitions of his special dancing, and where his incredible control over them led critics to compare him to the ringmaster of a circus.

The Second World War caused a suspension of Gurdjieff's activities; he lived throughout the war in occupied Paris. Ouspensky moved from London to America and continued to run his group there. Yet when he returned to England in 1947, he seemed to have lost belief in the System. He had ceased to feel that it is possible for man to overcome his mechanicalness by strenuous effort, or that higher consciousness could be achieved, except in brief flashes. When he died in October 1947, Ouspensky was obviously a tired and disappointed man.

Gurdjieff experienced no such disillusionment. He continued to live in Paris and to travel to America; at his Paris flat he hosted enormous meals at which the guests had to drink endless toasts of various liqueurs that left them reeling. The aim seems to have been to make them reveal their inner selves. But by 1949, the strong liqueurs and even stronger cigars had taken their toll, and Gurdjieff died at the age of seventy-two.

Gurdjieff's is a particularly instructive case. No one who has read Ouspensky's account of his years with Gurdjieff—*In Search of the Miraculous*—can doubt that Gurdjieff was one of the greatest minds of the twentieth century. Was he a rogue messiah? It is impossible to answer with an unequivocal "no." He fathered many illegitimate children, and seems to have treated his female disciples as a harem. His follower John Bennett remarked: "He spoke of women in terms that would have been better suited to a fanatical Muslim. . . . " He was apparently even able to exercise certain magical sexual powers. Rom Landau tells how an attractive female novelist, sitting at the next table to Gurdjieff in a restaurant, suddenly went pale, and told her companion that Gurdjieff had "struck her through the sexual center" simply by staring at her.

Gurdjieff forces upon us the recognition that dominant males, like all dominant members of the animal kingdom, experience an urge, implanted by nature, to take sexual advantage of women. We have observed it in most of the messiahs in this book. All that can be said with certainty about Gurdjieff is that sex was not one of his prime motives in becoming a guru; he simply seems to have accepted it as one of the privileges of his position.

From the beginning, it is clear that Gurdjieff's central obsession was, unlike so many messiahs in this book, the mystery of human freedom, and how this can be achieved. He compares man to a coach and horses. Man's body is the coach, the feelings and desires are the horses, and the mind is the coachman. But the coach also has an owner, and it is only when he has achieved a higher degree of control and freedom that man can become the "owner" of his "coach," instead of merely its driver.

One of Gurdjieff's most important exercises was "self remembering." When I close my eyes, I become aware of myself. When I look at something—say, my watch—I become aware of the watch. The exercise is to look at the watch while remaining aware of myself looking at the watch. Anyone who tries it will discover that it can be done only for a few seconds; then we forget ourselves, or forget the watch. Gurdjieff taught his pupils to make continuous efforts of self remembering as they engaged in everyday activities.

Obviously, a man who has acquired so much interesting and original knowledge will feel the need to pass it on to other people. This Gurdjieff began to do about 1910. Soon he had a group of pupils in St. Petersburg and Moscow. They were not allowed to speak about "the work" to anyone who was not involved in it; Gurdjieff recognized that effort is easily dissipated in talk.

But from then on, he became, like most gurus, a slave of his own disciples. He took many of them with him when he left Russia in 1917. He even supported many of them at the Priory, his institute at Fontainebleau.

In 1924, there was the curious incident of Gurdjieff's motor accident. He was found lying beside his car, which had crashed into a tree, with his head on a cushion. Doctors diagnosed concussion; yet Gurdjieff's only injuries were cuts on his hands. When someone took his pulse, his fist clenched.

Many pupils subsequently left the Priory, and Gurdjieff was heard to say: "All my life I have lived for others. Now I will live for myself." It seems possible that Gurdjieff arranged his own accident to escape the role of guru and father figure. Yet within a few years, he was back in the familiar role, and remained in it until his death. His life had ceased to be his own. He was trapped in a kind of predicament that seems typical of messiahs.

The point is underlined by the career of one of the most bizarre gurus of the twentieth century, Edward Arthur Wilson. He was to become notorious under the name of Brother Twelve, sometimes referred to in the press as "British Columbia's Aleister Crowley." His story also raises again the fascinating issue of what constitutes the dividing line between a genuine teacher and a rogue messiah.

Born in 1878 in Birmingham, England, Wilson was the son of Irvingites. Edward Irving was a Scottish minister who was appointed to the Caledonian Church in London's Hatton Garden in 1822; convinced that the Second Coming was imminent, he induced in his congregation tremendous transports of religious fervor with sermons that were full of vivid imagery of the end of the world.

When, in 1830, they offered up prayers for some sign or miracle, Irving's congregation began speaking in tongues—that is, in strange languages, sometimes meaningless sounds, but sometimes foreign languages with which the speakers were unfamiliar. The "voices" told Irving that he was to be the new Isaiah, and that in forty days time, he would have the power to work miracles. But the forty days passed, and the miraculous power failed to descend. General disillusion followed; in 1833 he was dismissed, and in the following year died of tuberculosis.

In spite of this disappointment, many Irvingite congregations continued to meet, and the phenomenon of speaking in tongues became almost commonplace. Wilson and his two sisters were brought up in a strongly religious atmosphere; his father (a prosperous businessman) conducted prayers every morning and evening. The basic belief of the Irvingites (who preferred to call themselves the Catholic Apostolic Church) was that the Day of Judgement and the Second Coming would occur before the end of the nineteenth century.

Wilson was born at the time when Madame Blavatsky was achieving world fame, and it seems clear that he later came to pre-fer Theosophy to the religion of the Irvingites. Like Steiner, Wilson claimed to have been in touch with "invisible beings" from early childhood, and wrote: "I have often received visitations from high-ly developed Beings, and these always brought me help or comfort or instruction. At first I thought these were 'Angels,' but as I grew older . . . I learned of the Masters and their work for humanity."

Wilson went to sea as a teenager—he had trained on a Royal Navy ship—and wandered around the world for the next six years or so, even working as a "blackbirder," transporting kidnapped Negroes. In 1902, when he was twenty-four, he married in New Zealand, but would desert his wife and two children ten years later, claiming that he experienced a need to find himself. He also claims that it was in 1912 that he knew beyond all doubt that his life was to be dedicated to some important work. But for twelve years more he continued to wander in Africa, South America, the Pacific. In October 1924, he was living cheaply in a small village in the South of France when he had the vision that would transform his life.

"I was not feeling well, and had gone to bed early. At this time, I wanted to get some milk to drink, so I lit the candle which stood on a small table at the side of my bed. Immediately after lighting it, I saw the Tau suspended in mid-air just beyond the end of my bed, and at a height of eight or nine feet. I thought: "That is strange; it must be some curious impression upon the retina of the eye which I got by lighting the candle. I will close my eyes and it will then stand out more clearly.

"I shut my eyes at once, and there was nothing there. I opened them and saw the Tau in the same place, but much more distinct-ly; it was like a soft golden fire and it glowed with a beautiful radi-ance. This time, in addition to the Tau, there was a five pointed Star very slightly below it, and a little to the right. Again I closed my eyes and there was nothing on the retina. Again I opened them and the vision was still there, but now it seemed to radiate fire. I watched it for some time, then it gradually dimmed and faded slowly from my sight."

What he had seen was the Egyptian ankh, the symbol of life, and he recorded the next day that he felt that the five-pointed star symbolized adeptship. The next day Wilson heard a voice that repeated certain words which he felt to be passwords. A few days later, lying in bed in the dark, there was a sudden strange stillness, and he had a sense of looking down on "an immense vista of Time, a roofless corridor flanked with thousands and thousands of pillars. I seemed to be looking into both Time and Space at once." Then he again heard the voice, which addressed Wilson as, "Thou who hast worn the crown of upper and lower Egypt," and ordered him to prepare his heart, "for the Mighty Ones have need of thee."

Wilson now developed the faculty of automatic writing. He could place himself in a semi-trance state, and his hand would move quickly over the page. The short book that was dictated in this way was called *The Three Truths*; it declared that the soul is immortal, that the principle that gives life lives in everyone, but is perceived only by the man who desires perception, and that, "Each man is his own absolute Law-giver." After that, Wilson was told that he had now become a disciple of the Master who was the Twelfth Brother in the Great White Lodge, and that thenceforth he would be known as Brother Twelve.

An acquaintance who knew him at this period said: "He was one of the most fascinating personalities I have ever met. His knowledge of world religions was stupendous. He corresponded with spiritual and political leaders all over the world. He knew all kinds of prominent people."

In May 1926, Wilson arrived in London, to discover that his name was already known there. An article that he had mailed to *The Occult Review* from Genoa had been widely read and discussed. In it, Wilson foretold that a new spiritual cycle would commence in 1975, but that in the half century before then, "there stretches a veritable gulf of horror through which poor humanity must struggle as best it can." In retrospect, it seems an inspired prophecy. But skeptics will note that prophecies of horror and catastrophe are the stock in trade of messiahs, and that the year 1975 brought no new age of spiritual enlightenment.

Harry Strutton, the editor of *The Occult Review*, was impressed by Wilson, whom he described as a "natural seer," and liked a manuscript called *A Message from the Masters of Wisdom* so much that he agreed to have it printed. *The Message* repeated the prophesies of destruction and the unleashing of evil forces, but announced that the Masters of Wisdom were also about to do further work in the world. The result would be some "Great Work" that would usher in the year 2000.

Another article called "The Tocsin" led many readers of *The Occult Review* to accuse Wilson of scare-mongering. One of these was Sir Arthur Conan Doyle; Wilson had declared that Spiritualism, with its meddling in the "other world," had thinned the barrier and allowed evil spirits access to our universe.

The article also brought many admiring letters, and many requests for *The Message*. One of these was from Alfred Barley, an astrologer and a Theosophist, who was dissatisfied with the Theosophical Society (which at that period still regarded Krishnamurti as the future World Teacher).

Barley and his wife Annie visited Wilson, and were told that the Aquarian Foundation—Wilson's name for his organization—intended to move to British Columbia, in Canada, where Brother Twelve intended to set up a refuge from the coming catastrophe. This, Wilson had explained in a letter to members of the Foundation, had been chosen by his Master. The Barleys immediately sold all their assets and prepared to follow Brother Twelve to Canada.

In March 1927, Wilson electrified the Ottawa branch of the Theosophical Society when he told them that he had been appointed by Brothers of the Great White Lodge to create its counterpart on earth, and he invited them to become members. "The time left," he urged, "is terribly short." He added: "You are Knights of the Grail, or of the Round Table. You are pledged to your own Higher Self to lead His life, the Higher life." Most of the members of the Ottawa Lodge joined the Aquarian Foundation.

Wilson received the same enthusiastic reception at the Toronto Lodge, and repeated his success in Hamilton, London, and Windsor; he also found himself a publisher in Windsor. Then he caught a train to the West coast. He was headed for Nanaimo, on Vancouver Island. There he acquired another follower, a Vancouver lawyer named Edward Lucas, who noted: "I have met a Messenger . . . a direct personal Ambassador of the Great White Lodge."

Wilson charmed everyone. Like Steiner, he seemed modest and completely free of ego, but he talked with the deep conviction of one who has seen visions and heard voices. A small, slight man with a pointed beard and grey eyes, he had an air of compelling authority. Everything about him impressed people, yet he seemed completely a "man among men," wholly lacking in personal vanity. People who came to him prepared to find a charlatan went away charmed and convinced. Lucas later explained that he felt a powerful need to protect Wilson from harm, and "a strange uprush of love and loyalty such as I have not experienced in years."

Yet one Toronto host caught an ominous glimpse of another aspect of Wilson's personality. Wilson had given him a signed photograph, which his host lent to some friends. When he found out, Wilson flew into a rage and demanded the photograph back, declaring that he alone would issue photographs.

Wilson went on to California, where he was met by Will Comfort, a well-known writer of adventure novels; Comfort was impressed by the way Wilson delivered his message in a hotel hall, with a wedding going on next door so that his voice could hardly be heard; Wilson showed no sign of annoyance, and talked on steadily until the noise slowly subsided; by this time, everyone in his audience was with him.

Comfort was equally impressed by the way Wilson accepted criticism of an article he was writing for a New York newspaper, patiently rewriting it three times. Comfort noted that Wilson was "a man who had forgotten how to quit."

The trip to California was immensely successful. "Everyone loved him," Comfort's wife Jane noted; "He was stimulating and wise, and he always spoke carefully and with sensitivity." Yet after Wilson had returned to Canada, Jane received an odd letter from a woman who had given Wilson a lift back to San Francisco, and then invited him to stay at the home of her wealthy mother. They had talked about astrology until the early hours of the morning, when Wilson had suddenly proposed that he and she should have a child together, a future adept who would take over the work in the future. Wilson had even worked out the exact moment the conception should take place. The woman politely declined, and denounced Wilson to Jane Comfort as a fraud. Jane Comfort's faith remained unshaken.

It is an interesting story, for it seems to hint that, whether or not Wilson was a genuine mystic, sex might become his downfall.

In British Columbia, a group from England arrived, which included the Barleys, as well as a Scotswoman who called herself Elma Wilson. Years before she had nursed Wilson through a serious illness, and had become his companion, although they were unmarried. Wilson assured his followers that there was nothing sexual in the relationship.

A beautiful site for their new colony was found at Cedar-by-the-Sea, on Vancouver Island, and one hundred and twenty-six acres purchased at twenty dollars an acre. Seven "Governors" were appointed, and all members were asked to contribute to the building of the center. When it was finally completed, there was a special woodland retreat for Brother Twelve called the House of Mystery, where he could communicate with the Masters and write down their words. There he fasted for seven days although some of the disciples saw him walking in the woods when he was supposed to be in trance. Finally, on Wilson's forty-ninth birthday, everyone in the colony gathered under a great oak tree, where Wilson gave them an inspiring address that filled them all with an ecstatic sense of dedication.

Soon after this, Wilson explained to his followers that the world was in the grip of an "Empire of Evil," which had been causing problems for mankind since long before Atlantis, and which had inspired modern Bolshevism. He also felt that Jewish financiers were servants of the Empire of Evil, and that the Roman Catholic Church was another of its manifestations. The aim of the Empire of Evil was to set up a world dictatorship—here Wilson seemed to be anticipating Orwell's *1984*—but they would be frustrated at the crucial moment by the "Forces of Light," now being led by the Aquarian Foundation. Its six governors (Wilson was the seventh) would now begin to experience heightened consciousness as the Brotherhood sent its vibrations. In fact, all began to experience visions and an increase in their "spiritual powers."

Soon there was enough money to purchase land on the adjoining Valdes Island where Wilson proposed to build a monastery. This would be their place of refuge on the day of destruction.

Wilson announced that the machinations of the Roman Catholic Church had convinced him that he ought to try to acquire political influence. The governor of New York, Al Smith, was a Catholic, and he was also a presidential candidate. To have a Catholic president of the United States would, according to Wilson, be a tremendous victory for the Empire of Evil. So Wilson decided that the answer lay in creating his own political party—the Third Party.

His approach was practical, as he and another governor, Philip Fisher, went to Washington D.C. and lobbied congressmen, including Thomas Heflin, the unofficial spokesman of the Ku Klux Klan in Congress. Attracted by the idea of becoming president, Heflin announced that he was leading a Protestant crusade to prevent Catholics from gaining political influence. Wilson formed a Protestant Protective League that supported Heflin, and assured its members that twenty million Negroes—inspired by Jews—were planning a rebellion in the South in support of Communism; the Jews, he said, were hoping to set up a Rothschild as World Messiah.

In July 1928, Wilson went to Chicago for the Third Party's convention, and did his best to promote a coalition between three minor parties (including the Prohibition Party) and the Third Party. His efforts were a failure. No one was interested in the religious issue. In the event, the campaign was won by the Republican candidate Herbert Hoover, whom Wilson detested as much as Al Smith. Wilson's plans to become the *eminence grise* behind the president of the United States popped like a bubble.

He had, however, acquired something from his futile trip to Chicago. On the train there he met a divorcée named Myrtle Baumgartner, and before they reached Chicago, they were sharing Wilson's Pullman sleeper. Wilson told her that they had been lovers in ancient Egypt—as Isis and Osiris. He made her the same proposal that he had made the young woman in San Francisco, that they should collaborate in producing a child who would be the future messiah. Baumgartner accepted with enthusiasm.

On his way home from Chicago, Wilson stopped in Toronto to meet a wealthy member of the Aquarian League, Mary Connally, who had been deeply impressed by his latest publication, *Foundation Letters and Teachings*, and had contributed two thousand dollars. The elegant sixty-year-old woman, who had been twice divorced, was charmed and dazzled by Wilson, and promised him a large contribution—in due course he received from her a check for twenty-three thousand dollars.

Wilson and Baumgartner arrived back at Cedar in the middle of the night; she was immediately packed off the Valdes Island to give birth to the messiah. Her presence was kept secret, except from three disciples who were asked to go and live with her, and prepare for the accouchement.

But it was impossible to keep the secret for long. When it came out, Wilson explained to the scandalized disciples—including his common law wife Elma—that he and Baumgartner were soulmates, and that the Masters had ordered him to take her into his bed to give birth to Horus, the future World Teacher.

But when disciples heard that Baumgartner and Wilson were enjoying their spiritual union in the sacred House of Mystery, they waited outside and confronted them as they left. Wilson defended himself vigorously, and explained that their relationship was on a higher spiritual plane. But the disciples were deeply troubled; even an article by Wilson that explained his new doctrine of marriage—that it did not confer ownership of one partner by the other—failed to allay their doubts.

Will Comfort had already resigned over Wilson's violently anti-Catholic stand; now at least two other governors began to consider doing the same. They were even more concerned when they learned that Wilson had ordered a five thousand dollar tugboat so he could commute more easily to Valdes Island; the governors were supposed to ratify all expenditure.

Under this barrage of criticism, Wilson began to display signs of the paranoia that seems typical of rogue messiahs. Workmen on Valdes said he would fly into rages over trivial problems and give contradictory orders.

Finally, the other six governors met secretly in Lucas's office in Vancouver to discuss what could be done. Some wanted to have Wilson committed to an insane asylum. Others said they would be contented if they dissolved the Aquarian Foundation. Three days later, the rebel governors confronted Wilson and stated their criticisms, which included the issue of Myrtle Baumgartner.

Wilson was indignant. He accused them of being traitors, and flatly refused to dissolve the Foundation. Lucas finally persuaded him that he had no choice, but Wilson again erupted in fury when told that the assets of the Foundation—about forty-five thousand dollars—would have to be split between the governors. He declared that the twenty-three thousand dollars Mary Connally had given him was his own. Wilson went on to issue a general letter to all members, denouncing the small group of traitors and calling for support.

In late September 1928, one of the governors, Robert England, cashed checks for twenty-eight hundred dollars at the Foundation's bank, and vanished. He regarded the money as rightly his own; he had worked for the Foundation for an infinitesimal salary, and regarded this as back wages. Unfortunately, he had taken the cash from the twenty-three thousand dollars Mary Connally had given Wilson for his personal use. This gave Wilson the excuse he needed; England was arrested and thrown into jail.

As the Foundation crumbled, Wilson took to his bed in a state of nervous prostration. One of his governors, Philip Fisher, was showing signs of insanity, declaring that the Masters had appointed him the next leader; he was eventually confined in a mental home. Myrtle Baumgartner increased the confusion by having a miscarriage, which strengthened the skepticism of the doubters: after all, if the Masters had decreed the union, why had it ended in miscarriage? (Mary would eventually leave the colony after a second miscarriage.)

But Wilson was determined to fight back. When four rebel governors tried to dissolve the Foundation, Wilson arrived at the meeting with four governors he had just appointed, including the two Barleys, and out-voted them. The governors hit back by accusing Wilson of misappropriating thirteen thousand dollars of the Foundation's funds; a warrant for his arrest was issued, and he was taken off the steamer for Vancouver. Released on a bail of thirty thousand dollars, he returned to Cedar swearing vengeance on his enemies. He was even more enraged the next day when he learned that the rebel governors had obtained an injunction granting the freezing of the funds. After another appearance in court, Wilson suffered a minor heart attack.

The affair was publicized in the local press, as a result of which new revelations came to light. Wilson had always claimed that Vancouver Island had been selected by the Brethren of the Great White Lodge as a site for the colony, and that he himself had never been there. As a result of the publicity, a number of people now came forward who remembered that he had been there long before he became Brother Twelve. He had worked as a baggage clerk and as the driver of a delivery wagon, and had quit when refused a two-dollar raise. A woman whose father owned a stable recalled that Wilson had worked there, and that he had put on a show as a hypnotist in the local theater, in which he had demonstrated extraordinary powers of hypnosis.

All across Canada and America, Brother Twelve's followers were in a state of bewilderment; it seemed incomprehensible that a man of such obvious integrity should be accused of theft. Mary Connally traveled all the way from Asheville, North Carolina, to testify in court that she had given him twenty-three thousand dollars for his own use, even though she had made the check out to the Foundation.

The judge was impressed; instead of committing Wilson for trial, he merely placed him under bond and made him agree to appear at a future date. Wilson won another battle in court when the injunction freezing the Foundation funds was dropped.

But he suffered a setback in the case of Robert England. When England's trial began, England was mysteriously absent, but the jury nevertheless decided that he was not guilty. (In fact, England was never seen again, and his disappearance remains a mystery.) The next day, the same jury acquitted Wilson on the charge of stealing the Foundation's funds. The judge's view was that it was merely a quarrel among cult members.

The faithful disciples themselves had no doubt that something far more serious was going on. All of them took it for granted that Wilson conversed with the Masters and possessed occult powers; he himself often told them that he could leave his body at will and travel to any part of the world.

But England had tried to explain the sinister changes that had taken place in Brother Twelve as the result of evil forces on the astral plane; he described a vision in which he had seen a helmeted and evil-faced monk standing behind Brother Twelve, and two of the disciples had seen a black-cowled figure with "a face like smoked leather" in the vicinity of the House of Mystery. The only thing that puzzled them was why Wilson was failing to call his occult powers to his aid in his legal battles.

That question was answered in a dramatic manner at Wilson's next court appearance. This took place on December 6, 1928, and was, by the standard of earlier court battles, a fairly minor affair. A Los Angeles disciple named James Lippincott had done a great deal of construction work on Valdes Island, and declared that Wilson had failed to keep his promise to give him twenty five acres of land; now he was claiming four hundred and fifty dollars as a settlement. Wilson's counter-argument was that work for the Foundation was voluntary, and that he had made no promises.

After Lippincott had been questioned, his place in the witness box was taken by an ex-governor of the Aquarian Foundation named Coulson Turnbull. He had been one of the disciples that Wilson had trusted with the secret of Myrtle Baumgartner's presence on Valdes Island, and had lived there with his wife during Myrtle's pregnancy. His testimony about Wilson's promises to Lippincott was therefore vital. But as Turnbull stood in the box, he suddenly began to shake. A moment later, he groaned and collapsed on the floor. Several other people in the courtroom slid off their benches, apparently afflicted by the same fainting sickness. Turnbull was thrashing around as if wrestling with an invisible assailant.

A few minutes later it was the turn of the judge; when he tried to speak, he only succeeded in making a snarling noise, like a dog. Finally he succeeded in saying: "This court is adjourned." Turnbull was revived with smelling salts and helped out of the building.

When the trial resumed, Lippincott's lawyer stood up to summarize his case. But now he seemed to dry up, standing there with a bewildered expression on his face. He finally said: "This is ridiculous. I've forgotten what I was saying." The judge's prompting failed to restore his memory, and he returned to his seat.

The judge was forced to find in favor of Wilson, since he had heard no evidence to prove that Lippincott had been promised wages. As Wilson left the court in silence, his own chauffeur slipped on the steps and fell with a crash, dislocating his shoulder. This had the effect of convincing both believers and non-believers that Wilson had summoned some occult force, which had exploded out of control. Two of the British disciples fled that night.

The case for dissolving the Foundation now went before the cabinet of British Columbia, led by the Prime Minister. Wilson himself presented it, emphasizing, with some justice, that he had been the sole creator and architect of the Aquarian Foundation, and the others had no right to undo all his work. The Prime Minster promised a verdict in the near future.

But once again, a malign fate was against Wilson. One of his disciples, Thomas Smith, was accused of raping a cinema usherette named Gladys Barlow. Smith was a Los Angeles businessman who had become a resident at the colony in the previous spring. He had recently been divorced by his wife, who alleged brutality. At a high school dance he had met the twenty-two-year-old usherette, and the two had done some heavy petting in Smith's automobile; however, she had declined allow it to go further.

Smith begged her to marry him; she refused and broke off the relationship. After three months back in Los Angeles, Smith decided he had to possess her at any cost, and returned to Vancouver Island; Gladys reluctantly agreed to see him again when he threatened suicide.

Smith rented an empty house, and that evening—telling Gladys they were going to visit a friend—dragged her into the house, tore off her clothes, and raped her on a mattress on the floor. He forced her to say she loved him by squeezing her throat. After that, he took her home, where she agreed to announce their engagement to her parents.

Asking him to pluck her a rose from a bush in the garden, Gladys fled into the house, screaming to her parents to lock the door. The next day, Smith was charged with rape, and the case made headlines all across Canada. Smith was eventually sentenced to five years of imprisonment, although he was spared the whipping usually administered to rapists in British Columbia.

The Prime Minister, who had been on the verge of finding in Wilson's favor, now decided that there was obviously something in the accusation that Wilson was promoting immorality, and allowed the proceedings to mark time. A year later, the cabinet voted to dissolve the Foundation.

The Smith rape case seemed the last straw for the Foundation; Wilson was now so discredited that it was hard to see how he could continue. But those who expected to see him concede defeat were overlooking the stubbornness of this "man who had long since forgotten how to quit." He decided to transfer his activities to Valdes Island, and to the group of buildings he called the Mandieh Settlement.

Two new followers named Jefferson arrived from Toronto, handing over all their cash, and Herbert Jefferson, a commercial artist, was dismayed when Wilson gave him the task of clearing a path across the island. Many of the disciples he spoke to were disaffected, claiming, for example, that Wilson helped himself to their groceries without payment. When Jefferson and another worker were sent to work on nearby De Courcy Island, which Wilson intended to purchase with cash donated by Mary Connally, Wilson failed to show up to collect them for three days. Jefferson assumed it was a test.

A disciple named Roger Painter arrived from Florida, and was warmly welcomed by Wilson, since Painter was a millionaire "poultry king," and had ninety thousand dollars in his back pocket. Painter was accompanied by a combative red-haired woman named Mabel Skottowe, who had stolen Painter from his wife. She and Painter had been divisional secretaries for the Foundation in Florida, and Painter had contributed thousands of dollars.

Wilson instantly "saw" that Painter was a reincarnation of Jean de la Vallette, head of the Knights of Malta, who had worked with Wilson in a past existence. Soon after, Painter had a vision of knights riding down a winding road towards the Mediterranean.

But it soon became clear that Wilson and Mabel Skottowe were embarking on an affair; he was heard sneaking into her tent at night. One day there were loud screams from the tent, and Roger Painter rushed out; Mabel was found badly bruised and beaten.

Wilson ordered Painter to leave, and his authority was so great that Painter did so without any hard feelings, and continued to correspond with his fellow Knight of Malta. Elma, shocked at this new infidelity, rushed to stay with a friend in Vancouver, and was in due course sent off to Switzerland to establish another branch of the Foundation. As soon as she was gone, Mabel moved in with Wilson, and was soon supervising the daily labors, armed with a riding crop, which she often used when her temper got the better of her. She also decided to change her name to Madame Zee.

In September 1929, Wilson and Madame Zee moved to a newly built house on De Courcy Island, and he announced that, from now on, personal contact with the disciples on Valdes would be minimal because an adept required solitude. Left to themselves, the disciples grew more and more restive, and Wilson had to make a surprise appearance, at which he berated them and threatened them with dire penalties, also demanding whatever cash they still had; cowed and terrified of his "magical powers," they handed it over.

Mary Connally, who had just lost an expensive law case, decided to move out to the colony. She arrived in August 1930, to find that she had been assigned a house on Valdes Island, not on De Courcy, where she had expected to live in association with the Master.

Wilson was, in fact, on a visit to England with Madame Zee, where he had bought a trawler; he hired a crew and set sail across the Atlantic. This almost cost him his life; they were struck by storms, and ran out of food and drink. Saved at the last minute by a passing liner, they finally arrived back in England in early November 1930.

Mary Connally soon found that she was to be subjected to one of Wilson's tests; she was told that she had to do hard physical labor like everyone else. She was so under Wilson's domination that she did it without hesitation. She was told that she had to keep away from the other disciples, because her vibrations were so terrible that she would contaminate them. Elma, who had returned from Switzerland, was forbidden to rejoin the colony; Wilson was finished with her.

In the spring of 1931, another couple arrived in Valdes: Fermin Sepulveda, and his wife, an ex-opera singer named Isona. They also brought their son Dion, and two daughters, Valea and Sereta.

Wilson was greatly attracted by the sex-hungry Isona, and lost no time in seducing her. It is not clear how Madame Zee reacted. He also seems to have been strongly attracted to the boy Dion, and moved him into his house.

Things began to go wrong when Wilson told Valea, who was twenty-one, that he had selected an elderly farmer to be her lover; she fled her bedroom, scrambling down a tree, when she heard his footsteps on the stairs. Valea was even more upset when her thirteen-year-old sister Sereta told her that a disciple named Bill had tried to rape her.

Wilson's affair with Isona soon came to an end as he tired of her sexual demands, and there was a quarrel, during which he threatened to maroon her on a deserted island without food or water. She took a boat and rowed to a town ten miles away. Wilson sent her husband and children to bring her back, but she refused. And eventually, she persuaded her husband to complain to the police about the attempted rape of Sereta.

Again, it looked as if Wilson's reign was about to end. And then, incredibly, the Sepulvedas changed their minds and returned to Valdes Island. Dion was later to claim that he had been hypnotized by Roger Painter, who had returned, and given post-hypnotic suggestion always to report back to Wilson. (One disciple would later report how she had once seen Madame Zee halt Dion in his tracks, as he was running towards Wilson's house, by purely mental suggestion.)

The cabinet of British Columbia had finally decided against the Foundation; they felt that Wilson was an undesirable resident, and looked for an excuse to order his expulsion. Aware of this, Wilson began to show signs of increasing paranoia. He ordered the disciples to break off their construction work and build forts instead. He bought a case of rifles, and kept six of them mounted in his office. The disciples were made to do sentry duty.

The Sepulvedas fled again, this time for good. The remaining disciples were overworked and exhausted. Wilson and Madame Zee became increasingly arbitrary; Annie Barley wondered if they were insane, or were on drugs.

When Madame Zee ordered a seventy-eight-year-old woman to drown herself, and abused her violently for failing to do so, matters came to a head. Alfred Barley drew up a letter demanding a meeting in which their complaints could be discussed; Wilson angrily refused. But he noted the names of the rebels, and a few days later announced that they were being expelled to Cedar. He took them there in twos and threes on the trawler.

As soon as all were present, they held a meeting and decided to hit back. Mary Connally, to begin with, wanted some of the cash she had handed over to Wilson. They were all still terrified of Wilson's "magic," until a friendly reporter assured them that Wilson's Egyptian magic had no power on Indian land. Their minds relieved, they decided to proceed with the law suits. In April 1933, a judge finally awarded Mary Connally twenty-six thousand, five hundred dollars, plus ten thousand dollars costs, and the ownership of De Courcy Island. The Barleys were awarded over fourteen thousand dollars.

Alas, it was too late. Wilson and Madame Zee had fled, leaving the buildings on De Courcy Island wrecked; one cabin had had a tree felled on it. A year earlier, Wilson had secretly bought some land up the coast, and two faithful disciples had built a cabin on it. They hid there until the results of the trial revealed that they now owed fifty thousand dollars. Then they fled east, taking their gold with them—well over half a million dollars in cash.

For a while they lived in a rented farmhouse in Devon, then moved to Switzerland. On November 7, 1934, Edward Wilson died in his apartment in Neuchatel, at the age of fifty-six. He was cremated there, and Madame Zee lived on in luxury hotels for the remainder of her life.

Was Edward Wilson slightly insane to begin with? Almost certainly not. His books—their style is exceptionally clear and pungent—reveal a remarkable mind. His lectures were powerful, and left no one in any doubt that he was a genuine mystic. As a personality, he was as hypnotic and charismatic as Rudolf Steiner. Reading the extraordinary account of his life in John Oliphant's *Brother Twelve* (1991), it is impossible not to be aware that he could easily have lived the remainder of his life among adoring disciples, and that the colony could have turned into been a kind of Eden.

What was it that possessed him to throw it all away and destroy his life's work?

The answer, as is usual among rogue messiahs, seems to have been sex.

The change became apparent after he had met Myrtle Baumgartner, on his way to Chicago. It seems relatively certain that his sexual experience up to that point had not been wide, restricted to his wife, and (possibly) to Elma. Now he had been accepted as a prophet, he felt he had the right to choose himself a bride, and make up for his lack of sexual experience.

As we have seen, his downfall began after he smuggled Baumgartner to Valdes Island; that was the point at which the disciples began to doubt, and his fellow governors to defect. The affairs with Madame Zee and Isona Sepulveda reveal the same Achilles' heel.

Perhaps the most puzzling thing about Wilson is the apparently "magical" powers. Before the final court case, one disciple, Kaye Kirchner, declared: "I was paralyzed by Brother Twelve for six weeks, and walked around like a drunken man for some time." A workman who was spying on Wilson described how, as he was about to get into his car, "I was suddenly stricken. It was just as if I'd been hit on the head. I couldn't drive; my arms were dead, my head felt the size of a balloon. I was paralyzed by the power of black magic. It didn't leave me for an hour, and for days I had a sore head."

These—and similar claims by disciples—could be dismissed as hysteria, except that the court episode, in which even the judge experienced similar symptoms, suggests that Wilson's powers were real. It would seem that genuine psychic powers are no guarantee that the guru is not "human, all too human."

NINE

THE GOSPEL OF FREE LOVE

It would be simple but facile to dismiss Brother Twelve as a man who lied and deceived his way to a fortune. It is true that he did; but the problem is more complex than this. His own accounts of his early life suggest a man who was driven by a deep dissatisfaction with himself. Like most religious figures, he started out as a man with a kind of psychological thorn in his side.

In a similar manner, the founder of Quakerism, George Fox, talks in his journal about his own youth: "I fasted much, walked abroad in solitary places many days, and often took my Bible, and sat in hollow trees and lonesome places until night came on; and frequently in the night walked mournfully about by myself; for I was a man of sorrows in the time of the first working of the Lord in me. . . . "

What are such men hoping to find? The answer can be found in a passage quoted by William James, in which a man describes his sensations standing on mountain tops: "What I felt on these occasions was a temporary loss of my own identity, accompanied by an illumination which revealed to me a deeper significance than I had been wont to attach to life."

This is not necessarily a religious experience. For example, it is a good description of what a football enthusiast feels when his team wins: loss of personal identity, and a sense of a deeper significance than he finds at home. Men like Brother Twelve and George Fox experience a need to lose their identity in something of wider significance than a football match. This craving for something of wider significance is the religious function that Jung talks about.

Outbreaks of religious fervor seem as mysterious as outbreaks of a new strain of flu. One of these, the so-called Great American Revival, swept across America in 1832, and even crossed the Atlantic to Europe. It burned so relentlessly in New York that parts of the state became known as the Burnt Over Region.

The most popular doctrine was called Perfectionism, and it was based on the belief that with enough moral effort, men and women could become perfect while still on this earth. The chief obstacle to perfection was sexual desire, so the Perfectionists preached that men and women had to observe a strict vow of chastity.

At a meeting of Perfectionists in Manlius, New York, in 1834, those who took the doctrine seriously decided to call themselves Saints. They preached that the Day of Judgement was not far off, and that this would be succeeded by the Kingdom of Heaven, in which the chosen would be happy for eternity.

One of the most enthusiastic converts was a good-looking young woman named Lucina Umphreville, who declared that women should turn their backs on love and that men should cease to try and tempt them into marriage. But spiritual love, of course, was a different matter. If a man and woman who were true soulmates came together, they could spend their time gazing into each other's eyes, or even allow themselves the occasional chaste kiss or embrace, provided they remained faithful to their vow never to succumb to physical temptation. The knowledge that they belonged to one another would sustain them, and the realization that they were successfully wrestling with the demon of sexual desire would bring them spiritual exaltation.

Not surprisingly, it worked. This was an age of idealism, when men put women on pedestals. So as they held hands, gazed into each other's eyes, and talked about their souls, these spiritual husbands and wives could enjoy a sense of delightful intimacy while congratulating themselves on defying the devil. After all, one of the problems of physical sex is that it can become mechanical and anticlimactic, turning into mere familiarity. No one would allow the smell of a rose to lure him into eating it. So why should two spiritual soulmates, enjoying the intoxicating scent of romance, want to lose it in mere animal contact?

Women, in general, found it easier to live up to Lucina Umphreville's teaching than men. Young virgins in any case were inclined to find the thought of sex alarming and disgusting, and it gave them a feeling of virtue to talk religion with other young virgins, and treat men with coldness and disdain. Lucina's male critics called her "Miss Anti-marriage." Lucina rejected this, for she was united in spiritual marriage with one of the Saints—he was also a popular revivalist preacher—called the Rev. Jarvis Rider.

It sometimes happened, of course, that these spiritual soulmates succumbed to temptation and coarse physical passion. If that happened, it only proved they were not true soulmates, and each was expected to go on searching for his or her pre-ordained partner. In fact, Lucina's Perfectionism was more fun than it sounded. The doctrine of spiritual husbands and wives was a pleasant way of breaking down the Victorian inhibitions about sex.

One of the men swept up into this religious revival was a young New Englander named John Humphrey Noyes. He differed from the founders of most religious cults in being a member of Vermont's upper class; his father was a successful businessman and a Congressman, and his cousin Rutherford B. Hayes was the nineteenth President of the United States.

Until he was twenty, Noyes studied law at Dartmouth College in Hanover, New Hampshire. Then, in 1831, he attended a revival meeting, and was swept away by the powerful preaching of the Rev. Charles Finney. From then on, there was no possibility of pursuing his father's profession of politics; he had to become a minister. His father, who was familiar with his son's rebellious temperament, told him that if he became a minister, he would have to behave himself, otherwise "they will whip you in." "Never!" said his son emphatically, and he proved to be a man of his word.

Studying theology at Yale, Noyes again revealed his tendency to rebellion when he embraced Perfectionism. He announced that it was possible to become perfect in this life through will-power. His professors, whose job was to turn out well-mannered clergymen who would fit into New England society, were outraged, and expelled him from school.

For the next four years Noyes spent most of his time in New England, particularly New Haven, one of the major centers of the revival. He mixed with other Perfectionists, crystallizing his own view of religion. This was based on the unorthodox notion that he himself was free of sin and in a state of perfection. Noyes's problem was that, unlike George Fox and other religious converts, he lacked the feeling that he was a "miserable sinner." His attitude to the world was cheerful and realistic. The reason he felt no pangs of conscience, he decided, was that he was not a sinner.

One day in 1833, Noyes received a revelation that explained exactly why. He was reading the Gospel of St. John when he came across Jesus's words: "If I will that he tarry till I come, what is that to thee?" That surely meant that Jesus's second coming would be within a reasonable time span of his remark—fifty years at most, Noyes thought.

The same was true of the quotation, found in Matthew, Mark and Luke: "There be some standing here which shall not taste of death till they see the son of man coming in his kingdom." Unless Jesus was mistaken—and that was surely impossible—this meant that the Second Coming must have already occurred. The precise date, Noyes worked out, was A.D. 70. In that case, the sinners had already been divided from the saved, and that explained why Noyes felt no sense of sin.

He soon learned that this doctrine could cause problems. A preacher named Simon Lovett, from Brimfield, Massachusetts, asked him to explain his ideas to the congregation there. Arriving in March 1835, Noyes found it full of pretty and brilliant young women who were more than ready for his assurance that guilt was unnecessary. They looked at the young preacher—he was twenty-four—with deep admiration, and subsequently pressed his hands and made it clear that they regarded him as their spiritual father and teacher.

Noyes was intoxicated with all this yielding femininity. He was also slightly alarmed, for he sensed that he could not control the enthusiasm that he had released. Halfway through the night, he realized that if he stayed there, he would inevitably be tempted to taste some of the "sweets" on offer, and leapt out of bed. He left the house on tiptoe and hurried across country through the snow. It took him twenty-four hours to walk the sixty miles to his home in Putney, Vermont, but there he felt safe.

The women of Brimfield, cheated of their opportunity to kill shame, decided on a kind of martyrdom; since Noyes was no longer there to help them, two of them went into the bedroom of the Rev. Simon Lovett at midnight and woke him up. They made so much noise that they were quickly interrupted, and they soon had their wish for social martyrdom granted.

Few people believed that they simply wanted to make a kind of public gesture. While everyone agreed that the Rev. Simon Lovett was hardly likely to sin with both of them at the same time, it would have been too anticlimactic to believe that nothing had occurred. So from Boston to New York, the gossip declared that the three had been caught engaged in "bundling"—embracing while fully clothed, probably in bed. People began to refer to Lovett and his close friend the Rev. Chauncey Dutton as the head of the "Bundling Perfectionists."

One of the women, Mary Lincoln, was sent away to stay with a female friend, but the other young ladies soon joined her to commiserate. Mary began to rave, and declare that the town of Brimfield would be consumed with fire like the cities of the plain. She then rushed out, followed by a friend called Flavilla Howard, and they threw off most of their clothes and climbed to a nearby hilltop to await the Day of Judgement.

Finally convinced that their prayers had caused the Lord to relent, they set out to look for shelter. It was so dark that Mary, who was leading the way, had to throw her dress (her only garment) over her head so that Flavilla could follow the glimmering of her body. They finally found shelter in a farmhouse, and went home the next morning, tired but unharmed. At least they had their fill of denunciation and public abuse.

The Saints continued to cause scandal. Mary Lincoln and the Rev. Chauncey Dutton decided that they were spiritual mates, and began to travel the country together, preaching Perfectionism, and assuring their hosts that they lived in the same purity as St. Paul and the female companion who accompanied him on his wanderings.

Eventually, they succumbed to public disapproval and married, after which they became ardent followers of a new prophet called William Miller, who was convinced that the end of the world would occur in 1843. Miller—we shall meet him again—became the founding father of the Seventh Day Adventists, the sect to which David Koresh belonged.

Maria Brown went to New York and became a close friend of Lucina Umphreville, who was still bound in spiritual marriage to the Rev. Jarvis Rider. She was invited to stay at the home of an ardent Perfectionist called Thomas Chapman, whose beautiful wife was immensely popular among the Saints. She took with her Lucina Umphreville, the Rev. Jarvis Rider, and the Rev. Charles Lovett. Thomas Chapman was away from home much of the time, digging a canal, but he had complete confidence in the Saints.

It proved to be unjustified. As all five knelt in prayer, the Rev. Jarvis Rider decided that Mrs. Chapman would make an even better soulmate than Lucina, and told her so. Since this was all on a high religious plane, Mrs. Chapman felt no shame in admitting that she also felt a spiritual affinity for Rider. Lucina was soon being consoled by Lovett.

When Thomas Chapman came home, he was enraged to find that his wife had taken another spiritual mate, and committed violent assault on Rider with a horsewhip. Although Chapman later felt ashamed of himself, and apologized to Rider, it was too late to save the marriage; he separated from his wife, who died soon after. The affair provided even more fuel for scandalous gossip than the Bundling Perfectionists of Brimfield.

Meanwhile, back in Putney, Noyes was allowing his own ideas to mature. His first converts to his views were his mother, two sisters and a brother. He married the granddaughter of a governor of the state, and his wife joined the congregation, as did the husbands of his two sisters and his brother's wife. But it was in 1836 that the full consequences of his belief that the Second Coming had already arrived dawned on him. George Bernard Shaw once described Noyes as "one of those chance attempts at a Superman which occur from time to time in spite of the interference of Man's blundering institutions," and the idea that now occurred to him had a boldness that certainly places Noyes among the most original minds of the nineteenth century.

If the Kingdom of Heaven had arrived in A.D. 70, that meant that the institution of marriage was eighteen centuries out of date, for in heaven "they neither marry nor are given in marriage." Lucina Umphreville was clearly wrong. Sex was not gross and immoral; it was, on the contrary, innocent and permissible.

"Amativeness," Noyes argued, was starved in monogamy, "which gives to sexual appetite only scanty and monotonous allowance, and so produces the natural vices of poverty, contraction of taste, and stinginess or jealousy." There was a sense in which all men were married to all women, and vice versa. When believers in this doctrine came together, they could indulge freely in sex without any feeling of guilt. In the marriage supper of the Lamb, every dish is free to every guest. "In a holy community," Noyes wrote in a letter of January 1837, "there is no more reason why sexual intercourse should be restrained by law, than why eating and drinking should be; and there is as little shame in the one case as in the other. . . . I call a certain woman my wife; she is yours. . . . She is dear in the hands of a stranger."

When published in a magazine called *The Battle Axe*, this letter caused outrage and scandal. But those who denounced Noyes as a libertine were ignoring one important sentence: "God has placed a wall of partition between the male and the female during the apostasy for good reasons, which will be broken down in the resurrection for equally good reasons; but woe to him who abolishes the law of apostasy before he stands in the holiness of the resurrection." In other words, *The Battle Axe Letter* (as it became known) was not an excuse for licentiousness; in order to enter into its spirit, men and women should believe that the Second Coming has already occurred, and that they are in a state of spiritual perfection.

Little by little, the Putney Association grew. One of the converts was another man who had been converted by Charles Finney, and who had also had a traumatic experience at the hands of a Bundling Perfectionist. George Cragin was a young Wall Street clerk who ran Bible classes when he met a pretty schoolteacher named Mary Johnson and married her. They were soon converted to Perfectionism, and when Mary read an article by Noyes on the power of faith, she felt that her life was changed. Their house became a center of Perfectionists in New York.

But George was worried by the adoration his wife seemed to arouse in the males. Feeling that this was a sign of his selfishness, he turned for help to a disciple of Noyes, the Rev. Abram Smith, an unusually charismatic and powerful preacher. They became close friends, and when Cragin's lease ran out, Smith invited them to go and live in his house near the village of Rondout, on the Hudson River.

It was a bleak place, and the Cragins were expected to work hard. Mrs. Smith (Smith's second wife) did not like them, and soon the lack of sympathy between her and her husband widened into a rift, and he threw her out to go and live with relatives.

George and Mary Cragin both regarded Smith as a father figure; Mary was completely under his spell. An enthusiastic believer in the teachings of Noyes, Smith soon decided that Mary was his "spiritual wife," and began asking her to come to his room for instruction. George was jealous, but felt that he was again under the influence of the devil. While he was outdoors, engaged in hard physical labor, Mary Cragin became Abram Smith's physical as well as spiritual wife.

Cragin found out by accident. He had urged Mary to spend a week in New York, while Smith was supposed to be on a "mission" in Pennsylvania. When he heard that Smith had delayed his trip to Pennsylvania, and spent the same week in New York, he began to suspect the worst. A visit to some Perfectionist friends in New York confirmed his suspicions; Smith and Mary had occupied the same room.

Back at home, Mary confessed her infidelity. When Smith returned from Pennsylvania, he summoned all his preaching talent to convince George Cragin that he and Mary were spiritual soulmates. Looking at the man he knew to be his wife's seducer, Cragin was unmoved. Finally, Smith said he would go off to Putney to ask Noyes's advice; he asked Cragin to write a note to Noyes saying that he had no unkind feeling towards Smith, and Cragin did as he asked.

When Smith arrived in Putney, he found that the Perfectionist in whose house he and Mary had committed adultery was already there, and that Noyes knew the whole story. Noyes told him he was a rogue, and ordered him to go away and sin no more. Smith returned to Rondout and took back his evicted wife. The Cragins left, and went to join Noyes and his Putney community. But Mary, who had obviously taken Smith as a lover because she felt some dissatisfaction with her husband, sadly decided that from now on, she and George would only be spiritual soulmates.

But Noyes was also running into trouble. By now, the community had taken over five hundred acres of land, and begun to live communally, farming in the afternoon and studying in the evening. Although Noyes was still faithful to his wife—he had never known another woman—he continued to preach communal love.

This doctrine raised an obvious problem. If men and women slept together as they felt inclined, what about getting pregnant? Contraception was virtually unknown; the only male contraceptives of the period were cardboard or rubber sheaths that removed most of the pleasure from sex.

Once again, Noyes came up with an inspired idea. He called it male continence, but this did not mean that the male had to remain sexually abstinent. It meant that he had to remain in contact with his partner for only as long as he felt certain that he was not likely to impregnate her. At that point, he was honor bound to withdraw.

What was so inspired about this idea of *coitus interuptus?* Simply that Noyes had once again seized on the essence of the interaction that made the doctrine of Perfectionism so potent. There is a sense in which physical intercourse is the least important part of sex. Women are inclined to prefer the romantic delights of courtship, and even males have to admit that the pleasures of increasing attraction, increasing intimacy, have a flavor that tends to evaporate in the act of sex. It is too easy to take sex for granted, so that it degenerates into physical repetition. If sex is to remain exciting, it must not be allowed to degenerate in this way.

What Noyes was suggesting was that sex should be a highly disciplined activity, requiring a high level of focused concentration and self-control. Of necessity, it could only be enjoyed in brief installments, since after more than a few minutes, the male is in danger of producing semen. If this was to be avoided, and the woman satisfied, he had to attain a high degree of detachment and vigilance. This in itself would guarantee that sex could never degenerate into a mere habit.

Noyes finally formulated this idea in 1846, and his followers now embarked upon the practice of "complex marriage" (in which any male or female could become sexual partners) and male continence. For the first time, Noyes had experience with a woman other than his wife, and his wife of other males besides her husband.

His other followers adopted the same practice with enthusiasm. This was more than mere communal wife-swapping. It combined all the idealistic delights of Perfectionism, such as the sense of living on a higher spiritual plane, with the pleasure of being able to choose between two dozen partners. (By this time, the community numbered about fifty.) Prayer meetings and a practice called "mutual criticism" helped to maintain a high level of religious self-awareness.

Regrettably, their neighbors in Putney were scandalized by what they heard, and complained to the authorities. In 1847, Noyes was indicted on grounds of adultery. Too sensible to waste energy on fighting entrenched prejudice, he sold the Putney property and moved to twenty-three acres of land at Oneida, in New York State, twelve miles from Oneida Lake. There, in 1848, he set up his experiment in what he called Bible communism.

Life at first was hard. Eighty-seven people lived in two log houses, and their workshop was an old sawmill. They worked from dawn till dusk, but it was twelve years before they stopped running at a loss. But their sexual communism made it all worthwhile, for, as one of Noyes's sons commented: "The opportunity for romantic friendships . . . played a part in rendering life more colorful than elsewhere. Even elderly people, whose physical passions had burned low, preserved the fine essence of earlier associations."

In other words, life at the Oneida Community had the atmosphere of a village dance or social, where the sexes came together with a view to getting better acquainted. A few experienced sharp pangs of jealousy—it is hardly natural for either male or female to reflect that their lifelong partner is now in bed with someone else—but no one doubted that Noyes was right, and that this was merely the old Adam suffering for his sins.

The young also found the atmosphere exciting. Noyes taught that it was a disgrace that young people, who were ready for sex from their early teens, should have to wait ten years or so to satisfy their curiosity. So teenage virgins were introduced to amativeness by older people of the opposite sex.

It was by no means a sexual free-for-all. Those proposing to take advantage of complex marriage had to declare their intentions, and do it with everyone's approval. Consent had to be mutual; unless both partners were willing, there could be no coupling.

Understandably, large numbers of people wanted to join the Oneida Community and share the fun; by the end of the first year, the number had doubled. There were farmers, lawyers, mechanics, doctors, even clergymen. Within two years, the log huts had turned into respectable-looking timber houses, one of them with four stories; in the early 1860s, a large brick mansion with several wings, which could have been mistaken for a university, was completed. Pregnancy was by no means forbidden, but was carefully controlled by the community.

Noyes himself seems to have been an extraordinary man. While obviously the dominant figure there, he was by no means a tyrant; rather, he was a benevolent headmaster. If the basic philosophy of Oneida was a rationalization of Noyes's desire for sexual variety, he differed from most other messiahs in having no desire to reserve the best for himself. If members of his flock required admonition or correction, this was administered by "mutual criticism," practiced in groups. The result seems to have been a lack of the kind of discord that has marred most other attempts at religious community.

It is unfortunate that we possess so little detailed knowledge of the working of the Oneida Community. The Victorians were naturally reticent about sex, so that even if someone had decided to write a book, it would probably have been devoid of the kind of details provided by Jeannie Mills in her book on Jim Jones. But since such books are usually written by disgruntled ex-disciples, and there are no recorded instances of quarrels or bitterness at Oneida, we have to be content with the accounts of the community published in the *Oneida Circular*. From this we learn that the mansion had a library of five thousand volumes, including works by Darwin, Huxley and Herbert Spencer; that they had an excellent orchestra; that they performed plays; and that they often had picnics at Oneida Lake.

The Community's finances began to improve when they were joined in the mid-1850s by Sewell Newhouse, an inventor of steel traps. The Community began to manufacture them at Oneida. They also made furniture, wove silk, and made traveling bags; the Oneida trademark became a sign of quality.

Children passed into the care of the community as soon as they were weaned; the parents were allowed to visit them as much as they liked, but possessiveness was discouraged. The children were allowed to get up when they felt like it in the morning, and encouraged to learn a trade or craft. Many were sent away to college and university, and most returned to offer their services to the community.

Yet, oddly, the main problem encountered by the community as the years went by was the attitude of the young. They had had no experience of the revivalism that had filled the older members with religious fervor; one of Noyes's sons, a doctor named Theodore, was openly an agnostic. Many of the younger members felt that complex marriage was immoral, and that the normal family was far more natural.

By the time he was in his sixties, Noyes was ready to retire; he moved to another branch of the community at Wallingford, leaving his son Theodore in charge. But Theodore lacked his father's charisma, and when his attempts at regimentation caused rebellion, Noyes was forced to return.

But the harm had been done; seeds of discord had been sown. The community had always been subject to violent attacks from the world outside—usually it was on the charge of immorality—but its inner unity had prevented these attacks from causing problems. When Noyes heard that some of the younger people actually supported one of Oneida's harshest critics, Professor Mears of Hamilton University, he decided that it was time to go.

On June 23, 1876, Noyes left Oneida secretly, and went upstate to Niagara, where he remained for the final ten years of his life. But he recognized that Oneida's sexual practices would always cause rage and envy, and in 1879, he advocated that they should give up complex marriage "in deference to the public sentiment which is evidently rising against it."

The community accepted his advice, and there were dozens of marriages. Two years later, communism was also abandoned, and the community reorganized as a joint stock company. When Noyes died in 1886, the Oneida Community was as financially successful as ever, and branches had been established in many other parts of the country.

Why was Oneida such a startling exception to the rule? The answer lies, again, in the personality of its founder. As far as we can tell, Noyes was completely lacking in the paranoia that seems to characterize rogue messiahs. He had a strong sense of purpose, but lacked the element of aggression and the need to dominate that has undermined every messiah in this book.

In fact, the Oneida experiment throws an interesting new light on the whole problem of rogue messiahs.

To begin with, we might consider the question: why did Noyes decide to retire to Wallingford, then Niagara? He must have known that his withdrawal would lead to serious problems. Even if he decided to take no more active part in the life of the community, there was no reason why he should not spend his retirement there.

Why did he leave secretly in the middle of the night? This sounds not unlike his nocturnal flight from Simon Lovett's congregation at Brimfield nearly forty years earlier. On that occasion, he was fleeing from attractive young women who wanted to make him their spiritual mentor. Some instinct told him that this would be playing with fire, and that succumbing to temptation would bring about his downfall. Undoubtedly he was correct.

But Noyes had nothing of the sort to fear at Oneida, which had been his whole life's work. Then why leave secretly? Because, I suspect, he had come to face another truth about himself, that his whole concept of "communal love" was pure self-deception.

Noyes was a man with a powerful sexual impulse, as we can see from his comment that marriage starves the sexual appetite with "only scanty and monotonous allowance." He had seen friends like Jarvis Rider and Abram Smith almost destroyed by scandal. He was not a hypocrite, yet it seemed to Noyes that there should be some way of reconciling religious feeling with the appetite for more variety of "food" at the Feast of the Lamb.

As we have seen, he came to feel, in all honesty, that the solution was for all men and women to regard members of the opposite sex as spiritual husbands and wives. When the Oneida Community immediately doubled its membership, Noyes saw that other serious and respectable members of the community felt as he did.

What happened during the course of the next thirty years, as his sexual impulse became less urgent, was that he realized that this was fundamentally self-deception. At least, if this is not what happened, then Noyes was neither as intelligent nor honest as I believe he was.

It suits the life-force that members, particularly males, of the "dominant five percent" should have powerful sexual appetites since they are more likely to produce dominant and healthy offspring. (It is more difficult for women, since bearing and rearing a child is far more demanding than fathering one.) In nature, dominant males often have a harem. Moreover, the dominant lion often kills off the cubs of his predecessor, to make sure his own cubs have the advantage. When David Koresh announced that all the women in the sect were his property, he was simply behaving as nature wants dominant males to behave.

In order to ensure the continuance of the species, nature has made us slaves of the sexual illusion. This is the instinct that fills us with the conviction that sexual fulfillment is as important to our personal well-being as food or shelter. This is in fact untrue; no one ever died of sexual starvation. Yet when human beings are in the grip of sexual desire, whether romantic or purely physical, the satisfaction of that desire seems as important as breathing to someone who is gasping with suffocation.

In fact, the satisfaction of very powerful sexual desire often leaves us in an odd state of ambivalence, a feeling of, "What was all that about?" The satisfaction of other desires—food, drink, physical or intellectual excitement—can leave us glowing and fulfilled; but sexual satisfaction always carries a trace of disappointment, due to a dim awareness that it has failed to deliver what it has promised.

I should add immediately that this is not true for close personal relations, since the sexual contact draws strength from a wider network of affections. I am speaking only of the impersonal sexual appetite that aims at "possession," that is, at "conquest." This is dependent on a kind of illusion, which in males takes the form of Casanovism—a simple desire to make love to any attractive female. It could be called "symbolic response," since it is an attraction to a symbol rather than a person. ("She was just my type—a woman.") This is, in fact, basically the attitude of the rapist and the sex killer.

As Noyes grew older, he must have recognized that all his self-justification about the Second Coming and the end of marrying and giving in marriage was merely a rationalization of the dominant male's desire for a harem, and that this desire was a consequence of the sexual illusion, which causes dominant males to feel that their amativeness is starved in monogamy.

Now that this illusion had weakened, and Noyes found himself responding to attractive women as fellow creatures rather than potential bed-partners, he probably felt ashamed, as far as he allowed himself to feel ashamed, of the ideals that had led him to form the Oneida Community, and which had caused so many teenage girls to lose their virginity.

It seems at least likely that Noyes outgrew the illusion. Most of the messiahs in this book allowed themselves to be totally possessed by it until it led to their downfall.

The story of Noyes requires a postscript. We have seen how two Perfectionists named Mary Lincoln and the Rev. Chauncey Dutton became disciples of a revivalist preacher called William Miller. Miller, who was a farmer and a student of the Book of Daniel, had arrived at the conclusion that the end of the world was due on October 22, 1843.

Like so many revivalists of that period, he was an impressive man in the pulpit, and soon had a following amounting to fifty thousand. As 1843 approached, they began to sell all they had and to prepare for the Second Coming. On the great day, thousands gathered on a hilltop in Massachusetts. One man wore a pair of turkey wings and climbed a tree, so as to be ready to fly to heaven; unfortunately he fell and broke an arm. Some of the faithful carried umbrellas to aid them in their flight; one woman tied herself to her trunk of belongings so it would accompany her to heaven.

The sage Ralph Waldo Emerson, who was walking nearby with his friend Theodore Parker, asked what all the commotion was about. One of the faithful replied: "Don't you know the world is going to end today?" "That doesn't affect me," said Parker, "I live in Boston."

Midnight came and passed, and when it was clear that Armageddon was not going to arrive after all, they all went ruefully home. Most had sold all they had; one farmer had given his farm to his son, a non-believer, who now declined to give it back.

In his despair, Miller had an inspiration. His calculations had been based on the Christian year, and no doubt he should have used the Jewish calendar. In that case, Judgement Day would arrive on October 22, 1844. Once again everyone assembled for the last trump, and once again everyone went home feeling sadder and wiser when it didn't happen.

This time, Miller had the sense to recognize that he had been misled by his own enthusiasm. "We were deluded by mere human influence, which we mistook for the Spirit of God." So when one of his closest friends, Hiram Edson, told him that he had had a vision in a cornfield that Miller had been right after all, but that the Day of Judgement had taken place in Heaven, Miller refused to be tempted. He died five years later, chastened and disillusioned.

Edson, on the other hand, continued to preach his new doctrine—that Christ was even now sorting out the sinners from the saved in heaven, and that the faithful had to redouble their efforts to be worthy. They would have to celebrate the Seventh Day (Saturday) as the Sabbath, and strictly observe the dietary laws of the Old Testament. So Seventh Day Adventism was born, and has flourished to this day.

A series of prophets would take up where Miller had left off— notably Hiram Edson, Ellen White and Victor Houteff. It was Houteff who came to believe that he was an incarnation of King David, and who broke away from the Adventists to form his own Branch Davidian Sect, with its headquarters in Waco, Texas, where, as we have seen, David Koresh induced his followers to join him in a fiery suicide.

TEN

THE SEXUAL WATERSHED

In 1867, long after Perfectionism had been forgotten, and the religious revival of the 1830s was only a memory, an author named William Hepworth Dixon began to write a history of the sexual scandals of the past few decades. Dixon was a man before his time, a kind of investigative journalist, and his two-volume work *Spiritual Wives* is a remarkable monument to his curiosity and his patience. He had interviewed Noyes, Brigham Young, and even the unfortunate George Cragin, and although the conventions of his time prevented him from being as frank as a modern journalist, he still managed to tell the story with a lack of reticence that must have shocked his Victorian readers.

In the previous year, Dixon had succeeded in interviewing a man whose notoriety in England was as great as that of Noyes in America. The Rev. Henry James Prince presided over his own version of the Oneida Community, which was known as the Abode of Love—he preferred the Greek word Agapemone—at Spaxton, near Bridgewater in Somerset. There was one major difference between Prince and Noyes: Prince was a hypocrite who preferred to keep his lively interest in the opposite sex a secret.

In fact, Prince would hardly be worth a mention in this rogue's gallery of messiahs if it were not for the fact that, for the purposes of this book, he may be seen as the watershed between the old age and the new. In the messiahs of previous ages, there is seldom any suggestion of sexual duplicity, (although a few have taken mistresses whom they regarded as their own equivalent of Mary Magdalen).

Rather, there is a tendency to regard sex as a temptation of the devil.

The Skoptzy, a Russian sect founded in 1770 by a messiah called Kondrati Selivanov, made male converts submit to castration, and females to having their breasts amputated and, if they could bear it, their genitals mutilated. We have seen that the Perfectionists of the 1830s believed that they could become saints by total abstention from sex. Noyes's doctrine of free love may have been based on genuine religious conviction, but it led to widespread scandal and caused the downfall of the original Oneida Community.

Yet the moralists were fighting a rearguard action. The nineteenth century was the age of romanticism and self-expression. Its men of genius no longer believed in subjugating themselves to the Church or to its patrons. Besides, sex was too delightful, too exciting, to be ignored or swept under the carpet—a lesson the Perfectionists had to learn the hard way. When Goethe wrote that "the Eternal Feminine draws us upward and on," he had announced the beginning of a new age in which the distinction between sex and religion was slowly being eroded.

In fact, the Rev. Henry James Prince began his career as a man with a deep and sincere religious impulse. As with Brother Twelve, the interest to us of his story lies in trying to guess at precisely what point he surrendered to the siren song of the sexual illusion.

Prince was born in Bath in 1811, the same year as Noyes. A sickly child, he was brought up by his widowed mother and by a lodger named Martha Freeman, a Catholic. He was a pious child, and spent a great deal of time reading the Gospels.

At the age of eighteen Prince went to Guys Hospital in London to study medicine; he became a doctor three years later, and returned to Bath to practice. Three years after that, he became so ill that he came close to death. In this state his mind returned to the religion of his childhood, and he decided that he had to join the priesthood.

Prince studied at St. David's College in Lampeter, Wales, a school that was run by a fox-hunting clergyman who enjoyed his food and wine. There, the ascetic Prince soon became the center of a group of students that preferred prayer and theological discussion, and his gravity, purity, and quick intelligence led them to regard him as something of a saint. These high-minded enthusiasts became known as the Lampeter Brethren.

At this time in the mid-1830s, England was going through much the same religious convulsions as America, due in part to the activities of a young Oxford clergyman called John Henry Newman, whose sermons and tracts were causing much heart-searching in the Church of England. Prince was also swept away by religious fervor, and none of his friends had any doubt that his own sermons and tracts would have as great an influence as Newman's.

Unfortunately for Prince, there was one major difference beyond his control. In Oxford, Newman had a highly intelligent, receptive audience. In the Somerset parish of Charlinch, to which Prince was assigned as curate, the churchgoers were hard-headed farmers and hard-working country folk, and most of them were accustomed to sleeping peacefully through the sermons. They were at first puzzled, then irritated, then bored by Prince's religious fervor. Prince's wife—he had married the aging Martha Freeman—did her best to make friends among the poor of the parish, but it was uphill work.

Then Prince made an important convert—no less than his own vicar. The Rev. Samuel Starky was seriously ill in the Isle of Wight, and not expected to recover. On what he thought was his death bed, Starkey read a printed sermon that "fell upon my soul like rain on a thirsty glebe." He soon began to recover, and was delighted to learn that the author of the sermon was his own curate, whom he had never met. He hurried back to Charlinch, and became Prince's first convert.

Little by little, with painful slowness, Prince began to make headway among his unlettered flock. At his Bible classes and prayer meetings he gradually built up a small but enthusiastic band of admirers, mostly women. But the local farmers and laborers resented the devotion of their womenfolk. Many of them locked up their wives rather than allow them to go to the vicarage. There were threats and quarrels, and finally, Prince's bishop decided he had to go; he was packed off to Stoke, in Suffolk. Prince made the move without his wife, for Martha had died in Charlinch, worn out by her duties. Shortly before he left for Suffolk, Prince married Julia Starky, the aging sister of his vicar.

In Stoke the story repeated itself. Bringing religious fervor to a "coarse and loutish population of farmers" (as journalist Dixon calls them) was like trying to light a damp bonfire. Then the farmer's wives and dairymaids began to attend Prince's prayer meetings, and infuriated their husbands. After two years, the bishop decided that Prince had caused enough trouble, and had to be sent away.

This time Prince revolted. He had had enough of rural parishes. He consulted with some of his old Lampeter Brethren—most had remained close friends—and decided to strike out on his own. Fortunately, he was not destitute; his first wife had left him money, and his new one, Julia, had a small annuity which would have kept them in comfort if the worst had come to the worst. Prince moved to Brighton, hired a church hall, and tried the effect of his oratory on an urban congregation.

They were far more receptive than his rural auditors, and he now began hinting that he was receiving direct guidance from the Holy Spirit. A number of the Lampeter Brethren joined him, and accepted him as their leader. Only one of them, Arthur Rees, was unable to accept the notion that his friend was the new messiah, and broke with him.

But Prince had certainly struck the right note with his congregation. His following increased dramatically. At this point, he invited them all to a meeting in the Assembly Room of the Royal Hotel in Weymouth, and made a dramatic announcement. The Day of Judgement was near, and those who had accepted salvation at his hands would live for ever. All others would perish. Those who wanted to live forever should follow Prince.

It was a bold stroke and it paid off. Did Prince really believe it? The question, as this book has shown, is not as simple as it looks. He had struggled for years to become the new John Henry Newman, and had failed. The sense of defeat and frustration must have been enormous. Now, at last, he had what he needed: an audience, a band of the faithful, who regarded him as a saint. He had to bind them to him with chains of iron. When he told them the end of the world was nigh, he was only repeating what preachers have said—and believed—throughout the ages. Prince probably had a perfectly clear conscience.

Among those who decided that Prince was the way of salvation were the five Nottage sisters, who had become converts in Suffolk; each of them had inherited six thousand English pounds from their father, a wealthy merchant. They now agreed to follow Prince wherever he chose, and to contribute their inheritance to building an "Ark of Refuge" from the wrath to come.

For the moment the band of faithful disciples moved into a house in Weymouth, but it was inconveniently small. Prince decided to return to Spaxton, near Charlinch, and build an "Abode of Love" in a beautiful wooded valley among the Quantock Hills. Three of the Nottage sisters were married off to male disciples— Prince simply announced the decision to them—but they were warned that, in the new kingdom of heaven, sex was strictly prohibited. In 1840, when Prince was twenty-nine years old, they all moved into the Abode of Love. The Rev. Starky and his wife accompanied them.

We know little of the early years in the Abode, except that one of the Nottage sisters, Agnes, rebelled against the no-sex rule and became pregnant; Prince cast her out as a sinner, and she had to live with her mother. Her husband stayed behind. The youngest sister, Louisa, who was forty, tried to join the community, but was kidnapped by relatives and thrown into a mental home. Eventually, she was released and lived at the Abode, where she handed over her money to Prince.

If Prince had continued to shepherd his little flock and superintend the building of cottages and outhouses, he would never have come to public attention, or been featured in Dixon's *Spiritual Wives*. But after a few years, he seems to have tired of his elderly wife, and decided that the Chosen of God deserved someone younger.

He suddenly announced to his followers that the Abode was still full of sin, and that a sacrifice was needed. This sacrifice would be a virgin, who would become the Bride of the Lamb, and purify them all. God had promised him that he would reveal the identity of this Bride in His own good time; meanwhile, they could only wait.

Prince had the cunning to keep them in suspense for many months, as if waiting for the command from God. But finally it was announced that God had spoken. Everyone in the Abode was summoned to the chapel, where Prince sat on a throne dressed in trappings that were gorgeous enough for an archbishop. The organ played softly and incense filled the air. Then Prince rose solemnly to his feet, crossed the chapel, and held out his hand to a sixteen-year-old orphan named Zoe Patterson. Zoe, together with her widowed mother, had been in the Abode since she was a baby, and her mother had died there. Now she only blushed and bowed her head, and as the organ pealed, she allowed Prince to lead her off to his private apartments. The community was now sinless.

No one entertained the slightest doubt that the marriage would remain pure and sinless. So six months or so later, everyone was shocked and puzzled as Zoe showed unmistakable signs of pregnancy. It could not be Prince, of course, so the inference was that it was some other man. Some thought it must be the devil himself. Only one of the old Lampeter Brethren, Lewis Price, drew the sensible conclusion—it had all been a masquerade so that Prince could finally enjoy the embraces of a virgin; Price and his wife Harriet (formerly a Nottage) left the Abode, and withdrew their money.

Other members of the faithful also defected. After all, if they were to be denied sex, why was Prince to be allowed to enjoy a virgin? The scandal spread to the village, then to the national newspapers. The Victorians loved a sex scandal as much as their less inhibited descendants, and the words "Abode of Love" became a synonym for sin practiced in secret. It was naturally assumed that every woman in the place was Prince's mistress. In fact, although there were other attractive women in the Abode, there is no reason to believe that Prince was interested in anyone but Zoe.

Prince lived to be eighty-eight, and when he died in 1899, his followers were shocked, for he had assured them that they had all become immortal once they abandoned everything to follow him. Of course, there had been other deaths in the half century since Prince had become their leader, but he had always explained them by saying that they were the result of sin. Now they had to accept that Prince himself was a sinner, and they hastened to bury him in the grounds by night.

It was almost the end of the Abode. Many followers left, and others turned to Spiritualism, hoping to contact Prince in the afterlife. Those who remained felt lost without a leader. The secretary of the Abode, Douglas Hamilton, decided that he had to act quickly if disintegration was to be avoided. A new messiah was urgently needed.

It was probably at this point that Hamilton heard of a middle-aged clergyman whose powerful sermons had an overwhelming effect on his audiences, particularly on young girls. His name was John Hugh Smyth-Piggott, and he was forty-eight years old; he was at present in Dublin, Ireland, having recently married an attractive member of his congregation who was many years his junior. Hamilton hurried to Dublin, and was impressed to find a handsome man with a weather-beaten complexion who looked more like a sailor than a vicar; in fact, Smyth-Piggott had been in the merchant navy. He had what his admirers called a fine gift of oratory, but his detractors dubbed a gift of the gab.

When Douglas Hamilton told him that the women of Spaxton were awaiting a new "Heavenly Bridegroom," Smyth-Piggott replied: "Go and tell them your search is ended."

Before going to Spaxton, Smyth-Piggott decided to test out the powers of his oratory in London, in a small church in Clapton, which was affiliated with the Abode of Love. On Sunday September 7, 1902, he stood up in the pulpit and announced: "I am the Messiah. In me you behold Christ in the flesh."

A few worshippers fell on their knees; the others gaped in astonishment. But when, the following Sunday, Smyth-Piggott arrived to follow up his announcement, a crowd of six thousand booed, jeered and threw stones; as the police held them in check, the "messiah" fled. Smyth-Piggott was told that if there were any more disturbances like this, he would be charged. He decided to move to the Abode of Love, where gaining acceptance was easier.

In fact, no one turned a hair when, at their first service in the chapel, he told them he was the messiah. Under Prince they had become accustomed to accepting the presence of someone who talked to God on a daily basis.

Smyth-Piggott proved to be a charismatic leader, full of vigor and new ideas. His efforts at fund-raising swelled the depleted coffers, and brought in new residents, among whom, as usual, there were a number of young women. Smyth-Piggott installed his wife Catherine in a cottage in the garden, and spent a great deal of his time instructing the younger females.

Unlike Prince, Smyth-Piggott was a man of the twentieth century. Prince had dreamed longingly of virgin brides as he read the Song of Songs; Smyth-Piggott, the ex-sailor, faced the fact that he loved women, and saw no reason why he should not take advantage of those who wanted to become his soulmates.

But, as a man of the world, he knew that open seduction would cause problems. One of his biographers accuses him of running a kind of oriental harem. But the truth is that we do not know. The likeliest scenario is that he took a number of "brides," but urged upon every one the need for discretion to prevent other women becoming jealous, and to prevent scandal from spreading to the village, and thence to the scandal-hungry newspapers.

After a mere two years, Smyth-Piggott dropped all pretense. In July 1904 he came back from a trip to the "outside world" with a beautiful young girl called Ruth Anne Preece, and announced that she was the Bride of the Lamb. She was dignified, gentle, and fairly well off. In June 1905 she gave birth to a boy who became known as Glory, and in the following year to another boy called Power. These were joined in due course by a sister called Life. In 1906, his bishop defrocked him, but it made no difference; Smyth-Piggott's congregation at the Abode regarded him as the Master who could commit no sin.

One young Russian girl who moved into the Abode to share its atmosphere of peace described how, after several weeks, Smyth-Piggott asked her to his room and paid her many compliments. After that, he took her arm and made passes across her forehead which made her feel faint. But when he told her that she was his "soul bride," and that he could do no wrong, she fled, and left the Abode soon after.

Fresh problems arose when Smyth-Piggott seduced a new arrival known as Sister Grace. Ruth showed herself to be a woman of spirit and confronted him about it. His reaction was to summon all the members to the chapel, and to tell them that Sister Ruth had sinned against them. As Ruth stood there in her ceremonial robes, other sisters came forward and stripped her of them, leaving her half naked. After that, Sister Grace was installed as the Bride of the Lamb. Ruth, fifteen years older and wiser than when she had taken part in the same ceremony, left the Abode of Love.

Like Prince's "marriage" to Zoe Patterson, this ceremony proved to be a mistake. It got into the newspapers, and they made the most of it. Villagers began to hiss and boo when Smyth-Piggott showed his face outside the Abode. A group of youths from Bridgewater decided that he deserved to be tarred-and-feathered and climbed over the wall one night; they grabbed a respectable-looking man who emerged from the front door. Unfortunately, it was an elderly resident named Charles Read, and he found the experience of being tarred-and-feathered so traumatic that he died soon afterwards.

Smyth-Piggott made his greatest mistake when he cast his eye on the attractive wife of one of the London followers. Like so many other women, thirty-seven-year-old Dora Bedow found him irresistible, and lost no time in abandoning her husband and child and moving to Spaxton. Her husband refused ever to see her again.

But once installed as the Bride of Christ, Dora proved to be less pliant that previous occupants of that position. She had a strong character, and sometimes spoke sharply to other disciples. Smyth-Piggott began to spend an increasing amount of time in travel, particularly in Norway, where he had set up another Abode of Love. From there he often sent pretty flaxen haired women back to Spaxton.

But even as a seducer, Smyth-Piggott was losing his old skill and vigor. In his sixties, time was taking its toll; his sermons were becoming incoherent, and his hypnotic passes were failing to subdue young women. Early in 1927, when he was seventy-four, he took to his bed with influenza, and remained there until March, when he died. Douglas Hamilton, who had brought him from Dublin, officiated at the funeral, while outside, police held back the curious crowds, who wanted to see for themselves how many beautiful young women were in mourning.

Smyth-Piggott's wife Catherine died in 1936, and the first Bride of the Lamb, Ruth (who had been allowed to return), died in 1956. Two years later, the Abode of Love finally closed its gates. Its past twenty years, without a Spiritual Husband, had been a dull time.

Looking back over the history of messiahs, from Simon Bar Kochbar to David Koresh, we become aware of how much the word messiah has changed its meaning.

Originally, it meant a military leader who would lead his people to triumph. In the Middle Ages it came to mean a God-King who would restore social justice and bring a reign of plenty. By the time of George Fox and John Bunyan it had come to mean a prophet who denounced the "worldly wisemen" who had lost sight of the true meaning of religion.

It was also taken for granted that sexual desire was a manifestation of the lower self. Noyes and Joseph Smith changed all that; it was they who added the sexual dimension to the concept of "messiah." Since then, most messiahs have been lechers, or at least, have added sexual potency to their list of godlike qualities.

The obvious explanation—most messiahs are human beings who are a prey to the sexual impulse—is true but simplistic. Sabbatai Zevi, whom no one has ever accused of libertinism, became a "messiah" when he was in his manic moods, flooded with a sense of exaltation that made him feel godlike. Smyth-Piggott, Jim Jones and David Koresh used sex for the same purpose. It reinforced their sense of power, of being more-than-human.

When some future historian looks back over the centuries, he will see the nineteenth century as a sexual watershed. This was the age when humanity became increasingly obsessed by sex, and when sex crimes first began to appear. (Oddly, the sex crime, in our modern sense of the word, was relatively unusual until the last quarter of the nineteenth century.) By the second half of the twentieth century, the historian will note that civilization was dominated by sexual obsession. Certainly, this was the age when the fairly innocent lechery of Prince and Smyth-Piggott took on darker and nastier undertones.

The career of Rock Theriault, sentenced in 1993 to life imprisonment for the torments he inflicted on his disciples, brings home the full impact of this contrast.

At the age of twenty, Rock Theriault, a French Canadian born in 1947, seemed the last person in the world to turn into a paranoid messiah. He was good-looking, popular, amusing, resourceful, and a charmer of the opposite sex. His education was incomplete—he dropped out of school at fourteen—but he made up for it with natural intelligence and a gift for self-expression. He seemed the type who was meant for success.

His problems seem to have started when he married at the age of twenty, and became the father of two sons. With a menial job in the Montreal fire department, he may have felt that life had suddenly turned into a treadmill. Theriault developed gastric ulcers that necessitated the removal of half his stomach. His wife also noted that his interest in sex seemed to increase; he wanted her to wear miniskirts, and he tried to persuade his in-laws to allow him to open a nudist colony on their property; they indignantly refused.

In his mid-twenties, Theriault became involved in local politics, and gained a seat on the city council. He was an articulate and committed councilor, but too hot-headed; his plans for new roads, playgrounds, and houses would have bankrupted the council. When it became clear to him that making a career in local politics would require patience and hard work, Theriault stopped attending meetings and was voted out of office.

The same thing happened when he joined a local rotary club; he worked his way up until he became president of a committee, then tried to change everything. The club threw him out. Rock Theriault was clearly the kind of man who needed to dominate, but was not sure where to begin.

In 1976 he seduced a woman named Gisele Tremblay, whom he had met at a dance, and deserted his family. Gisele found him charming and charismatic as he talked about his wood-carving business, his career in politics, and his knowledge of medicine; he did not tell her that the wood-carving business had gone bankrupt and that his career in politics had ended after one year. Gisele was fascinated by the way that he could strike up friendships and charm strangers, and she loved his wild sense of humor and his practical jokes. Yet it was clear that the easy-going exterior concealed a troubled mind. Theriault had bouts of alcoholism that occasionally landed him in the hospital.

He was also violently anti-Catholic, having been brought up in a Catholic household, yet now he began to read the Bible, particularly the Old Testament, declaring that he found it a "more honest and pure source of spirituality."

In 1977, Rock Theriault attended a meeting of Seventh Day Adventists, who had launched a local crusade about "the future of civilization." Within weeks he professed himself converted, and was soon knocking on doors and trying to convert others. His fellow Adventists found him charming but boastful; "Rock was the type of person who claimed to know everything," said one of them.

Nevertheless, he proved to be an excellent salesman of Adventist literature, and Gisele, who often accompanied him, was again fascinated by his ability to charm strangers. Allowed a commission of forty percent on the books he sold, he was soon making a good income. He proved to be equally gifted at running week-long workshops to teach people how to give up smoking.

The Adventists launched another "crusade" in the town of Plessisville; the message was that the world was becoming increasingly wicked and that the Second Coming could not be long delayed. Among the young people who became interested were Jacques Fiset, and three girls, Solange Boilard, Chantal Labrie and Francine Laflamme. Rock Theriault was introduced to them, and soon all four were under his spell as he talked about God's blueprint for humanity and the decadence of the modern world.

He began inviting them to spend weekends in the one bedroom apartment of Gisele, who found it cramped, but enjoyed seeing her lover so happy. Four more bored and unhappy young people soon joined the fold: Nicole Ruel, Marise Lambert, Josee Pellettier and Claude Ouelette. Every weekend the apartment became an overcrowded doss house.

On a week-long religious seminar at Lake Rosseau, Theriault invited his crowd of young disciples. There he met another admirer, a twenty-eight-year-old nurse, Gabrielle Lavallee, who also succumbed to his charm, confidence, and air of omniscience. From the time she had been gang-raped as a child, Gabrielle's life had been unhappy; she felt she was a born victim, and Theriault's air of command dazzled her. It was during this seminar that Rock Theriault claimed that he had had a vision; alone on a hilltop he had seen the sky turn white, and God had spoken to him.

With his crowd of disciples now amounting to a dozen or so, Theriault began to spend weekends running his no-smoking classes in nearby towns. Not long after, the group set up a Healthy Living Clinic in the town of Ste-Marie, south of Quebec City. They sold books on natural foods and vitamins and holistic healing, as well as organic food, fruit juices, and vitamin pills. The girls wore sack-like dresses and, at Theriault's request, no bras.

One local resident was so charmed by these enthusiastic young people that he sold his house and gave them five thousand dollars. But Giselle noted with alarm that Rock tended to put their profits straight into his own bank account. She also felt misgivings about the fact that all the women were obviously in love with him, and wondered how long he could hold out. To soothe her jealousy, Rock Theriault married her.

Problems began when local residents complained to the police that bills were being left unpaid. Then a girl with leukemia, whom Theriault had persuaded to move into the colony for "natural healing" died, and he was blamed. At this point, the Seventh Day Adventists decided that Theriault was making converts for the satisfaction of his own ego rather than for the church, and voted him out. He was not concerned. He was now the messiah of his own religion.

On June 5, 1975, the group—it was by now ten women and four men—drove out of town just before dawn, leaving behind their unpaid bills. For a month they drove northwest towards the St. Lawrence River, halting to hold non-smoking seminars. It was on July 6 that Rock Theriault announced his revelation: the wrath of God would be unleashed on the earth in February 1979, but God had appointed him his emissary, and told him to take his disciples to some remote spot, far from civilization, and live the simple life until the disaster came.

They finally selected the spot, a brush-covered mound near a small lake; it was half an hour from the sea, and a four hour walk from the road. The nearest village, Saint-Jogues, was fifteen miles away. They carried their bedding and cooking utensils from the road, cut down trees with a chainsaw, and began to build a log cabin. Some hauled rocks to make a fireplace; others dug a well. It took nearly four months to build the cabin; until then they lived in tents. To symbolize their break from society, Theriault gave them all biblical names like Esther, Rachel, Ruth and Nathan. Theriault called himself Moses.

It seems to have been a happy time. The group indulged in theatricals, and listened to Theriault's lectures on the corruption of modern civilization. The nurse Gabrielle said later: "We really believed that he was a representative of God."

In their book *Savage Messiah*, Paul Kaihla and Ross Laver comment: "On the surface it seemed simple: a dominant figure taking advantage of a lot of weak-willed acolytes. But on a deeper level, Rock and his followers had developed a kind of mutual dependence. His entire adult life had been spent trying to impress others and gain their approval. Now he was surrounded by a group of people whose admiration for him knew no bounds."

He grew a long black beard, and devoted even more time to reading the Bible. Then, after Gisele had told him that it was unnatural for young women to be without a man, he decided that it was time to try to be a husband to them all. A few days later, he slept with Nicole—she was married to Jacques Fiset—in a loft. When Gisele found out, she became hysterical; Theriault knocked her to the ground and shouted: "My name is Moses and I am your master. You will obey me." Since she was six months pregnant, Gisele decided that it would be prudent to obey.

Theriault was fascinated by the Jonestown massacre in Guyana on November 18, 1978. But the suicide of Jones's nine hundred followers also led to problems as the Quebec authorities began to wonder about their own commune in the wild. Four policeman arrived at the camp, and to avoid trouble, Theriault agreed to accompany them to Quebec City for psychiatric tests. He assured the doctor that he was not the leader of the group, that it was run on democratic principles. But he talked frankly of his religious visions, leading the doctor to conclude: "He is suffering from a mystical delusion . . . but never showed himself to be aggressive or menacing towards others, and I do not believe that hospitalization is necessary."

Theriault returned to the commune with a new confidence. Soon after that he announced that all the marriages in the group should be annulled (the only exception being Maryse and Jacques

Giguiere, who had been together when they joined). Then, one by one, he took the women in the group into his own bed. When the nurse, Gabrielle, was summoned, he told her that she was not allowed to kiss him, only to fellate him. Moreover, he would not penetrate her unless he wished to make her pregnant. She could, however, if she liked, masturbate while she gave him pleasure.

Possibly because of the increased demands on his energy, Theriault returned to eating meat. Gabrielle was ordered to have sex with a local shopkeeper in return for food. (This was not because of any shortage of cash; the fourteen hundred dollars a month the group received in welfare checks went straight into Theriault's account.)

He also went back to alcohol, which he had abandoned for two years. The effect on his character was disastrous. He began striking his disciples, and punishing what he regarded as transgressions by ordering them to strip and stand outside in the cold for hours. He punished a crying baby by ordering the child's parents to roll him in the snow. When Maryse Giguiere talked about leaving, her husband was ordered to discipline her by cutting off one of her toes with an axe. When he burst into tears, Theriault seized the axe and threatened to cut off all her toes; finally, Jacques Giguieres obeyed, and chopped off one of Maryse's small toes.

When the end of the world failed to arrive in February 1979, Theriault explained that the problem was that God experienced forty years as a single second, and therefore could easily make a mistake, and the disciples accepted this odd explanation.

When the police took Theriault into a Quebec hospital for another psychiatric examination, the authorities also seized the opportunity to fly relatives of the disciples to the commune, hoping they could break Theriault's hold over them. It was hopeless; without their leader, the disciples were like drug addicts deprived of their fix, and awaited his return in a state of dumb misery. Many refused even to speak to their parents.

In March 1981 there was more serious trouble. An ex-mental patient named Guy Veer had joined the group, and when Samuel, the child of Maryse and Jacques Giguiere, was found dead, Theriault explained that Veer had lost his temper because the child kept him awake, and had hit him in the face. It was revealed later that Samuel had been circumcised with an unsterilized razor blade, after which raw alcohol had been poured on his penis; his death was probably due to the results of the anesthetic Theriault had squirted into his mouth. The child's body was incinerated.

That September, after another drinking bout, Theriault decided that Guy Veer should be castrated to cure his headaches. Veer was given several glasses of alcohol, then made to lie down on a table with a rubber band around his scrotum, while Theriault and Gabrielle removed his testicles. His scrotum bled for a week. Soon after that, Theriault tied Veer to a tree, beat him with a leather belt, then ordered his followers to stab him to death; it was only as they were preparing to obey that he laughed and called them off.

Veer was so terrified that he made for the nearest village and reported the death of the baby, which he said had been kicked by a horse. The result was another police raid on the commune, and the arrest of Theriault and most of his followers. The children were seized and placed in care. On September 29, 1982, Theriault was sentenced to two years in prison, and five other followers to shorter periods. The commune buildings were burnt down and the ruins bulldozed.

Even this failed to break up the group. Those who had escaped jail moved into accommodation in New Carlisle, where the trial had taken place. Gisele was placed in charge of them, and received Theriault's instructions by telephone. Theriault even succeeded in impregnating three of his "wives" while out on weekend passes.

When he was released in February 1984, the group was still intact. On May 2, Theriault and his followers once more headed for the wilderness, this time for a bleak and remote stretch of forest in northern Victoria County, Ontario, thirty miles from the town of Lindsay. Theriault had paid a one-hundred-dollar deposit on the two hundred acres, with a promise to pay the remainder of the purchase price—twelve thousand dollars—over five years. Now the labor of building a home began all over again.

This time, the local authorities refused to allow the group to live on welfare. Theriault's response was to order his followers to shoplift. Throughout the winter of 1984, this was highly successful, but when four of them were caught in January 1985, they were ordered never to return to Lindsay.

Now drinking once again, Theriault's innate aggression began to surface. He chastised transgressions by hitting the offender with the flat side of an axe; once he hit Marise Lambert on the forehead with a hammer, and the gash had to be sewn up with needle and thread. He sometimes ordered offenders to lie on the floor, then urinated in their mouths. When Jacques Giguiere fought back and struck the Master, his punishment was to be circumcised with a knife. Theriault often summoned several wives to sex sessions—sometimes all eight; he liked to have several of them massaging his back and shoulders as he made love to another. After orgasm, he would order the women to have lesbian sex while he watched.

In January 1985, the authorities once more began to take an interest in the commune when Gabrielle's five-month-old baby died; the child had been left outside in a wheelbarrow for almost two hours, in a temperature of minus ten degrees Fahrenheit. When a Toronto group called COMA (Council on Mind Abuse) began to monitor the commune, Theriault became increasingly paranoid. After his outbursts of violence, he would explain that it was not he who was responsible, but a sinister Master of Life and Death who took him over and ordered punishment.

Theriault's obsession with holding on to his followers was justified when Maryse Giguiere left. Georgia Brown, co-founder the Council on Mind Abuse, could hardly believe her ears as Maryse poured out stories of beatings, sacrifice of animals, and tales of sexual orgies in which children participated.

On December 6, 1985, snowmobiles descended on the commune and the fourteen children were taken away. They verified the tales of sexual orgies. One boy described how he saw three of his half sisters pushing the skin of Theriault's penis up and down; another little girl described how, "Pappy likes me to pull on his penis and make the white stuff come out of it." One girl had torn genitalia, while another described how one of Theriault's sons had tried to rape a five-year-old girl and hurt her.

With so much evidence against him, it seemed inevitable that Theriault's days as a messiah were numbered. But charges were never brought; the authorities decided that they lacked sufficient evidence.

By 1988, Theriault's paranoia had increased to the point where his followers were subjected to continual violence. *Savage Messiah* contains three pages that list thirty-three individual atrocities. These included blistering the back of one of his wives with an oxy-acetylene torch, aborting another by kicking her in the stomach, burning the breasts of another with a welding torch, breaking every toe on the foot of a male follower, then pulling out eleven of his healthy teeth with a pair of pliers, and cutting off half a woman's finger with wire cutters.

In the autumn of 1988, he decided that Solange Boilard needed a stomach operation. He began by inserting an enema into her rectum, then forcing a plastic tube down her throat. He then made an incision in her right side with a knife, reached in, and began to pull out chunks of flesh. During all this time, the girl lay fully conscious and unmoving. Finally, he ordered someone to sew her up, then made her stand and walk about the room. The next day, blood began to gush from her mouth, and later that day, she died. Oddly, Theriault was shattered, and asked one of the male disciples to shoot him. Solange's body was buried in the commune.

A few weeks later, in one of his drunken bouts, Theriault ordered her to be dug up, then had her cut open, and some of her organs placed in a jar. After this she was reburied; but a day or two later, he had her exhumed again, and removed more body parts. Finally, after he had repeated this process several times, and the body was beginning to decompose, it was incinerated

After that, it was the turn of Gabrielle. When she complained of a toothache, Theriault forced open her mouth, and pulled out eight healthy teeth with pliers. Then, as he tried to attack her with a knife, she gripped the blade, and sustained a deep cut. She ran away and obtained hospital treatment; Theriault followed her and begged her to return.

But in July 1989, in another drunken rage, he pinned her hand to the table with a knife. After making her sit like this for nearly an hour, he decided that her arm had to be removed. He took a carpet knife, and began to hack away at her shoulder, slicing through flesh and tendons. When he tired, he called upon other women to help him, and they gradually exposed the bones on all sides. Finally, with a meat cleaver, Theriault severed the arm. As Gabrielle lay bleeding on the floor, he fell into a drunken sleep on a couch.

A few weeks later, when the stump was only partly healed, Gabrielle was held down while Theriault cauterized it with a red hot iron bar.

For Gabrielle it was the last straw. On August 16, 1989, she fled to a hospital. Even in agony, she remained loyal to Theriault, explaining that her arm had been crushed in a car accident, and that her boyfriend had amputated it to save her life. But the doctors called the police, who pointed out that even if the purpose of the operation had been to save her life, it was still illegal.

When the police arrived at the commune, they found it deserted. Theriault's final orgy of violence had convinced everyone that it was time to leave.

Gisele, Theriault's first mistress, fled to the town of Orillia, in Ontario. There she became friendly with Gordon Manktelow of the Social Services Department. But it was many weeks before she finally told Manktelow the full story of Rock Theriault's commune, and of the appalling death of Solange Boilard. By coincidence, it was on the same day—October 6, 1989—that Theriault was recognized by two police constables and arrested.

In a court in Lindsay a few weeks later, Theriault was sentenced to twelve years for amputating Gabrielle's arm. But it was not until January 18, 1993, that he was sentenced to life imprisonment for the murder of Solange Boilard.

Some of Theriault's acquaintances are on record as saying that he was insane. If so, it was the kind of insanity that appears with monotonous frequency in messiahs. In Theriault's case, it is easy to trace its growth.

He was a man whose fragile self-esteem depended on making an impression on other people. Dominating a group of disciples was the fulfillment of his dream, and became as addictive as a drug. This much is easy enough to understand. What is far more puzzling is why he then turned into a sadistic alcoholic.

The clue may lie in the fact that his decline began after he began to take the other women as his "wives." He clearly expected this to be some kind of ultimate fulfillment, an experience that would infuse him with certainty and leave no more room for self-doubt.

What seems equally plain is that this failed to happen. The supermale seems to have discovered that, in practice, dominating eight women is no more satisfying than dominating one. The alcoholism also indicates an attempt to escape a tormenting sense of unfulfillment. The outbursts of sadistic violence can be seen as merely another response to the same problem.

What seems clear is that the murder of Solange Boilard and the mutilation of Gabrielle Lavallee only made the problem worse. Like Jim Jones, Jeffrey Lundgren, David Koresh and Brother Twelve, Rock Theriault seems to have found himself trapped in an endless cycle of negative feedback.

ELEVEN

THE MASK OF POWER

Four days after his marriage in October 1917, W.B. Yeats was startled to discover that his wife could produce automatic writing. She would go into a trance with a pencil in her hand, then her hand would write strange and fascinating fragments. After a while, the "communicators" began to speak through her mouth when she was asleep. Their aim, apparently, was to describe all the possible types of human beings—there are twenty-eight, they said—and to relate these to the twenty-eight phases of the moon.

It took three years for the "communicators" to outline their complicated system, and when it was finished, Yeats wrote it all down in one of his most puzzling books, A Vision.

Each of the twenty-eight types is described in terms of four sets of characteristics, which are called Will, Mask, Creative Mind, and Body of Fate. Will is a person's basic type—the Emotional Man, the Concrete Man, the Receptive Man, etc. The Mask is the front he chooses to show the world, often the opposite of his basic type. Creative mind is the way he expresses himself creatively: intellectually, emotionally, physically, and so on. Fate is his destiny, what is "written in the stars."

The aspect that Yeats obviously finds most fascinating is the Mask, the person we want the world to believe we are. This was because Yeats himself was basically a shy and timid man, who regarded himself as a failure. As a youth he had played the dreamy poet, wearing his hair long and dressing in shirts with large collars and a floppy bow tie. As he grew older, and became more involved in the theater and politics, something more practical was required. The new personality was more dominant; in spite of his shyness, he became a formidable speaker, learning to outface hostile audiences. He had learned to wear the mask of power.

According to Yeats, the mask should not be regarded as a deception; if we wear it long enough, it turns into reality. Was Yeats a shy person who developed a mask of dominance, or was he a dominant person who took a long time to outgrow his shyness? Yeats would say that both views are equally true.

Looking back over the messiahs in this book, we can see that the mask theory applies to most of them, probably to all. Koresh started off feeling weak and vulnerable; then, step by step, he created the mask of dominance. So did Lundgren and Wilson and Prince and Theriault. So did the three Christs of Ypsilanti. Each of these men felt defeated by life, and escaped the defeat by claiming to be omnipotent. But madmen obviously represent an extreme; they are at the opposite end of the spectrum from Yeats's realistic attempts to remake himself. The others can all be placed at some point between these two extremes.

Yeats began as a disciple of Shelley, with his "dream of a young man, his hair blanched with sorrow, studying philosophy in some lonely tower, or of his old man, master of all human knowledge, hidden from sight in some shell-strewn cavern on the Mediterranean shore." He soon learned that the mask of the unworldly poet had certain disadvantages, particularly in romantic relationships. Shelley is essentially passive, almost masochistic:

> *Oh lift me from the grass!*
> *I die! I faint! I fail!*
> *Let thy love in kisses rain*
> *On my lips and eyelids pale.*
> *My cheek is wan and white, alas!*
> *My heart beats loud and fast;*
> *Oh! press it to thine own again,*
> *Where it will break at last.*

Most women are too practical to want a lover who needs soothing like a tearful child. The woman Yeats loved, Maude Gonne, preferred to marry a man of action, who died in the 1916 Irish uprising. Although Yeats had described him as a "drunken, vainglorious lout," he had to admit that women, in their perverseness, seem to prefer drunken vainglorious louts to poets.

Another of Yeats's colleagues, also in the Order of the Golden Dawn, began by trying on the mask of the poet. Edward Alexander Crowley, was born in 1875 into a family of Plymouth Brethren. The result was a lifelong detestation of Christianity, which led him to formulate his own religion—Crowleyanity—which he believed would one day conquer the world.

Although Crowley had been writing verse since the age of ten, it was not until he was twenty in his first year at Cambridge that he discovered Shelley. The influence was immediate and profound. Shelley's anti-authoritarianism deeply appealed to Crowley; he had been expelled from Oxford for writing a pamphlet called "The Necessity of Atheism." So did Shelley's romanticism, particularly that of his first mature poem, "Alastor, or The Spirit of Solitude."

This tells the story of a poet who falls asleep beside a stream, and dreams of a beautiful girl who sings as she plays on a harp, then moves towards him and "folds his frame in her dissolving arms." Unable to forget his vision, Alastor spends his life in search of her, and finally dies, prematurely old, under the full moon. Crowley wrote: "Already I was aware, in the abyss of my heart, secret and silent, that I was Alastor, the wanderer in the wilderness, the Spirit of Solitude."

He symbolized his new identity by changing his name from Alexander to Aleister. His first volume of poems, *Aceldama*, was published under the pseudonym of "A Gentleman of the University of Cambridge," in imitation of "A Gentleman of the University of Oxford" on the title page of Shelley's *Necessity of Atheism*. A few years later, he would even imitate Shelley to the extent of eloping with (and marrying) a woman whose parents were trying to force her to marry a man with whom she was not in love.

Apart from publishing volumes of poetry, which remained unread and unrecognized, Crowley's first attempt to act out his poetic ideal was to join a group known as the Celtic Church, which "lived and moved in an atmosphere of fairies, seal-women and magical operations." They apparently regarded *Le Morte D'Arthur* and *Parsifal* as Christians regard the Bible.

Although he had been obsessed by sex since his adolescence, Crowley decided, as did the American Perfectionists of the 1830s, to commit himself to an ideal of chastity and pursuit of the Holy Grail. Unfortunately, he had no idea where to start looking.

At this point he came upon a book about magic by A.E. Waite, and wrote to ask Waite to expand his hints about a secret church. In reply, Waite urged him to read a book called *The Cloud Upon the Sanctuary* by an eighteenth century mystic called Karl Von Eckartshausen, which was about just such a secret church. Crowley read it several times. "The sublimity of the idea enthralled me; it satisfied my craving for romance and poetry." He "appealed with the whole force of my will to the adepts of the Hidden Church to prepare me as a postulant."

No adepts answered his prayer; but in 1898 Crowley met an analytical chemist who told him about the existence of the organization that Waite was probably hinting at: the Magical Order of the Golden Dawn. Like Yeats, Crowley became a member, in a ceremony at the Mark Mason's Hall in London.

So far, Crowley's pursuit of the "mask" had followed much the same course as Yeats's: poetic idealism and rebellion, the quest of the Holy Grail and a church of secret adepts. But the mask of the dreamy and unworldly poet no more suited Crowley than it did Yeats. The son of wealthy parents, Crowley had been able to realize his sexual dreams in the arms of maidservants and prostitutes from an early age, so he soon outgrew Alastor's vision of a beautiful harpist. But like Yeats, he was firmly convinced of the reality and efficacy of magic. While Yeats remained, in essence, the poet dreaming in his lonely tower, Crowley exchanged the poet's mask for that of the magician.

Calling himself Count Vladimir Svaroff, he took a flat in Holborn and constructed a mirror-lined room for the practice of white magic; there was also a temple dedicated to black magic, in which Crowley kept a skeleton to which he sacrificed small birds. He shared the flat with an ascetic friend called Allan Bennett, another member of the Golden Dawn.

When Bennett moved to Ceylon, in an attempt to cure his asthma, Crowley rented a mansion on the edge of Loch Ness, in Scotland, and began to practice magic (or, as he preferred to spell it, Magick), attempting to conjure up his Holy Guardian Angel, with the aid of an old book of spells by Abra-Melin the Mage. Crowley claims in his autobiography that the house soon became populated with shadowy shapes. A few years later, when he returned to Scotland, he found that locals regarded the mansion as haunted, and refused to pass it after dark.

After a spectacular quarrel with the London Lodge of the Golden Dawn—they regarded him as a boastful charlatan—Crowley set out in 1900 on an around-the-world tour, on which he had some interesting adventures. He studied magic under a shaman in Mexico, had an affair with a married woman in Hawaii (and wrote a volume of poems about it called *Alice: An Adultery*), visited Allan Bennett in Ceylon (and left him installed in a Buddhist monastery), tried to climb Chogi-Ri, the world's second highest mountain, but was beaten back by the weather, and eventually arrived back in Paris, where he met Somerset Maugham, who painted an unflattering portrait of him in a novel called *The Magician*.

In Scotland, staying at the house of his painter friend Gerald Kelly, he met Kelly's sister Rose, a divorcee who had scandalized her family with her love affairs. They were now pressing her to marry one of her suitors, which aroused Crowley's Shelleyan indignation. He persuaded her to elope with him, and they were married by a lawyer. In spite of his initial misgivings, he found her bedroom techniques so exciting that he was soon convinced that he was in love with her.

His devotion was increased by the discovery that she enjoyed being spanked—Crowley always had a streak of sadism about him. They went to Cairo on their honeymoon, where they spent the night in the King's Chamber of the Great Pyramid. There Crowley claimed he was able to read aloud a magical invocation by a lilac glow which he recognized as the "astral light." On a visit to Ceylon, Rose discovered she was pregnant, and they returned to Cairo, where Crowley studied magic under an Arab sheik.

At this point, Crowley claims, his wife told him that he had offended the god Horus, and since her knowledge of mythology was minimal, he was intrigued. When, in the museum next door, she showed him a stele with an image of Horus, he suddenly became convinced that the Secret Chiefs of the Golden Dawn were trying to contact him. He begins the chapter of the *Confessions*, a book in which he describes his magical exploits, with the words: "This chapter is the climax of this book. Its contents are so extraordinary, they demand such breadth and depth of preliminary explanation, that I am in despair."

In a semi-trance state Crowley's wife instructed him on how to invoke Horus, and when he did so, he was told through her that the Equinox of the Gods had come, that a new epoch in human history had dawned, and that he was to be the link between these celestial forces and mankind. In other words, Crowley was given to understand that he had been chosen as the messiah.

On three days in April 1904, he entered his workroom at precisely midday, where he heard a "musical and expressive voice" which dictated to him a new scripture called *The Book of the Law*, which "claimed to answer all religious problems," and, according to Crowley, could lead human beings to the achievement of transcendental insight. To the modern reader, *The Book* reads like a mixture of the Song of Songs, Nietzsche's *Thus Spake Zarathustra* and the poems of Swinburne. "Beauty and strength, leaping laughter and delicious languor, force and fire, are of us. We have nothing with the outcast and the unfit: let them die in their misery. . . . "

Is *The Book of the Law* a deliberately conceived fake? The obvious answer is yes. But, as we have seen so often in the case of rogue messiahs, the obvious answer may be too simplistic. Crowley used magical rituals to induce a form of heightened consciousness, and he may well have believed that there was a sense in which *The Book of the Law* was dictated by a voice, perhaps from inside himself. The case of Kirk Allen and the jet-propelled couch makes us aware that imaginative obsession can be transformed into an apparently solid reality.

It is also necessary to recognize that people who try to contact spirits often obtain convincing results, although it is beyond the scope of this book to decide whether they are real or self-delusion. All that can be said with certainty is that for the rest of his life, Crowley continued to believe that *The Book of the Law* was divinely inspired, and that it was the basis for a new world religion called Crowleyanity.

The difficulty of accepting *The Book of the Law* as any kind of religious text is that, unlike every other world scripture, it makes no attempt to tell the aspirant how to transform his life. Its most famous sentence is: "Do what thou wilt shall be the whole of the law." Crowley explained that its aim was "the emancipation of mankind from all limitations whatsoever."

Crowley's followers have explained that, "Do what thou wilt" means far more than, "Do what you like." It refers to the true will that lies deep inside us, the expression of the true self, which we spend our lives trying to uncover. But in Crowley's case, it seems to have meant doing whatever *he* felt like doing, no matter how much misery and inconvenience he caused.

This was demonstrated on his next around-the-world trip, when he deserted a mountaineering expedition that was attempting to climb Kanchenjunga in the Himalayas, ignoring the cries of companions who were half-buried in snow in a crevasse. Crowley had quarreled with them, and felt that the accident served them right. It was on this same trip that he also deserted Rose and her daughter in Asia in order to see an ex-mistress in Shanghai. When Crowley returned home he found a letter from Rose saying that the baby had died of typhoid in Rangoon. It was after this trip that Rose showed the first signs of the alcoholism that would eventually kill her.

Crowley's conviction that he was a messiah seems to have caused a deterioration in a character that was already overly self-indulgent. He had a feverish appetite for acclaim, for recognition, for disciples. But most of those who were unwise enough to become intimate with him discovered that Crowley also had an incredible capacity for wrecking other people's lives.

The health of the poet Victor Neuberg—he performed magical rituals with Crowley in Morocco in 1909—was seriously undermined when Crowley made him sleep on a bed of gorse in a freezing cold room for ten nights. His biographer, Jean Overton Fuller, believes that this is how Neuberg contracted the tuberculosis that killed him at fifty-seven. Raoul Loveday, a young Oxford graduate, died after swallowing a cup of the blood of a cat sacrificed by Crowley in a magic ritual. Another disciple, Norman Mudd, committed suicide by drowning after Crowley's rejection. Several mistresses died insane, or under tragic circumstances. The death of Loveday caused the press to label Crowley "the wickedest man in the world," and after that, his self-chosen title, "the Beast, 666" suddenly began to take on more sinister overtones. There were many who believed that he was possessed by the devil.

In 1929—by this time Crowley was fifty-four—an Oxford student named Arthur Calder-Marshall decided to ask him to lecture to the Poetry Society. Crowley suggested a talk on the sadistic child-murderer Gilles de Rais. Calder-Marshall went to meet him in a restaurant, and found an overweight man who looked like a stock-broker. "He had the same dewlaps as actors who play corrupt senators in American films, a skin that was a rough as a calf's tongue, a tired, used face, sagging with satiation."

In fact, the authorities banned the lecture. Crowley insisted on it being printed, although it was so bad that Calder-Marshall had difficulty persuading the printer to set it up. Nevertheless, Crowley saw Calder-Marshall as a possible disciple, and invited him down to a cottage near Knockholt in Kent.

Calder-Marshall arrived with a girlfriend, and Crowley lost no time in sending her out with his wife—an exotic and plump Brazilain woman—to walk around the estate. As soon as they were alone, Crowley gave Calder-Marshall a large brandy and a toxic Brazilian cigarette, and asked him what he meant to do when he left Oxford. Calder-Marshall said he wanted to be a writer. Crowley then offered to employ him while he was learning to write. At the same time he leaned forward and stared into his eyes.

Calder-Marshall wrote: "I suddenly realized . . . that he was trying as quickly as possible to hypnotize me. His (eyes), weak and rather rheumy, were trying desperately to shine, like the bulb of a torch whose battery is failing." Calder-Marshall experienced a wave of disillusion and revulsion. For years he had assumed that Crowley was the devil incarnate. "When I came down to it, all it amounted to was this shagged and sorry old gentleman, trying to outstare me across a table."

Calder-Marshall's disappointment led him to rudeness. When Crowley asked if he had read his works, Calder-Marshall replied: "I have. They may be wonderful as magic, but I can't believe that anything that is so badly written could be." When Crowley's wife returned and asked what they had been doing, Crowley replied acidly: "I'd say I'd been wasting my time."

Calder-Marshall summarizes: "I realized that for all these years I had been looking for Milton's idea of Satan, a figure of Pure Evil; and that this impure character, trying rheumily to hypnotize me, was the genuine article. Evil is never Pure."

By the beginning of the Second World War, Crowley was an alcoholic and a drug addict. Yet when he died in a Hastings boarding house in 1947 at the age of seventy-two his belief that he was the messiah of a new religion was undiminished. To have abandoned it then would have been a form of psychological suicide.

Crowley's career is of interest largely because he was so much more intelligent than most messiahs.

Like most of them, he was driven by an obsessive desire for "a place in the sun." But he went about it in a more subtle and roundabout way than Jim Jones or Ervil LeBaron. His interest in Shelley led him to identify with Alastor, and to attempt to become "the Spirit of Solitude, the Wanderer in the Waste." If he had, as he liked to claim, been recognized as "the one poet in England," he would probably have been content to play the part for the rest of his life. But no one read his poetry.

It was the same muddled idealism that led Crowley to join the Celtic Church, then to dream of becoming a kind of monk. It argues an odd lack of insight into his own oversexed and self-indulgent personality that he even thought of it. Which makes us aware that Yeats was right: the mask is usually the opposite of the everyday personality. Crowley was nothing like Shelley or Alastor. He was spoiled, egotistical, and spiteful. But when he joined the Golden Dawn, he realized that he had found an even more suitable mask. The magician is *supposed* to be a man of power, and Crowley badly wanted power.

Yet he wanted more than that. Crowley believed deeply in magic; it was as close as he ever came to religious belief. As in the case of Brother Twelve, there seem to be indications that he developed certain magical abilities, including hypnosis. In Sicily, where he set up an "Abbey of Thelema," he decided to sacrifice a cat that had scratched him. Raoul Loveday's wife Betty May described how he made the sign of the pentagram over the cat with his magic staff and ordered it to remain there; the cat became transfixed. Betty May carried it away and put it outside; it returned and sat in the same place, immobile, refusing food. Later, with Crowley presiding, it was "sacrificed" on an altar.

But being a magician demanded more dedication than Crowley possessed; he never succeeded in finishing the six month ritual of Abra-Melin the Mage. (One biographer believes that it was his failure to complete this rite that led to his lifetime of bad luck.)

The voyage around the world that followed was a search for identity. It was in Cairo, in April 1904, that Crowley believed he had finally found his true identity: messiah, guru, world teacher. Equipped with this new mask, he began his assault on the world.

Although he proved a better magical guru than poet or magician, his inherent weakness of character again caused success to elude him. One infuriated disciple walked out after shouting: "I'm sick of your teaching—teaching—teaching—as if you were God Almighty and I were a poor bloody shit in the street."

Crowley's problem was that he was obviously not God Almighty, or even a genuinely inspired teacher. Yeats had declared that a man who wears the mask for long enough ends by becoming the mask. "Seeming that goes on for a lifetime is no different from reality." But Crowley lacked the patience to maintain seeming for a lifetime, or even a few years. What he really wanted—Arthur Calder-Marshall realized this—was power, immediate power. The history of messiahs reveals that this is the quickest way to psychological self-destruction.

The basic problem of the mask is that it condemns its wearer to hatred and resentment. Why? Because a mask implies defensiveness, and we are bound to hate the things we feel threatened by. Even Yeats loved to quote Ruskin: "As I walk to the British Museum, I see the faces of the people become daily more corrupt." He had to see the faces of the people become more corrupt in order to justify his own feeling of superiority.

This combination of resentment and superiority is, of course, the essence of criminality. The French murderer Lacenaire, guillotined in 1836, wrote in his *Memoirs*: "A victim of injustice from infancy . . . I had created a view of life very different from other men's. . . . Oh, I concede, I became wicked and even cruel. Woe betide anyone who offended me if I could snatch a favorable moment. I was the more dangerous because I never avenged myself until I was certain of success; I never showed my hatred until the instant propitious for satisfying it."

This kind of resentment, of sitting in judgement on society, is typical of the criminal. More than a century later, Bobby Beausoleil, a friend of Charles Manson, told Truman Capote: "I have my own justice. I live by my own law, you know. I don't respect the laws of this society. Because society doesn't respect its own laws. I make my own laws and live by them. I have my own sense of justice."

Beausoleil, according to Capote, was the unwitting cause of the Manson murders. He had stabbed to death a musician named Gary Hinman, in an attempt to extort money, and in an effort to mislead police into believing that Black Panthers were responsible, scrawled "Political Piggy" in blood on the wall, with a sign like a panther's claw.

A week later, Beausoleil was arrested as he drove Hinman's car. It was because of this, according to Capote, that Manson decided to begin a series of copycat killings, in the hope of convincing the police that Hinman's killer was still at large. The obvious objection is that other murders, even with bloody graffiti, would hardly convince the police of anything of the sort (as, in fact, they didn't—Beausoleil was sentenced to death).

The murders committed by the Manson "family" were typical cult murders, like those of Jeffrey Lundgren or Ervil LeBaron. The main difference—the one that concerns us here—is that Manson was not a manic messiah who believed he had a message for mankind: in fact, he was quite positive about not having a message; he believed in letting people do as they liked.

But, like Crowley, he also felt more comfortable living behind a mask. The most famous photograph of Manson shows him staring demonically into the camera, with a swastika slashed on his forehead. In fact, most people who met Manson found him a quiet, unthreatening little man, with a touch of Charlie Chaplin about him. Film footage of interviews taken in jail confirm this.

When Charles Manson arrived in San Francisco in 1967, he was thirty-two years old, and had spent most of his adult life in prison or reform school. His mother, Kathleen Maddox, was fifteen when she became pregnant with him; a few years later she was in jail for armed robbery. Manson was placed in a children's home when he was twelve, and began his career of burglary soon after. By the time he emerged from a ten year jail sentence in 1967—it was for car theft, check fraud, and pimping—he was institutionalized, and would have preferred to stay in prison.

San Francisco in the decade of the Flower Children proved to be a revelation. Suddenly Manson was no longer an ex-jailbird but a member of the Beat Generation. He was well qualified, having learned to play the guitar from the gangster Alvin "Creepy" Karpis. Busking outside the University of California in Berkeley, he met a librarian named Mary Brunner, and soon moved in with her. He acquired a second girl—Lynette Fromme—when he found her crying on the pavement after a quarrel with her family. Manson told her "I am the god of fuck." After years in prison he was as sexually active as a rabbit.

Young women were attracted to him because he had a striking personality, yet seemed unthreatening; he was almost a father figure. Manson told a friend: "I'm a very positive force . . . I collect negatives." A prison report on him had stated: "Charles Manson has a tremendous drive to call attention to himself." But now he no longer had to call attention to himself; teenage girls stuck to him as if they were fragments of colored paper and he possessed some kind of static electricity.

Another woman he picked up was nineteen-year-old Susan Atkins, who had left home at sixteen and served some jail time for associating with criminals. She invited him back to her apartment, and as they lay naked, he told her to imagine that it was her father who was making love to her. She claimed that it was the greatest orgasm of her life. Later she was to say of him: "He is the king and I am his queen. And the queen does what the king says."

The drugs undoubtedly helped. Manson and his "family" never used heroin; they preferred pot and psychedelics. It was on an LSD trip that Manson saw himself as Christ, and went through the experience of being crucified. It made a deep impression. His followers later said that he had "Christlike vibes." He liked to point out that his name meant "Son of Man."

He somehow acquired a battered Volkswagen bus, and with his family of young women, now grown to half a dozen or so, he shuttled around between California, Oregon and Washington, gradually acquiring more followers. They exchanged the Volkswagen for a yellow school bus and removed most of the seats so they could sleep in it.

Then how did this mild, inoffensive, guitar-playing hippie turn into the maniac who ordered the murder of half a dozen people he had never met?

At this point in our book, that question should be easy to answer. When Manson came to San Francisco, he saw himself as a gentle pacifist, trying to spread the gospel of love and understanding. Within six months he had a group of followers over whom he exercised almost absolute control. He found the role of leader hard work; at one point he even announced the dissolution of the group and sent most of them away. But they soon drifted back, and he realized that, whether he liked it or not, he had to play the role of patriarch and guru.

But what is a patriarch and guru figure supposed to do? He has to *demonstrate* his power. Most of the messiahs in this book, from Smyth-Piggott to David Koresh, harangued their followers for hours at a time, claiming to be in direct contact with God, and making awesome prophecies. Manson never claimed to be God, or even Moses—although his sermons on modern corruption could also last for hours. He merely claimed to be a good musician—he said as good as the Beatles—but no one in the music business seemed to agree with him.

Little by little, he became accustomed to wearing the mask of power. When he and a disciple named Paul Watkins came upon a rattlesnake, Manson ordered Watkins to sit in front of it. Watkins did ("I must have been crazy, but that's the kind of effect he had on me."), and the snake rattled and slid away; Watkins was convinced Manson had some strange power over animals. When a man named Melton, whom they had robbed of five thousand dollars, came in search of his money, Manson handed him a knife and said he was welcome to kill him if he had a quarrel. Melton said he hadn't, but he wanted his money. Manson said that in that case, he had better kill Melton, to prove that death did not exist. Melton decided to leave without his money.

When a drug dealer named Crowe came in search of twenty-four hundred dollars worth of marihuana he had paid for, Manson pointed a revolver at him and pulled the trigger. Nothing happened, and he fired again; this time Crowe collapsed with a bullet in his torso. Manson left, convinced that he had killed Crowe; in fact, Crowe survived, but did not report the shooting. Again, Manson had proved his ability to protect his own.

When Bobby Beausoleil was ordered to persuade Gary Hinman to give them twenty thousand dollars, Hinman refused, and Beausoleil rang Manson. Manson came over with a sword, with which he slashed Hinman's face, half severing his ear. After this, Manson left, leaving Beausoleil to try to beat Hinman into divulging the whereabouts of his money. When this failed, Beausoleil rang Manson again and asked what he should do; Manson ordered him to kill Hinman. Beausoleil didn't hesitate; he stabbed him twice in the chest, and Hinman died of loss of blood.

So Manson became accustomed to wearing the mask of power until it blended into his own face. He had always believed that he and his "children" were victims of a rotten, uncaring society. Now, as he identified with the mask, he became more violently anti-authoritarian. Like all messiahs, he justified his rejection of society by announcing the end of the world, or rather, of capitalist civilization. He began keeping death lists of people who deserved to die when the great "crash" came; he expected America's blacks to rise up and slaughter the whites. In the typical manner of messiahs, anti-authoritarianism turned into paranoia and ruthlessness.

Two weeks after Hinman's death, on August 8, 1969, Manson ordered four of his followers—Tex Watson, Susan Atkins, Patricia Krenwinkel and Linda Kasabian—to commit murder at a house in Cielo Drive, where an acquaintance in the music business had lived. They encountered a friend of the houseboy about to leave the drive, and Watson shot him in the head. After this, they went into the house and held up its inhabitants at gunpoint, including film star Sharon Tate (who was pregnant) and three friends who had come to dinner. When the Manson clan left, all four were dead, stabbed or shot.

The following night, Manson walked into the house of supermarket owner Leno LaBianca, held up LaBianca and his wife Rosemary at gunpoint, and tied them up. After that, he left, and Tex Watson and Patricia Krenwinkel stabbed the LaBiancas to death.

Two months later, Susan Atkins was in custody, being questioned about the Gary Hinman murder. She confided in a fellow prisoner, revealing her part in the Sharon Tate killing; the prisoner told someone else, who told the police. In early December 1969, Manson, Watson and four of the women were charged with the murders. In March the following year, Manson and four of his followers were sentenced to death; one of them, Linda Kasabian, turned state's evidence. This was reduced to life imprisonment when the death penalty was abolished in California in 1972.

The similarities between Manson and Koresh are obvious. Both began as unaggressive, undersized children who saw themselves as victims. But Koresh began to throw off this image at an earlier age than Manson, when he won a race at school and began to see himself as an athlete. Koresh's religious background also gave him an advantage; it made the religious route to domination the obvious choice. Yet even so, Koresh, like Manson, spent years trying to achieve success as a guitarist and pop singer; a healthy instinct told him that it would be better to be Bob Dylan than Jim Jones. When it came to the test, neither Koresh nor Manson was strong enough to escape the whirlpool created by their power over others.

It is tempting to believe that the solution of the problem may lie in intelligence. With the exception of Yeats, and possibly Crowley, none of the figures in this book has been notable for intelligence, or been interested in ideas for their own sake (Manson even banned books from his commune.) Would a Koresh who was interested in other books besides the Bible still have turned into a violent monomaniac?

The answer could well be yes. One of the most intelligent and sensitive of modern writers chose to escape his sense of inadequacy through the creation of a mask of power, and ended in the self-destruction that seems so typical of messiahs.

The suicide of Yukio Mishima, disemboweled with a ritual sword, seems to indicate that even literary talent cannot halt the messiah's downhill slide into resentment and violence.

Mishima—his real name was Kimitake Hiraoka—was not, as he liked to claim, born a samurai. That was part of the mask of power he cultivated later. His ancestors were peasants, and he was an undersized and sickly child, brought up by an intensely neurotic and possessive grandmother, even though his mother and father lived in the same house. He spent much of his childhood in his grandmother's windowless room.

Play was restricted, and even then he was only permitted to play with girls; but he was allowed to read as much as he liked, and loved the fairy tales of Oscar Wilde and Hans Andersen. He soon became conscious of his morbid streak; he did not like the princesses, but was fascinated by princes who were murdered or fated to die.

Andersen's "Rose Elf" affected him deeply. It is an account of a prince who, while kissing a rose, is decapitated by a villain with a big knife. "My heart's leaning towards Death and Blood and Night would not be denied," wrote Andersen. In fact, such a preoccupation is already present in Japanese literature, from *The Tale of Genji* to the works of the Nobel Prize winner, Yasunari Kawabata.

Later, when Mishima experienced erections at the sight of males in bathing costumes, he realized he was homosexual. When he experienced his first orgasm looking at a picture of Saint Sebastian pierced by arrows, he also recognized that he possessed a strong sadistic streak. He daydreamed of massacring young white males on a large marble table and eating parts of their bodies.

In certain respects, his development paralleled that of a younger Japanese contemporary, Issei Sagawa, whose daydreams were of killing and eating a white woman, and who became notorious in 1981 when he murdered a female fellow student at the Sorbonne and ate parts of her body.

As a teenager, Mishima wrote his first novel, *The Forest in Bloom*, as a serial for a literary magazine edited by his teacher. It is a remarkable work, covering three epochs in the past, each of which describes an episode in the life of an aristocratic heroine. The mood is heavily romantic, and pervaded with a death-eroticism reminiscent of Wagner's *Tristan und Isolde*; the tone is remarkably assured, reminding a European reader of Francoise Sagan's *Bonjour Tristesse*. With its rich evocation of the past, it seems to be turning its back on the twentieth century, with its ugliness and soulless technology, to dream of nobler times. Published when its author was sixteen (under his pseudonym Mishima) its first edition sold out in one week.

Oddly, Mishima's father was outraged to learn that his son was a writer, and made him promise to give it up. He often raided the boy's room, and destroyed manuscripts he found while his son looked on. Mishima had to persuade the sister of a schoolfriend to keep them for him. The opposition deepened his determination to become a writer and, naturally, his feeling that a writer is someone who has to be prepared to face persecution.

During the Second World War, the teenage Mishima worked in a factory manufacturing kamikaze airplanes, and dreamed of dying for his emperor. Yet when called up in 1945, he succeeded in avoiding military service by convincing the doctor that he was tubercular, even though he felt guilty about it for the rest of his life. He was always a mixture of realistic caution and romantic fervor.

Kawabata, the Nobel Prizewinner whose work has a melancholy-tinged flavor not unlike Proust, became an admirer after reading a story by Mishima about homosexuality; Mishima became his protege.

Mishima's autobiographical first novel, *Confessions of a Mask*, made him famous at the age of twenty four, in 1949. It is a frankly narcissistic account of Mishima's childhood and teens (including the period in the aircraft factory) and its central episode is a largely fictional account of his involvement with a young girl named Sonoko.

But it is the last scene of the book that catches the essence of Mishima. He and Sonoko have gone into a cheap dance hall on a hot summer day, and the hero is fascinated by the sight of a young gangster, sitting stripped to the waist among his friends, black tufts of hair sticking out from his armpits. He experiences intense sexual desire, and when the youth has gone, imagines him walking out into the street and becoming involved in a fight, which ends when someone drives a knife through his belly.

What is poignant here is the contrast between the innocent Sonoko, the young Japanese girl who dreams of a husband and family, and the sadistic imaginings of the man she is thinking of marrying.

In Japan, Mishima's novels continued to be hailed as works of genius, although when they were translated, Western critics were less sure. They admired the beauty and self-assurance of the style, but noted the underlying unpleasantness of the themes, particularly the touch of cruelty in his attitude towards women. There is a hatred of normality that is reminiscent of the early Graham Greene; in a story called "Sunday," the writer's pleasure is unmistakable as he describes how a conventional young couple are pushed on to the track by the crowd at a railway station, and decapitated by an oncoming train.

In Mishima's highly successful novel *Thirst for Love*, a middle-class city woman becomes obsessed with a young farmhand—he sounds like the gangster in *Confessions of a Mask*—and during a Shinto festival, has the opportunity to make his back bleed by scratching him with her nails. But when he begins to show signs of responding to her obsession, she stabs him through the neck with a mattock. It is as if Mishima is at once identifying with the woman, and at the same time trying to punish her.

In 1950, Mishima began to frequent gay bars—he claims that it was simply to gather material for his portrait of an embittered homosexual novelist—and to mix with female impersonators. It was when dancing with a young transvestite one day that he was stung by a joke about his thinness, and decided to take up body-building.

It took him more than three years, but by the time he had finished, the undersized youth had turned into the muscular athlete of one of his most famous photographs; in fact, Mishima had turned himself into the young gangster of *Confessions of a Mask* or the farm laborer of *Thirst for Love*. "My body became for me just like a new sports car for its proud owner." Flaunting his new attractiveness, he had many love affairs with female impersonators in the Kabuki theater.

In 1950, a psychopathic young novice had burned down the Temple of the Golden Pavilion (Kinkakuji) in Kyoto, declaring that he hated its beauty; Mishima used this as a basis of his novel *The Temple of the Golden Pavilion* (1956), which led critics to declare that he had achieved a new maturity.

Mishima's novice monk Mizoguchi is not really the central character; it is his friend Kashiwagi, a club-footed monk, who dominates the book. Kashiwagi is a cynic who justifies himself by invoking Zen. He demonstrates his techniques of seduction by stumbling and falling as a beautiful girl approaches; she helps him into her home and bandages his leg. He seduces her, then teaches her how to disguise the loss of her virginity from her future husband; after which he abandons her.

Clearly, Mishima's old attitudes are as strong as ever. This also emerges in a story told by Kashiwagi about how the monks of two temples dispute about who shall take charge of a stray kitten, and a monk named Nansen asks them if they can give him a good reason for not killing the kitten. When they are unable, he kills it. Later, when he tells the story to his friend Joshu, Joshu answers his question by placing his muddy shoes on his head. This is supposed to symbolize the sheer absurdity of believing that the kitten's beauty can be killed by killing the kitten. Nansen admits that, if the monks had perceived this solution, he would have allowed the kitten to live.

This kind of intellectualism gives the novel its specious air of profundity; in fact, it is clear that what is wrong with Mishima is his inability to operate on the level of intellect. He remains an emotionalist, trapped in his own inner contradictions. The tormented emotions of his characters often remind us of Dostoevsky, but he lacks Dostoevsky's passion for ideas.

By the early 1960s, the Japanese critics had also begun to perceive Mishima's limitations; so far his novels had always been best-sellers, often adapted for the screen, and his plays were equally successful; now they began to encounter coldness and real hostility. His friend Henry Scott Stokes has written: "Mishima's aim—his fundamental aim in life, it might be said—was to shock."

But shock tactics inevitably run into the law of diminishing effects. *Kyoko's House* (1959) was his first total failure. Its four characters are nihilists, people who feel that life is meaningless or who have no idea why they are alive; two die by violence, and the total effect is to leave the reader feeling he has been taken on a journey to nowhere.

The attacks on the book shook Mishima deeply; he set immense store by success, and had had little else for ten years. Now, by 1960, he began to feel that his life had ceased to move forward. When he appeared as a gangster (*Yakuza*) in a "B" film called *A Dry Fellow*, the public was baffled; to act in a first rate film would have been understandable, but this seemed simply a lapse of taste. His next lapse seemed even more baffling. In a novel called *After the Banquet*, about a restaurant owner named Kazu, he decided to satirize a former Foreign Minister, in the person of a politician who has an affair with Kazu. The politician sued for libel, and Mishima lost.

Soon after this, Mishima took offense when an old friend told him that he was a snob who took himself too seriously. He broke with a literary group with which he had been friendly for many years. He was beginning to display the paranoia of a man who has projected himself into a mask in exchange for emotional security, and who begins to feel this security threatened.

The 1960s saw the beginning of the rebellion of youth against the establishment; there were huge political demonstrations against the government. Mishima, who had never been interested in politics, followed all this with fascination. But typically, Mishima's reaction was deeply conservative. He wrote a story called "Patriotism," about an army officer who decides to commit *seppuku* (ritual suicide) after the rising of right wing young officers in 1936; although he has played no part in the rebellion, he cannot bear to take part in suppressing the rebels. The story describes at length all the preparations for suicide, then the ritual disembowelment. Subsequently, the story was turned into a highly successful film, with Mishima playing the part of the officer, in which the suicide is accompanied by the *liebestod* from Wagner's *Tristan und Isolde*.

In a novella, *Voices of the Heroic Dead* (1966), Mishima makes the ghosts of *kamikaze* pilots reproach the Emperor for having betrayed them when, in 1946, he declared he that he was a human being, not a god; he reinforced the point with criticism of the Emperor in a television interview. Among Japan's literary establishment, this made him virtually an untouchable. But Mishima's romanticism demanded that the Emperor should be a god, whether he was or not. He was moving into the realm of pure fantasy.

His novel *The Sailor Who Fell from Grace with the Sea* is a return to the morbid death-romanticism and sadism of earlier work. It is about a boy who peers through a hole in the bedroom wall, watching his mother make love with a sailor. When the sailor decides to remain on shore and live the unheroic life of the bourgeoisie, the boy and two friends plan to murder him, drug him, flay him alive, vivisect him with a scalpel. The last scene of the novel shows the sailor drinking the glass of drugged tea. It is one of the nastiest stories Mishima ever wrote, and reveals a total enslavement to his darker impulses. The book was a failure in Japan.

His biographer Henry Scott Stokes recognized Mishima had chosen to wear a mask, recording that he "always seemed high spirited in public, gesturing, joking, and laughing the raucous, rather ugly laugh which he is said to have been taught by his overbearing grandmother. His 'mask' was firmly in place: a stranger might have classified him as a former amateur boxing champion turned night club owner or band leader. For there was something coarse about his 'mask'; he projected an air of deliberate vulgarity. . . . "

There was the same air of vulgarity about a volume of photographs for which he posed called *Torture by Roses*, with pictures of Mishima lying naked on a beach with a rose in his mouth, and even more so in a subsequent set of photographs, one showing him as a Saint Sebastian pierced by arrows, another wearing nothing but a military cap and a jock-strap and leaning against a motorcycle. Other photographs taken at the same time depicted gruesome road accidents, executions, duels, and ritual suicide. It began to seem that exhibitionism was turning into buffoonery.

By 1969 Mishima had formed a group called the Shield Society, made up of right wing students whose initiation consisted in drinking blood flavored with salt. He designed gaudy uniforms for them—yellow, green, and brown, with brass buttons and wasp-waists—and they were allowed to train with the army. Stokes, who went "training" with them on the slopes of Mount Fuji, described it as "kitsch exemplified."

Mishima's second-in-command, Masakatsu Morita, was also his lover. He was a fairly late comer to the Shield Society. In fact, by the 1970s nearly all the original members had left in disgust or disillusion. Mishima became Morita's protector, and Morita gave acquaintances the impression of being Mishima's fiancee. Mishima often told friends: "Remember him; he's the one who'll kill me."

By this time, most Japanese had ceased to take Mishima seriously; the way he was behaving made them want to avert their eyes. His last novel, a huge tetralogy called *The Sea of Fertility*, which began to appear in 1969, was almost universally ignored by critics. The hero dies at the end of each volume and is reincarnated in the next; but Mishima's attempts to convince the reader that he believes in reincarnation are only half-believable, and explain why this novel, which he intended as his masterpiece, is as oddly inconclusive and unsatisfying as the early nihilist novel *Kyoko's House*.

The old literary skill is still there, but Mishima seems to have no idea where he is going. A Kabuki play written and directed by Mishima, with a *seppuku* scene that featured gallons of blood, was criticized as "a failure, but an impressive one." Mishima's biographer John Nathan calls it "dazzling in its way, but hollow." This also seems to summarize the spectacle that Mishima's life was turning into.

Mishima seems to have decided to restore his reputation with one dramatic act that would confound the critics. He had decided on suicide at least a year before he put the plan into effect. He seems to have seen it as a kind of romantic *liebestod* with his lover Morito.

In January 1969, police had stormed the University of Tokyo, where the students were on strike, and driven them out. Mishima was disgusted that none of the students had chosen to die for their beliefs; he told his cadets: "There was not one of them who believed in what he stood for enough to hurl himself out of a window or fall on a sword."

At eleven o'clock in the morning of November 25, 1970, Mishima and four of his cadets, including Morita, entered the Eastern Army headquarters in Tokyo, and seized the commander, General Mashita (who was a friend of Mishima's). The general was bound, and Mishima explained that the condition for his release was that all the soldiers should be assembled in the courtyard and listen in silence to a speech. Mishima then appeared on the balcony, and addressed about a thousand soldiers, exhorting them to rise up and throw off the degrading democracy that had sapped Japan's spirit. His basic theme could be summarized this way: back to pre-war imperialism. Apparently his audience was unconvinced; there were jeers and cries of "arsehole."

After eight minutes, Mishima went back into the room, rolled up his clothes, and tried to disembowel himself with a samurai sword; he only succeeded in making a cut two inches deep. Morita then tried to cut off Mishima's head, but the blows were feeble, and the head fell off only at the fourth attempt. One of the other disciples sliced off Morita's head with one stroke. Then the general was released, and the riot police admitted. The three survivors were charged only with minor offenses, since *seppuku* is legal in Japan; they received four year sentences.

Mishima's death failed to release the storm of right wing sentiment he had hoped for. The Prime Minister expressed the general view when he declared that Mishima had gone insane, although there were many who felt this was merely a suicide pact between lovers. Mishima's books ceased to sell; the final volumes of *The Sea of Fertility* met the same indifference as the earlier ones. There was a general feeling that the curtain had come down on an extremely bad play, and that the sooner it was forgotten, the better.

Looking at Mishima in retrospect, it is still impossible to take him seriously. The photographs he preferred show him as a muscular athlete, or as a samurai warrior, his arm outflung as he shouts *Banzai!* But the photograph that seems to contain the essence of Mishima is the one that shows him sitting on horseback at the age of four, looking into the camera with an expression of doubt and mistrust.

This was the real Mishima, the truth behind the mask: Peter Pan, the boy who never grew up. Mishima's tragedy was that the mask never began to even approximate the reality; inside he remained a child who wanted to play games.

The conclusion to be drawn from this chapter is that Yeats was mistaken: the mask never becomes a reality, no matter how long it is worn. All that happens is that the person behind the mask remains trapped like a fly in amber.

Yeat's own practice was far better than his theory. He abandoned the mask and allowed his poetry to grow through questioning, self-doubt, and the exploration of ideas. The result is that, of all the poets of the twentieth century, he strikes us as the one who most succeeded in developing until the very end.

TWELVE

THE SECOND STREAM

The only messiah figure with whom I ever came into personal contact was a woman called Charlotte Bach. Hers is as instructive and fascinating a case as any in this book.

I first became aware of Charlotte's existence in the autumn of 1971, when a heavy parcel landed on my deep freeze. It proved to contain a huge typescript, around six hundred pages long, entitled obscurely *Homo Mutans, Homo Luminens* which (she told me later) meant "Man the Changer, Man the Light Bringer." It was subtitled *An Introduction to Human Ethology.* I had to get out my dictionary to learn that ethology is an approach to the study of animal behavior that combines questions about its causation, development, and evolution. That left me none the wiser.

The book was written in a completely incomprehensible jargon, full of references to zoologists like Desmond Morris and Niko Tinbergen, and Konrad Lorenz; and psychologists like Jung and Freud. When I replied politely, asking Charlotte to explain herself, she sent another typescript, equally huge and unreadable. It seemed that the original one had been merely the prolegomena.

But a few days later, stuck in bed with a cold and sore throat, I made a determined attempt to read the prolegomena, and ended by feeling that, whatever the shortcomings of her style, Charlotte was possessed of a vast and impressive erudition. What she was saying seemed to me new and important. I wrote to tell her so, and got a letter that began "Thank you, thank you, thank you . . . " She told me later that when she read my letter she burst into tears.

226

I met her subsequently in London. She was a huge, bosomy woman with a deep voice and a Hungarian accent, and I took her and some friends to dinner. My first assumption was that she was a lesbian, but when one of my other dinner guests told me she had stuck her tongue down his throat as he kissed her goodnight, I had to admit that it was unlikely.

During dinner that evening, Charlotte told us how she and her husband had left Hungary during the Communist takeover of 1948, and settled in England. In 1965 she had been involved in a double tragedy when her husband had died on the operating table, and her son had been killed two weeks later in a car crash. As she told us this story she sobbed into her handkerchief. She repeated the story and the sobbing a few weeks later when I introduced her to another friend.

Two years later, a magazine called *Time Out* asked me to interview Charlotte, who had apparently acquired dozens of disciples. The problem was that I still found her theory incomprehensible. So I took her to lunch at the Savage Club, then sat her in an armchair and said, "OK, now explain your theory from the beginning."

It had started, Charlotte explained, after the death of her husband, when she needed something to take her mind off the tragedy. Her training, she explained, had been in psychology, so she decided to compile a dictionary of psychological terms. But when she came to the definitions of various sexual perversions, she began to encounter difficulties. Where did normality end and perversion begin?

Charlotte advertised in a magazine saying she wanted to meet people who suffered from odd sexual anomalies. As she met sadists, masochists, homosexuals, transvestites, and so on, it struck her that transvestites were quite unlike the others. One tweedy university professor asked if she minded if he behaved normally, and when she said no, stripped off his trousers, revealing that he was wearing women's panties, garter belt, and stockings. Then he sat there, quietly puffing at his pipe as he answered her questions.

Then there was a transvestite named Derrick Alexander, who felt that he was a woman trapped in a man's body; Charlotte actually persuaded him to have a sex-change operation. Here was obviously a case, she told me, where nature itself had made a mistake. Could that be the case with other so-called perversions?

One day, Charlotte read a paper by Desmond Morris on the zebra finch. It seemed that if a male finch, intent on courtship, is rejected by the female, it will proceed to do the female courtship dance. Apparently ten-spined sticklebacks react in the same paradoxical way; if a male cannot find a female, it often begins to behave like a female. It is as if frustration induces homosexual behavior.

Now among zoologists, such odd behavior patterns are called "displacement activities." Two angry male fish look as if they are going to tear one another apart, but instead bury their heads in the mud and waggle their tails in the air. It is nature's way of preventing bloodshed.

In the same way, bored human beings drum their fingers on the table or tap their feet. It is a way of finding an outlet for the energy of frustration. This is a displacement activity, or, as Charlotte preferred to call it, "spillover activity." But while a bored male may drum his fingers on the table or start clipping his nails, he does not usually put on a woman's underwear. So why should zebra finches and sticklebacks behave like the opposite sex?

The answer, Charlotte claimed, came to her in a flash of revelation. It is because all of us are really half-man and half-woman. In some of us, the male seems to have won the battle, in others, the female. But such balanced people, Charlotte thought, are uninteresting; they find a member of the opposite sex and settle down to a lifetime of mediocrity.

Far more interesting, she told me, are males like Michelangelo and Leonardo. The male-female conflict in them remains unresolved. Nietzsche once said that we must have chaos within us to give birth to a dancing star. The people with sexual chaos within them are more likely to give birth to great art. Why have so many artists and poets been homosexuals?

One day, a young man in the grip of religious obsession told her that he had experienced a sexual orgasm that had gone on for eight hours. Reading a book about tribal shamans by Mircea Eliade, Charlotte learned about shamans who experience ecstasies that last for hours. Suddenly, enlightenment dawned. Charlotte told me she jumped to her feet and shouted: "*That's* what it's about—evolution!"

She had always recognized that human beings differ from other species in their constant striving for happiness and fulfillment. They hate stagnation. This constant striving is a desire to evolve. Human beings, she concluded, differ from other species in being fundamentally sexually unstable. But there is a good, sound biological reason for this. It's is called neotony. This might be renamed Peter Panism. A neotonous species never grows up; it dies before full biological maturity. There is a Mexican lake salamander called the axolotl lizard which is actually a baby land salamander.

A Dutch zoologist called Ludwig Bolk suggested in the 1920s that humans may be neotonous apes. The ape embryo reaches the same state of development as a fully developed human embryo, then goes on developing brow ridges, body hair, specialized teeth, and so on. Human beings may be the Peter Pans of the ape world.

Charlotte saw human beings as an essentially child-like species, who never grow properly into men and women, but remain half-and-half. "Normal" people are people who have put a kind of unconscious stopper on their inner chaos. But "abnormal" people, those who possess the possibility of *interesting* development, remain essentially immature.

On the other hand, a highly creative person, like Beethoven, seems to feel a curious reluctance to accept normality. His relationships with women never seem to work out because he has an unconscious urge not to curtail his development by settling down. The result is personal unhappiness, and masterpieces like the symphonies.

The core of Charlotte's theory is that there is no such thing as a man or a woman, except in a crude physical sense. We are all men/women. (Jung had reached a similar conclusion, arguing that all men have a female component called the *anima*, and all women a male component called the *animus*.) The main difference between human beings is simply how far each of us accepts or rejects that "other self" of the opposite sex. Charlotte calls the acceptors "asseverationists," and the rejectors "denialists." According to Charlotte there are eight basic types, eight ways of coping with our sexual ambiguity.

In a basic sense, we are obviously determined by whether we happen to have been born male or female. This forms the basis for two types. But there is also the question of whether a person is psychologically male or female. There are men who feel they are really women, and vice versa. That adds two more types.

A person who is psychologically of the same type as his/her body, Charlotte calls positive. Those who are a different type from their body she calls negative. So a homosexual, for example—a woman in a man's body—would be called male negative.

The most important characteristic for Charlotte was how people react to that basic tug to become the opposite sex. So you might have a person who is physically a man, psychologically a woman, and who resists the tug to become the opposite sex (in this case, male, since "he" is psychologically a woman). Or you might have a person who is psychologically a woman, physically a man, and who affirms her masculine aspect. Rephrasing a distinction cited above, Charlotte called the resisters "denialists" and the affirmers "asseverationists." This obviously doubles the number of possible types to eight.

These three factors—a person's physical sex, a person's psychological sex, and whether he or she accepts or rejects the tug to become the opposite sex—make up eight types.

A "normal man" is a male soul in a male body, feeling quite happy about his maleness, and denying his female side (male positive denialist). A normal female is a female soul in a female body, enjoying her femininity, and denying her male side (female positive denialist). Charlotte had a low opinion of "normal" people, feeling that they are cowards who prefer to blind themselves to their basic potentialities.

Oddly, she had an equally low opinion of two other sexually stable types. There are some female souls in female bodies, who assert their desire to become male. These are "butch" lesbians who wear male clothes and smoke cigars. Then there are male souls in male bodies, who affirm their femininity. These are transvestites, who try to look and sound like women. Because these two types have accepted the pull towards their opposite, they are also uncreative, stable and therefore uninteresting.

What interests Charlotte are the four unstable types. "Femme" lesbians, who often seem intensely feminine (so that men wonder irritably why they are wasting themselves on other women), are male souls in female bodies, asserting their femininity. But a man's soul in a woman's body can also deny her feminine aspect, and become a bossy and overbearing female. Then there are men who are psychologically female, but who prefer to assert their maleness by throwing their weight about—Charlotte thought many leather-jacketed motorcyclists fit this type, which is basically homosexual. Finally, there is another type of male who is psychologically female, but who denies the pull to become male, becoming a drag queen or "raging queer."

All these types are unstable and subject to change. The leather-jacketed rowdy may stop denying his femininity and become a pouf. A femme lesbian (who is psychologically a man) may become a normal housewife. The drag queen may get tired of denying his maleness and take on a more positive role; Charlotte knew one who became an artist. She also knew a femme lesbian who grew tired of denying her male aspect, and became a writer.

So, according to Charlotte, creativity is a reaction to this inner cat's-cradle of tensions between male and female. I recall her telling me that Hemingway was a female soul in a male body, preferring to assert his/her maleness.

To me this all sounded highly convincing, and I reported it in my article for *Time Out*, which had the effect of bringing Charlotte even more disciples. I met some of these one evening, and found them an interesting crowd, many highly intelligent, with a large proportion of brilliant and articulate homosexuals. By now, Charlotte was teaching at a polytechnic school in central London, and was permanently surrounded by admirers. Her self-esteem had always been enormous, and now it became stupendous. She told me that she expected not one Nobel Prize but two.

Undoubtedly, her popularity was based on the fact that she brought a new meaning and self-confidence to the lives of so many people who had considered themselves social outcasts. With her scientific theory, backed by formidable erudition, she made them feel important. In fact, by linking religion and evolution with sexual deviation, she was making them feel superior to the so-called normal person. They were potentially creative and normal people weren't. In fact, they were the spearhead of evolution. No wonder her disciples treated her as the messiah.

A couple of years after the *Time Out* article, I went on to write a section about Charlotte in my book *Mysteries* (1978), in the chapter about evolution, and she was so pleased that she had this section printed and bound up as a small book, which achieved wide circulation among her admirers. She was able to afford the printing because some of her new admirers were wealthy.

I should add that her work was highly combative and contentious; she spent a great deal of her time attacking conventional science and scientists, all in highly emotive terms—an attitude scientists understandably associate with cranks.

Then, one day in June 1981, Charlotte died, in her flat in Highgate. Someone noticed the accumulation of milk bottles outside her door, and when the police broke in, she had been dead several days. The cause was cancer of the liver.

The disciple who rang me up to tell me the news added another interesting piece of information. Charlotte was a man.

It was then that I began to learn the really interesting side of Charlotte's life.

His/her real name was Carl Hajdu (pronounced Hi-du) and, according to the papers he left behind, he was the son of a high-ranking civil servant in Budapest, and had inherited the title of baron.

But as more information came to light, it seemed that this was also fantasy. Carl/Charlotte, born 1920, was a product of a typical working class family, and although he had been to Budapest University, had shown no application whatsoever, and infuriated his teachers with his assumption of his own genius. During the war he became a junior lieutenant in the Hungarian army, and when Hungary became an ally of Hitler's Germany in 1944, was attached to the SS. In 1948 he escaped the Communist takeover and came to England.

Carl was already a transvestite. It seemed that one day, he had bought a girlfriend some nylon stockings, which he intended to present to her that evening. But she rang up to say she was unable to come, and he went to bed with a book; but as he lay there—no doubt regretting that his girlfriend was not beside him—he experienced an urge that surprised him; he put on the stockings, and masturbated. The result was an orgasm of unprecedented intensity.

Later, a friend left a suitcase full of his wife's clothing at Carl's flat, and Carl began dressing up in women's clothes, and once again experiencing a high level of excitement. Later, he began an affair with a married woman, who left her clothes at his flat, and he used to dress up in them, and experience more pleasure than in making love to her.

Carl posed as a psychiatrist, awarding himself a string of bogus degrees, wrote newspaper articles with titles like "Should big girls be spanked?" and "Why, oh why, do I steal?," and made a new career for himself under the pseudonym Michael Karoly.

An unpublished novel he wrote called *Fiona* left no doubt that he was not remotely homosexual. He had many mistresses, taking great pleasure in sexual conquest, and obviously satisfying them fully. But the novel made it obvious that he was a dreadful snob; *Fiona* is a general's daughter, while another mistress is a Colonel's wife, and the hero's career of seduction seems designed to boost his own ego rather than to achieve a satisfying relationship.

Carl apparently married one of these mistresses, a divorcee named Phyllis, who had a small son. Carl worked as a freelance estate agent, and was at one point in trouble with the law for collecting money for Hungarian refugees which remained in his own bank account, which may be why he changed his name to Michael Karoly. But Phyllis died, and so did her son. He locked himself in his flat and spent most of his time wearing her clothes. Bills remained unpaid, and he came close to suicide. The person who finally emerged from the flat dressed as a woman, and called herself Dr. Charlotte Bach.

A disciple named Bob Mellors supplied me with the facts of "her" life, and a strange new aspect emerged. Charlotte had a strong criminal streak.

In *Fiona*, the hero describes to his adoring mistress how he went into a shop to buy a wallet, but because the one he wanted cost slightly more than he was willing to pay, he stole it. After telling her this, he bursts into tears. He also tells her how, at the end of the war, he had gratuitously murdered a young soldier. He was out after curfew, and the soldier—he was only fifteen—told him he would have to come to the guardhouse for a check. His papers were in order, so he was in no danger of arrest; yet as the boy walked in front of him, the hero shot him in the back of the head.

Bob Mellors also discovered that Charlotte made a habit of stealing from stores. But ordinary stealing was not enough. She would look through the underwear, and slip a bra under her coat. The next day she would return to the store and explain that the bra was the wrong size, and ask to change it. When asked for the receipt, she would explain that she had lost it, and look helpless. Without exception, she was allowed to change the bra for another.

When I took Charlotte out to lunch in Camden Town one day, she took me to her printer; they were obviously greatly in awe of her. But she told one of her disciples that she never went into the printer's shop without stealing some small item.

When I learned of this, I realized that her relationship with me must have given her great pleasure. She was deceiving me, as she deceived everybody else. Crime gave her a kick, and her whole life was a long act of deception. She enjoyed pulling the wool over people's eyes as she enjoyed stealing. That was why she never followed Derrick Alexander's example and had the sex change operation, because then she would have *been* a woman, and there would have been no deception dressing in women's clothes.

Now I could see clearly why I disagreed with Charlotte's theory of evolution. This was based on the notion that evolution springs out of inner sexual conflict, and that this conflict is the result of being an immature species. As an argument, this amounted to double special pleading. Charlotte was not only making her own transvestitism the basis of her theory, but her own immaturity, this strange, childish element of crookedness, this delight in telling lies and thieving and deceiving. And this was a woman—or man—whose basic craving was to be a somebody, a celebrity, a guru: in short, like most of the other people in this book, a messiah. To some extent, I had helped to bring this about. For example, I allowed her, early in our acquaintance, to use a recommendation from me on her notepaper.

Yet there was, of course, a fundamental frustration in her newfound celebrity. It would have been risky, for example, to appear on television, because a real transvestite would have been sure to recognize that she was a man and say so publicly. Even her death was an illustration of the same problem. She had many doctor friends, but could not risk allowing any of them to examine her. So she died alone.

Charlotte's case sheds light on many aspects of the problems raised in this book. To begin with, sexual perversion.

Charlotte/Carl was a person with an abnormally powerful sexual drive. He mentions in one of his posthumous papers that he began masturbating at the age of ten, "and have not stopped since." At the age of fifteen he lost his virginity with a prostitute, and was not disappointed; it was as great a pleasure as he had anticipated. As he watched her pulling on her stockings afterwards, he became aroused, and wanted to start all over again, but he didn't have the money.

A psychiatrist told him later that if he had made love to the woman a second time, he would probably never have developed into a transvestite. This may or may not be true. What is certain is that like most highly sexed persons, a woman's underwear was an important element in Carl's enjoyment of sex.

In *Fiona*, he describes how his hero, watching Fiona strip to her panties, has an urge to "ask her not to undress any further, as the feel of the smooth slippery nylon, with the living, moving flesh underneath, aroused a greater sense of excitement than her bare body."

Suddenly it becomes possible to see why he turned into a transvestite. Sexual excitement seems to create a desire to unite with the opposite sex by interpenetration. When Carl was dressed entirely in a woman's garments, he had "united" even more intimately by "becoming" the woman he desired. There was no need for his sexual member to find its way inside her, for in a sense, he was already inside her. Being in her clothes made him feel as if he had become her. He was, so to speak, having sex with himself. The result was probably a mild, continuous orgasm, like a low electric current.

We can see that no animal would be capable of such an odd mutation, for this is a peculiarly human use of the imagination, or rather, of what we have labeled the transformative faculty.

We can also see that there is an odd element of immaturity in the whole business. W.H. Auden once confessed that he found something indecent in a mutual homosexual relation. He felt that it was rather like two schoolboys being naughty in the lavatory. But it is very hard to separate human sexuality from this element of naughtiness. Child sexuality is, as Freud recognized, in some ways stronger than adult sexuality, for it is intensified by the feeling that this is naughty and forbidden. The child finds it inconceivable that his parents could do anything as "dirty" as having sex; as an adolescent, his notion of sex is heightened and exaggerated by frustration.

In practice, adult sexuality soon takes on a businesslike air, and loses all that adolescent fever and the feeling that sex will be an almost mystical experience. Adults who are determined to hang on to the fever soon find themselves behaving like children. Could anything be more absurd than a politician or businessman dressing up in baby's rompers, and asking a prostitute to administer a spanking? But then, could anything be more absurd than Jeffrey Lundgren sitting half-naked on a bed with a pair of knickers wrapped around his penis, as a disciple performs an erotic dance?

Charlotte recognized this element of absurdity in herself. Instead of condemning it as silliness and trying to outgrow it, she used her formidable cleverness to justify it as neotony, and set out determinedly to remain immature.

What is also clear in *Fiona* is that, sexually speaking, the hero behaves like most of the messiahs in this book. He would like a harem of sex slaves, but he has to make do with being a compulsive seducer. Even the adoring Fiona finally abandons him because he cannot resist cheating on her. He cheats, as he admits, because it is good for his ego. What he wants from a sex partner is that she should, as it were, inflate his ego with a foot pump. But the moment she stops pumping, his ego slowly deflates again, for it is full of slow punctures, due to a sense of inferiority, which he is unable to overcome.

In order to understand why this should be so, we must examine another concept: self-image.

To operate efficiently in the society of our fellows, we need a clear picture of ourselves, a sense of identity. A schoolteacher, for example, has a clear sense of identity because he (or she) has been assigned the task of teaching children something they do not know. So his self-image is of a teacher. A young married woman enjoys her self-image as a wife; when she has a baby, the self-image is further expanded into wife-and-mother.

Without such a sense of a well-defined role, many people live unhappy or disturbed lives. In effect, they are not sure who they are.

The essence of this problem was expressed with unusual clarity in a story called "The Looking Glass," by the nineteenth century Brazilian writer Machado de Assis.

A young peasant from a small village goes into the army for his national service. He becomes an officer, and when he returns home, his family is immensely proud of his lieutenant's uniform. His self-esteem increases by leaps and bounds as everyone admires him. One aunt keeps begging him to stay at her remote farm in the midst of the countryside. There he is treated like royalty, and the slaves are ordered to address him as *Senhor* Lieutenant.

But one day, his aunt's daughter falls ill, and she rushes off to nurse her, accompanied by her husband. The slaves seize this opportunity to desert en masse. The lieutenant is alone. After so much flattering attention, he finds the silence and solitude terrible. Suddenly, he does not know who he is. In his bedroom there is a full-length mirror, and when he looks in this, he feels that his image is less clear and sharp than it should be. He begins to experience compulsive anxiety. What if his image continues to lose clarity? What if it vanishes altogether? He will surely go insane. . . .

Then, in a flash, he sees the solution. He takes his uniform out of its drawer and puts it on. As soon as he looks in the mirror, he sees that his reflection has become firm and clear. Every day from then on, he puts on his uniform and looks at himself in the mirror, and in this way he is able to pass the days until his aunt returns, and he once again has someone to support his self-image.

Our society is the mirror that reflects our faces and gives us a sense of identity. We see our reflections in the eyes of other people. When we look our best, when we feel ourselves admired by our fellows (especially the opposite sex), our self-image becomes sharp and clear. When we feel low and unsure of ourselves, the image blurs. But we need a good, clear self-image as a matter of mental health. Otherwise, the ego deflates. A self-image is as important to us as food and drink.

Now we can see what was wrong with Carl Hajdu. He knew that he was lazy, dishonest, and unreliable. Instead of trying to find some way of increasing his self-esteem, he preferred a life of deception. He was a habitual thief and liar. But because he had a smooth and assured manner, women were inclined to admire him. He made them his chief bulwark against self-disgust. But they soon saw through him and left him, and he had to find yet another mistress.

Phyllis, the woman he married, seems to have admired him as he felt he deserved to be admired. When she died, it was as if his "looking glass" had been taken away. Like Machado's young soldier, Carl felt that his identity was dissolving. Like Machado's soldier, he solved the problem by putting on a "uniform," and becoming the scientist Charlotte Bach.

Yet he was continuing to live a lie. If he could have written his book as Carl Hajdu or Michael Karoly, and admitted that he was a transvestite, Carl's self-image would have become strong and clear, and his influence would have been far greater. But the habit of lying was too deeply ingrained. His very success as a messiah trapped him; for his disciples, he *had* to be Dr. Charlotte Bach, the great psychologist and scientist.

We can see how this concept of self-image applies to virtually all the messiahs in this book. They started out with identity problems, which they tried to resolve by setting themselves up as gurus and teachers. Their first clear self-image came when they found themselves surrounded by admirers. We can see the pattern repeating itself in Brother Twelve, Jim Jones, Ervil LeBaron, David Koresh, Rock Theriault, Jeffrey Lundgren, Shoko Asahara. But their underlying problem was the same as that of Charlotte: a basic lack of self-belief that gradually developed into the paranoia that brought about their downfall.

We can also see that the best "mirror" for most males is an admiring female. This is why sexual conquest is so important to messiahs. The eternal feminine draws us upward and on, "rising on stepping stones of dead selves to higher things." The most effective "stepping stones" are compliant females.

The problem with using sex as a flight of steps is that half the steps are missing. As we can see from the case of Charlotte, our sex lives are built on daydreams, and daydreams make unreliable ladders. The schoolboy who fantasizes about the schoolgirl next door has no conception of her as a real person. His expectations are pitched absurdly high. And since such fantasies condition our whole future, it is hardly surprising that sex is a distorting mirror that creates a kind of mild insanity.

Mrs. Thrale records that Dr. Samuel Johnson always ate like a pig, with gravy running down his chin. He explained to her that this was because he had never had enough to eat as a student, and now hurled himself on his food like a starving man. This explains why human beings are so illusion-prone about sex. Most of us have been starved for a long time before we have our first sexual experience, and our expectations are based upon years of unrealistic fantasy. That early conditioning in fantasy—it may begin years before adolescence—may stay with us for the rest of our lives, just as Dr. Johnson's appetite stayed with him long after he had become accustomed to three meals a day.

It should now be clear that most messiahs suffer from the same problem as Charlotte: an inner confusion that arises from their completely false estimate of the importance of sex.

One modern cult has, in fact, preached that sexual promiscuity is the quickest road to salvation. In the 1960s, a Californian named David Berg, who had been ejected from one religious sect for immorality, decided to found his own cult among the "Flower Children" of San Francisco. By 1972 Berg had two hundred "Children of God" colonies in fifty countries.

Berg's daughter Linda explained that her father—he had changed his name to Moses—preached total sexual freedom. "When I was just eight years old I had my first sexual encounter with my father. . . . As I got older I refused his advances, but my younger sister Faith did not." When she was seventeen, Linda was crowned "Queen of the Children of God" in Bromley, Kent, in England, as Berg had by now fled America to escape prosecution. "Later that September night, he approached me with the specific intent to have sexual relations with me. . . . In the early hours after that encounter, I fled. That was my first attempt to escape his influence. It almost ended in suicide. But after only a few days hiding out, lonely and afraid, in London, I went back to the cult. I saw no alternative but to surrender."

Linda's revelations continued, "My father always knew the right button to push, which weak points to attack, how to get through any defenses. By the time he had finished with me, I would believe that he was right and that I was totally wrong."

Another follower, eighteen-year-old Kristina Jones, described how she lost her virginity at the age of ten with a disciple she found repugnant, and who then raped her repeatedly; by the age of twelve, she had sex with twenty-five men. The children were expected to be sexually amenable—in submitting to the males they were displaying their "love of God"—and were punished if they showed signs of resistance.

The commune held regular "sharing" nights once a week in which couples would vanish to bedrooms while others indulged in group sex on mattresses in the middle of the floor. Children, some as young as five, had to perform strip teases to entertain them; these performances were videotaped and sent to other communes. The letters of "Moses" Berg were read aloud, detailing sex with his grandchildren. "Much of their content is sexual, and Berg preaches that virtually nothing is forbidden. Under headings of Revolutionary Lovemaking, he writes detailed encouragement of sexual freedom—and particularly sexual freedom of children."

Kristina Jones was finally rescued, at the age of twelve, by her mother, who had escaped the sect, but she found it extremely difficult to adjust to life in the outside world, where she was expected to think for herself. She also found it hard to say no to any sexual demands, having become accustomed to regard them as normal. She adds: "His prophecies never came true. If they had, California would have fallen into the sea by now, and Jesus would have been resurrected in 1993. Yet if Berg told his members to kill themselves tomorrow they'd do it."

Berg's "Revolutionary Lovemaking" goes even further than the Oneida Community. Noyes had only complained that "amativeness is starved in monogamy," and that this amounts to "scanty and monotonous allowance." Berg was suggesting, in effect, that sex was the road to salvation.

Now this was by no means unprecedented. Tantric yoga treats sex as a form of mind control. Crowley's *Ordo Templo Orientis* regarded sex as the central part of a magical ritual. But what Berg was suggesting was not sex as a discipline, but as a kind of free-for-all, in which even children should be available as sex toys. What he was saying, in effect, was that total sexual freedom would enable us to become fuller and more god-like human beings.

In short, Berg, like Charlotte, believed that sex is about evolution.

The idea certainly looks plausible. Evolution, in the personal sense, means growing up, and putting your immaturity behind you. This is why we all enjoy travel. It introduces us to new experiences and new horizons, and anyone will agree that this helps us to grow up. Is this not also true of sex? Every teenager is preoccupied with acquiring a boyfriend or girlfriend, because experience of the opposite sex is an important part of growing up.

But we also recognize that this is only true to a certain extent, and that promiscuity can become boring and self-defeating. This is because we cease to pay full attention to any repetitive experience, and it becomes mechanical. When we say that an experience has become mechanical, we mean that we have lost touch with its reality. It is happening merely inside our heads.

This is why autoeroticism cannot be used for personal evolution. It is essentially a self-enclosed circuit. And this is why Charlotte's notion that sexual perversion is about evolution is a fallacy. Charlotte's transvestitism was an elaborate game, which took place entirely in her imagination. The misapprehension here is what the philosopher Alfred North Whitehead called "the fallacy of misplaced concreteness."

Mark Twain put his finger on it in *Tom Sawyer*, in the chapter about painting the fence. Tom is resentful about having to paint the fence on a Saturday morning, when his friends are playing. But as friends gather round to jeer, he whistles, and looks as if he is enjoying it so much that soon they are all clamoring to be allowed to do it. Twain concludes: "Work is that which we are obliged to do; play is that which we are not obliged to do." Twain is pointing out that our notion of "work" is an example of the fallacy of misplaced concreteness. Work turns into play if you *want* to do it, and play turns into work if you *don't*.

Similarly, desire depends on whether something is easy or hard to obtain. Make something hard to obtain and it becomes, almost by definition, desirable. Make something easy to obtain, and it loses half its appeal.

The Second Stream

Our failure to understand that sex is largely "mental" depends on a false comparison with food. It is true that food, like sex, has its mental aspect. *Nouvelle cuisine*, for example, depends on decoration, and on making the food look attractive on the plate. But our need for food is nevertheless based on a real need, not on imagination. Without it, we starve. No one ever died from lack of sex.

Like whitewashing a fence, sexual excitement has its purely physical side. It depends on a kind of static electricity that accumulates in the loins, and which is discharged by friction. If too much of this "static" accumulates, it can become a perpetual distraction, turning a man into a satyr and a woman into a nymphomaniac. A person who walks around with a large amount of undischarged "sexual electricity" in the loins is in a kind of torment, like a starving animal whose only thought is food.

But no matter how strong this physical aspect of desire is, it is the mind that decides how it will be directed. Sex that was physical would be thoroughly boring. Sexual activity must be accompanied by the thought of what we are doing. The stronger this thought component, the more satisfying the sex. Without it, sex would be mechanical.

Now it is because of this thought-component that the idea of sex-as-evolution has become so fashionable in the twentieth century. Pornographers of the nineteenth century made the discovery of what I have labeled "superheated sex"—teachers seducing pupils, brothers seducing sisters, little girls losing their virginity to the butler, and so on—and the more "forbidden" the better. The Marquis de Sade, who spent most of his life behind bars, was one of the first to stumble on it. Confined in a prison cell, he spent his days in sexual fantasy which, after the manner of repetitive fantasies, became increasingly lurid and violent.

De Sade recognized that the essence of sexual desire was the thought-component of "the forbidden": the idea of purity being sullied. One of Sade's heroes, in the act of deflowering a virgin, shouts ecstatically, "Oh, I am a wicked villain!" He is deliberately amplifying the thought-component to intensify the sex.

Unfortunately, superheated sex is subject to the law of diminishing returns. Because it has lost its contact with reality, it can only be maintained by more and more lurid fantasies. It is trapped in a vicious circle, which is why Charlotte was mistaken to believe that superheated sex (i.e., sexual deviation) is the key to evolution.

The same criticism applies to that other disciple of mystical sex, D.H. Lawrence, who referred to the penis as "the rod that connects man to the stars." Lawrence was for a time an advocate of total sexual freedom, and an unfinished novel, *Mr. Noon* (started in 1920), is based on the philosophy of the German writer Otto Gross, who preached that "pleasure is the only source of value." The fact that Lawrence—he once wrote "What many women cannot give, one woman can"—should even contemplate the notion that complete sexual fulfillment lay in promiscuity, reveals the basic confused nature of his sexual philosophy.

Equally interesting is a scene from the original uncensored version of Lawrence's *Sons and Lovers*, in which the hero, Paul Morel, misses his train and has to spend the night in the home of a girl-friend, Clare Dawes, sleeping in her bedroom. He explores her room, notes her clothes, especially a pair of stockings on a chair. He begins to doze, then wakes up, "writhing in torment" with sexual desire. He takes the stockings and puts them on, and then "he knew he would have to have her."

Since Lawrence was writing in 1913, there could be no question of going further, as Carl Hajdu did, and allowing Paul Morel to reach a fetishistic orgasm. All the same, it is easy to see that this was the logical outcome, and that Lawrence's sexuality had the same powerful element of autoeroticism as did Charlotte's.

This becomes even clearer in a passage from *Sons and Lovers*: "Sex had become so complicated in him that he would have denied that he ever could want Clara or Miriam or any woman whom he knew. Sex desire was a sort of detached thing, that did not belong to a woman." What Paul Morel wants is "sex with the stranger." That is to say that, like Charlotte, Lawrence is pursuing the sexual mirage with an underlying conviction that it can be caught. This, as we have seen, this is a version of Whitehead's "fallacy of misplaced concreteness."

When we understand why this sexual mirage is bound to end in frustration, we can also grasp why most of the messiahs in this book became paranoid. Convinced that having a harem was the key to their personal evolution, they became increasingly frustrated to discover that it left them in a strange sense of unfulfillment.

Again, in *Sons and Lovers*, Lawrence writes: "He spent the week with Miriam, and wore her out with his passion before it was gone . . . there remained afterwards always the sense of failure and of death." Why does repeated lovemaking cause Morel's passion to vanish, leaving a sense of failure and death? Because his sexual frenzy is the pursuit of a mirage, and it leaves him empty-handed.

If evolution is not about sex, then what is it about?

Charlotte had glimpsed an important part of the answer when she wrote about men of genius, such as Beethoven, Leonardo, and Michelangelo. But she proceeded to the indefensible conclusion that their creativity sprang out of a desire to become the opposite sex. According to Charlotte, Michelangelo and Leonardo were creative *because* they were tormented by their sexuality. This sounds just plausible, since both were homosexual. But how does the argument apply to Beethoven, who was clearly heterosexual?

Looking through Charlotte's eight types, it is obvious that only one of them fits Beethoven, the type she called the male positive denialist. This is a male soul in a male body, denying its feminine aspect. Beethoven was certainly a male soul in a male body, and his music contains no trace of femininity. Presumably the same thing applies to many great composers, such as Bach, Handel, Mozart, and Brahms.

But according to Charlotte, this combination is stable, and therefore uncreative. In Charlotte's scheme, only the unstable is creative: homosexuals, drag queens, and femme lesbians (as opposed to butch lesbians, who are female souls in female bodies, asserting their desire to be male, and therefore quite stable).

There is clearly something wrong here. I felt flattered when Charlotte told me I was a male positive denialist—a male soul in a male body, denying its feminine aspect—until I noted that this would make me non-creative. When I saw that this would also apply to Bach, Handel, and Beethoven, I realized Charlotte must have got it wrong.

The truth, I now believe, is that Charlotte's whole theory—both sexes want to turn into their opposite—is nonsense. It sprang out of Carl Hajdu's need for self-justification. He wanted to believe that he was a male soul in a male body. So how could he explain his desire to dress up as a woman? He invented the notion that all males want to become females, and vice versa. Then he could tell himself that he was simply giving way to a universal urge which most of us are too dense to recognize. But his theory contained one fatal flaw. If he was a male soul in a male body, asserting his feminine aspect, then he was stable and therefore uncreative. And the same applied to hundreds of other men of genius who were obviously male souls in male bodies. It didn't make sense.

In my view, Charlotte was one of two things: either a female soul in a male body, who could have been "cured" by a sex-change operation, or a normal male whose sex drive was so powerful that female underwear was as important to him as the woman inside it, and wearing that underwear caused a permanent mild state of sexual excitement. Both these theories dispense with the need for a gender-conflict theory.

There is one respect in which she was correct. It is true that creativity springs out of conflict. But it is a different kind of conflict. Anyone can see what I mean by glancing at Beethoven's notebooks. Some of his greatest themes start off as completely boring and undistinguished. But he struggles on with grim persistence, and after perhaps a dozen changes—often far more—his unpromising "caterpillar" turns into a dazzling "butterfly." It is clear that the transformation has been effected by struggle and sweat, with more than a touch of despair.

This seems to be the law of artistic creation. It springs out of what a popular novel on Michelangelo called "the agony and the ecstasy." Among painters, Van Gogh is one of the most striking examples. So many of his paintings look oddly wrong; there is a clumsiness and distortion of perspective that made contemporary critics accuse him of incompetence. But in certain pictures the clumsiness is transformed into strength and intensity, and certain paintings—the "Road with Cypresses" or "The Starry Night"—surge with a kind of electrical vitality.

This explains why, at first, I found Charlotte's theory so plausible. Creativity obviously springs out of inner conflict; this had been the subject of my own first book, *The Outsider*. I had noted how often, in the case of nineteenth century artists and musicians, the conflict ended in suicide or madness. Van Gogh left a note that read: "Misery will never end," then shot himself in the stomach.

In that case, why should sexual conflict not produce great works of art?

We only have to think of Charlotte dressing up in women's clothes to see the answer. Charlotte could say, like Faust: "Two souls dwell in my breast." One soul was an intellectual male with ambitions to become a writer. The other was a self-indulgent female who loved stealing and telling lies. She was a Jekyll and Hyde, and her Hyde was locked into a vicious circle of autoeroticism. So in deciding to give Hyde precedence, Charlotte had ruled out all possibility of becoming creative.

In other words, there is an element of triviality in Charlotte's decision to devote herself to naughtiness. We sense this same element of triviality in all criminals. In deciding to lie and cheat and steal, they have condemned themselves to a kind of childishness. Crime is a form of selfishness, a decision to put yourself first, such as we see in spoiled children. It is the opposite of the kind of impersonality that creates great art or great ideas.

We can also see that this applies to most of the messiahs in this book. The fundamental triviality emerges in their attitude towards sex, particularly in their selfishness. They are, in effect, setting out to realize a childish daydream of absolute power. We can see, for example, the obvious similarities between Lundgren's Intercession ceremony, with its underwear fetishism, and Charlotte's need to dress in women's clothes. The messiah syndrome seems to be based on a kind of autoeroticism.

But all this only brings us back to the basic question. If evolution is not about sex, then what is it about?

Again, Beethoven's notebooks provide a clue, with their evidence of intense creative struggle. What seems to happen in this kind of struggle is that deep frustration builds up until it seems ready to explode. Then the unconscious mind comes to the rescue, and what seemed awkward and subtly wrong suddenly becomes graceful and perfectly right.

We have encountered the same process elsewhere in this book, such as in Lindner's case of Kirk Allen and the jet-propelled couch. We may recall that Allen preferred to spend most of his spare time in a daydream based on the Mars novels of Edgar Rice Burroughs. The turning point came when a predatory divorcée tried to seduce him, arousing traumatic memories of once having been the sex-toy of his nymphomaniac governess.

Why should this memory produce such a fit of revulsion? After all, most adolescent boys would enjoy being seduced by an attractive older woman. Because normal male sexual desire depends on the sense of conquest, the feeling that he pursues and the woman surrenders. Kirk Allen's first adult sexual encounter was with a woman who did all the pursuing; any magic she might have held for him must have dissolved in their first encounter. Thereafter, he was a kind of sex-slave, doing his best to satisfy her insatiable demands. She was a voracious pair of arms, a female octopus who wanted to devour him.

All this must have been shattering for his self-esteem. Yet because he could take refuge in the Mars fantasies, and because he was a brilliant student at college, Allen could hold at bay the unpleasant feeling that the bottom had fallen out of his world. It is even possible that he might have recovered his normal male self-esteem if he had been attracted by some shy girl who allowed him to do all the pursuing. Instead, he encountered another female "octopus" who reactivated all his traumas and once again raised the danger of a shattering loss of self-esteem. Allen's reaction was to rush back to his Martian identity. In effect, he begged his unconscious mind to send him to Mars, and the unconscious recognized the danger and stepped in like a fairy godmother with a magic wand, and did just that.

While most of us can understand the case of Kirk Allen in abstract terms, it is still virtually impossible to put ourselves in the place of a man who could make mental voyages to Mars. It is beyond our experience. We can understand a persistent fantasy, but not how it can take on total reality. We cannot imagine getting up from a real desk in a real room on Mars, and crossing to a real filing cabinet. In our normal world, there is always a clear dividing line between fantasy and reality. But if we can grasp the implications of this case, we see that they are tremendous.

Reality is not simple and unambiguous. There must be some sense in which it is dependent on the mind. When self-esteem is in mortal danger, the unconscious mind hastens to support it with delusions. If the three Christs of Ypsilanti had experienced an even greater degree of mental crisis, they would have been able to return to the Holy Land at will, deliver the Sermon on the Mount, and perform the miracle of the loaves and fishes.

All this ceases to be so baffling if we consider the strange miracle of hypnosis, when the conscious mind is sent to sleep, and the unconscious is persuaded to demonstrate its powers. Any good hypnotist could have sent Kirk Allen to "Mars" while he lay on a couch, and the experience would have been totally real. So all that happened in the Kirk Allen case is that his unconscious mind obeyed his desire to visit Mars rather than the orders of a hypnotist.

Kirk Allen demonstrated that the unconscious mind has the power not only to embrace a delusion, but to transform it into a kind of reality. Kirk Allen exercised the power of self-hypnosis. Now normal hypnosis is a state in which the hypnotist soothes the conscious mind into a trance (or mechanical) state, and then calls upon the powers of the patient's unconscious mind. Freud's master Charcot was able to make a patient believe that he had been touched by a red hot poker when he had actually been touched by an icicle, and the unconscious mind produced a blister. What is so extraordinary about Kirk Allen is that his conscious mind took over the role of the hypnotist, and persuaded his unconscious to transport him to Mars.

Of course, we make use of the powers of the unconscious mind every day. Most of us can use them as an alarm clock and tell ourselves that we have to wake up at a certain hour in the morning, and wake up at exactly that time. When we know we have to face some difficult challenge, the unconscious mind will provide us with the ability to meet it.

But a hypnotist can persuade the unconscious mind to accomplish far more remarkable feats. A nineteenth-century hypnotist named Carl Hansen used to order his subjects to become as stiff as a board, then lie with the head on one chair and heels on another, while several people sat on him as if he were a bench. Most of us would find this impossible if we tried to do it consciously. Yet clearly, the unconscious mind possesses the power to do it, and if we could learn to call upon that power we could perform even more remarkable feats, such as traveling to Mars, or experiencing life, as did Van Gogh, as a perpetual "Starry Night."

Why can I not persuade my unconscious mind to duplicate Carl Hansen's feat? Because I do not believe I can do it. So when my conscious mind gives the order to my unconscious, the unconscious senses my lack of conviction, and fails to provide me with the power. It was when Kirk Allen asked himself: "Why not?" that he suddenly found himself on Mars. He had recognized that he possessed the power to transport himself to Mars.

Equally bizarre and instructive is what happened to Kirk Allen's psychiatrist Robert Lindner. He was aware that Allen was suffering from delusions, but decided he would consciously enter these delusions as a form of participation therapy. Yet he found himself being inexorably sucked in, like someone who has ventured too close to the maelstrom. Lindner's clear understanding that it was all illusion made no difference. He had set out to persuade his unconscious mind to help him enter Kirk Allen's delusions, and it obliged so effectively that he felt himself being drawn into madness. He had miscalculated the awesome power of the unconscious mind, just as messiahs like Koresh, Jones, and Lundgren miscalculated it, and found themselves drawn into paranoia.

Man's main problem at this point in history is a lack of self-belief, which manifests itself in the need for messiahs. He feels that civilization has become too complex, that he has bitten off more than he can chew. The cause is plain. The complexities of everyday life tend to reduce him to a mechanical level, and at this level effort seems pointless. Sometimes, the mere thought of the complexity defeats him, like a rabbit hypnotized by a snake.

We can now see the full significance of Kirk Allen's trips to Mars. The immense power of his unconscious mind was capable of permanently transforming his reality. If Van Gogh had acquired the same knack, he could have experienced the exaltation of "The Starry Night" *whenever* he felt like it. Kirk Allen was using the faculty for defensive purposes, but there is obviously no reason why it should not be used positively and creatively.

This is what evolution is about: man's ability to make use of his hidden powers.

The reason we are so inclined to believe that sexual ecstasy can lead to individual evolution is that it seems capable of awakening hidden powers. Our basic human need is for what might be called "the flow experience." We recognize what this means on the crudest physical level: for example, the relief of going to the lavatory when the need has become urgent. Even scratching when you itch is an example of the flow experience; so is drinking when you are thirsty and eating when you are hungry. All these things release a flow of energy and relief.

When our energies are blocked and our purposes frustrated, we experience a feeling of stagnation, which can easily turn into a kind of energy-constipation, in which all our vital powers feel as if they have congealed into a leaden mass.

Human beings need the flow experience to change and evolve. Our energies could be compared to a river flowing over a plain. If the flow is too slow, the river begins to meander as it accumulates mud and silt. But a violent storm in the mountains can send down a roaring flood that sweeps away the mud and straightens out the bends, so that once again the river flows straight and deep.

That is why we all crave the flow experience. It also explains why we think of sex as the ideal flow experience, since it is a release of concentrated energy. But this leads to the mistaken notion that if we could experience enough of these floods of relief, the river would become an irresistible flood, and we would become godlike.

This fails to happen because of the power of habit. As a starving man ceases to starve, he naturally begins to take food for granted. Fulfillment causes the "robot" in us to take over. The notion that sex can transport us to mystical heights is then seen to be an exaggeration due to inexperience. The sexual elevator does not go all the way to the roof. It stops halfway, and if you want to get up to the roof, you have to walk up the stairs.

What is valid about the sexual experience is the intensity it is capable of achieving. A man who wants a woman badly enough focuses on her with total concentration, and is willing to achieve an enormous amount of energy and effort to achieve his goal. The classical hero, Paris, may well have achieved something close to ecstasy when he finally made love to Helen, but this was due to the effort it cost him. Sheer anticipation brought him close to what George Bernard Shaw calls "the seventh degree of concentration." It sprang from his own discipline and effort as much as from the object of desire. This is the opposite of habit, and is the only sense in which individual evolution can be "about sex."

Yet it is arguable that a more profound kind of evolution has already begun to happen.

It seems to have been H.G. Wells who first stumbled upon the idea that man has already taken a decisive new step in his evolution. It is interesting to consider how this insight came to him. It was during a night in 1932, when he was unable to get to sleep— sometime between two and five in the morning—that Wells began to pour his misery and frustration onto paper.

"I need freedom of mind. I want peace for work. I am distressed by immediate circumstances. My thoughts and work are encumbered by claims and vexations and I cannot see any hope of release from them; any hope of a period of serene and beneficent activity, before I am overtaken altogether by infirmity and death. I am in a phase of fatigue and of that discouragement which is a concomitant of fatigue, the petty things of tomorrow skirmish in my wakeful brain, and I find it difficult to assemble my forces to confront this problem which paralyses the proper use of myself. . . . "

"The proper use of myself"—this phrase started a new train of thought. What was the "proper use of himself"? Obviously, for Wells it was using his mind for creative purposes.

"There is nothing I think very exceptional about my situation as a mental worker. Entanglement is our common lot. I believe this craving for a release from bothers, from daily demands and urgencies, from responsibilities and tempting distractions, is shared by an increasing number of people who, with specialized and distinctive work to do, find themselves eaten up by first-hand affairs. This is the outcome of a specialization and a sublimation of interests that has become frequent only in the last century or so. Spaciousness and leisure, even the desire for spaciousness and leisure, have so far been exceptional."

Wells now begins to grasp the implications of these insights.

"Most individual creatures since life began have been 'up against it' all the time, have been driven continually by fear and cravings, have had to respond to the unresting antagonism of their surroundings, and they have found a sufficient and sustaining motive in the drama of immediate events provided for them by these demands. Essentially, their living was a continual adjustment to happenings. Good hap and ill hap filled it entirely. They hungered and ate and they desired and loved; they were amused and attracted, they pursued or escaped, they were overtaken and they died."

Here we have a picture of man tied down to the physical earth.

"But," says Wells, "with the dawn of human foresight and with the appearance of a great surplus of energy in life such as the last century or so has revealed, there has been a progressive emancipation of the attention from everyday urgencies. What was once the whole of life, has become to an increasing extent, merely the background of life. People can ask now what would have been an extraordinary question five hundred years ago. They can say, 'Yes, you earn a living, you support a family, you love and hate, but—what do you do?'"

Wells has recognized that man has started to live in a new realm, instead of being tied down, like any animal, to the earth, and he has recognized that this has happened fairly recently.

What he is stating, basically, is that "natural man" is passive and mechanical, but "conceptions of living, divorced more and more from immediacy, distinguish the modern civilized man from all former life." Artists, writers, philosophers, scientists, feel a need to subordinate primary needs to "these wider interests that have taken hold of them."

Wells further said, "The originative intellectual worker is not a normal human being and does not lead nor desire to lead a normal human life. He wants to lead a supernormal life."

This is what those Outsider-artists of the nineteenth century were seeking in their escapist fantasies. This is what the young W.B. Yeats was trying to express in his dreams of fairyland, and this is the true meaning of one of Yeats's favorite quotations, from de Lisle Adam's *Axel*: "As for living, our servants can do that for us." It is not a disgust with life itself: only with a "normal" life.

Wells points out that art and science are not a "suspension of primary life"; on the contrary, they are "the way to power over that primary life." Wells is quite clear that what we crave is power over our physical lives, so we can lead mental lives.

Now insights are coming in a flood, and Wells goes on: "We are like early amphibians, so to speak, struggling out of the waters that have hitherto covered our kind, into the air, seeking to breathe in a new fashion and emancipate ourselves from long-accepted and long-unquestioned necessities. At last it becomes for us a case of air or nothing. But the new land has not definitely emerged from the waters and we swim distressfully in an element we wish to abandon."

Here we sense that Wells is getting his imagery mixed up. To begin with, there is a sense in which the sea is a better metaphor for this new region of the mind, and the land for our old "primary needs." But having plumped for this nevertheless illuminating image, he fails to see that what is wrong with his "amphibians" is not that the land has not yet emerged from the waters, but that they have fins instead of legs. What they need to develop is legs.

Yet he is quite clear about what he wants. "I do not now in the least desire to live longer unless I can go on with what I consider to be my proper business. . . . I want the whole stream of this daily life stuff to flow on for me—for a long time yet—if what I call my work can still be, can be more than ever the emergent meaning of the stream."

After four pages of these blazing insights, the light begins to dim, and he returns to his original theme: trivial necessities prevent him from doing his "proper work," and with them, "the feeling of being intolerably hampered by irrelevant necessities" plagues him.

Wells has pinpointed the basic problem of modern man. He wrote elsewhere: "The bird is a creature of the air, the fish is a creature of the water, man is a creature of the mind." Yet he failed to fully grasp the consequences of his own insight.

This becomes clear when he explores it again in a short novel called *The Croquet Player* (1936), perhaps the most important of his later works.

The croquet player of the title is a conventional sportsman (Wells disliked sportsmen) who is staying in a French hotel. He falls into conversation with a Dr. Finchatton, who is convalescing there. Finchatton tells him a fascinating story about an evil force that pervades the marshes of East Anglia. He has encountered example after example of horrifying cruelty, and has come to believe that this is because archaeologists have disturbed the bones of ancient cave men, whose spirits now haunt the district.

The croquet player is enthralled. But he is less enthralled by Finchatton's psychiatrist, Dr. Norbert, who dismisses Finchatton's story as a fantasy. The truth, says Norbert, is that Finchatton is suffering from a plague, "a new plague of the soul," the angst of living in the twentieth century. The cave man is modern man, "invincibly bestial, envious, malicious, greedy."

"Animals live wholly in the present. They are framed in immediate things. So are really unsophisticated people . . . but we men, we have been piercing and probing into the past and future. We have been multiplying memories, histories, traditions; we have filled ourselves with forebodings and plannings and apprehensions. And so our worlds have become overwhelmingly vast for us, terrific, appalling."

Finchatton, Norbert explains, has invented his tale of the evil spirit of the cave man to enable his mind to cling on to something he can understand. But this is escapism. What man needs to do is to face the facts.

"Do as I have done and shape your mind to a new scale. Only giants can save the world from complete relapse and so we—we who care for civilization—have to become giants. We have to bind a harder, stronger civilization like steel about the world. We have to make such a mental effort as the stars have not witnessed yet."

Wells was inclined to think in terms of social changes, of improving civilization. He failed to grasp the purport of his brilliant insight about amphibians. It is not the world that needs to be bound like steel; it is the mind itself. It is the human mind that is too feeble, that tends to drift and come apart at the seams.

Yet what Wells had seen clearly is that man is in a new phase, the mental phase, of his evolution. In one sentence he hits the nail, almost inadvertently, on the head. "I want the whole stream of this daily life stuff to flow on for me . . . if what I call my work can still be . . . the emergent meaning of the stream."

Wells glimpsed that human life consists of two streams. The primary stream is the "stream of this daily life stuff." But the second stream is something else. It is a stream of pure mental activity, and it runs—it is supposed to run—parallel to the stream of ordinary life-activity. In fact, human beings have a habitual tendency to allow the two to get mixed up. When that happens, our efficiency is appallingly reduced.

Everyone has had the experience of feeling sick, and then getting rid of the sickness by thinking of something interesting. What happens here is that the two streams have been allowed to mingle, and thinking of something interesting causes them to separate, producing a sense of delight and relief. When the two streams are flowing in parallel, as they are intended to, we live at a far higher level of efficiency. This state, as Wells points out, is familiar to all "originative intellectual workers," and is so pleasant that it is deeply addictive. It is as if the mind takes off.

On December 17, 1903, the Wright brothers took their first crude motor-powered glider to the beach at Kitty Hawk, North Carolina, and succeeded in getting it into the air for about twelve seconds. It was the beginning of the age of flight. What they had discovered was that when their airplane flew fast enough, it took off. Now every air traveler knows the sensation: the increasing speed, then the lift-off into the air.

Intellectual workers like Wells usually make the discovery at an early age. They experience increasing excitement as they read something that fascinates them, then they get the sudden lift-off, the breathtaking sensation of flying, and looking down and seeing the landscape from a bird's-eye view. Sometimes the flight can last for hours, but it always ends with the wheels bumping down again on the ground.

What they are discovering is simply the ability of the mind to lift-off into the "second stream."

There is a moving example in Arthur Koestler's autobiography, which describes how he was sitting on a park bench, reading a book about the persecution of Jewish pioneers in Palestine, and grinding his teeth with rage. Then he read a phrase about Einstein. Relativity had led the human imagination "across the peaks of glaciers never before explored by any human being." Koestler experienced a vision of Einstein's formula hovering above snow-covered peaks; the feeling of rage dissolved into a "sense of infinite tranquillity and peace." The two streams had suddenly separated, and were running parallel, as they were intended to.

This is what happened to those Outsiders of the nineteenth century: lift-off, the sense of marvelous freedom and seeing the world from above, the intuitive recognition that this freedom is real, and that human beings possess the power to fly. Then back to earth, and the sudden doubt, the suspicion that it was merely a pleasant illusion, like getting drunk.

Wells had taken a decisive step beyond these tragic Outsiders; he had recognized that it is not a delusion, but a glimpse of a real but unrecognized aspect of the human mind. Yet he was still inclined to doubt whether man can learn to make use of it before his cave-man instincts reduce everything he has created to chaos.

Wells left out of account that man has an invisible ally, namely, the immense powers of the unconscious mind. But then Wells was unaware of a vital piece of research that casts an interesting new light on these powers—what has been labeled "split brain physiology."

Most of us nowadays are aware that the two cerebral hemispheres of the brain have completely different functions. The left brain deals with logic, language, and calculation; the right with intuition, and with recognizing forms and shapes. In short, you could say that the left brain is a scientist, the right brain an artist.

What is not so widely known is that ordinary consciousness lives in the left brain, and that the person who lives on the other side is virtually a stranger. This becomes clear when patients are subjected to the split brain operation (to cure epilepsy), which involves severing the knot of nerves called the corpus callosum, which connects the left and right halves. When this happens, the patient turns into two different persons.

For some reason no one understands, the left brain controls the right half of the body, and vice versa. The same, crudely speaking, applies to the eyes. Now if a split brain patient is shown an apple with his right eye (connected to his left brain) and an orange with his left, and asked: "What can you see?" He replies, "An apple." If asked to write with his left hand what he has just seen, he writes, "Orange." If asked what he has just written, he replies: "Apple." When a female split brain patient was shown a dirty picture with her right brain, she blushed; asked why she was blushing, she replied: "I don't know." Our "I" lives in the left brain (the scientist), while a stranger lives in the other side.

These two sides might be compared to Laurel and Hardy in the old films. Ollie, the fat one, is the you who lives in the left brain; Stan is the stranger who lives on the other side. Compared to Ollie, Stan seems stupid and vague. Yet he has an extremely important function: he controls our energy.

Imagine that Ollie wakes up on a gloomy day and groans: "Monday and it's raining!" Stan overhears, and since he has a tendency to exaggerate, howls: "O no! Monday, and it's raining!" As a result of his gloom, he fails to send up any energy. Then if Ollie cuts himself on his razor, spills the milk over the table, trips over the doormat as he leaves the house, he groans: "It's just one of those days!," and Stan wails: "O no! It's just one of those days." So again Ollie fails to receive the energy he needs for facing a hard day, and this means that things inevitably get worse. That is why, when faced with a whole series of disasters, we sink into depression. If it goes on too long, we may even develop delusional psychoses, like Bertha Pappenheim and the three Christs of Ypsilanti.

On the other hand, when a child wakes up on Christmas morning, Ollie exclaims: "Good, it's Christmas!," and Stan overhears and chortles: "Wonderful! It's Christmas!," and sends up a flood of energy—the peak experience. From then on, everything reinforces Ollie's delight: his presents, the lights on the tree, the smell of mince pies and roast turkey. By the end of the day, he may be in a state of "expanded consciousness," and as he goes to his grandparents for Christmas tea, the whole world looks like Van Gogh's "Starry Night."

One obvious objection to all this is that you and I are not split brain patients. But this is not entirely true. Mozart said that tunes were always "walking into his head" fully fledged, and all he had to do was write them down. Where did they come from? That other self in the right brain. If Mozart was a split brain patient, the rest of us certainly are.

Now the unconscious mind appears to be connected with Stan, the right brain. So for all practical purposes, the above comments on the left and right hemispheres can be applied to the conscious and unconscious minds.

We can see that when a hypnotist puts a patient to sleep, he is actually putting Ollie to sleep, and leaving Stan wide awake, and when he orders Ollie to become as stiff as a board and lie across two chairs, it is Stan who obeys the order.

When Kirk Allen fled back to his room, and felt a desperate need to visit Mars, the thought "Why not?" was a recognition that Stan could do it. Stan responded by creating a kind of waking dream of Kirk Allen's study on Mars which looked as solid as the real world.

It is in the relationship between Stan and Ollie that we can see how man could begin to make use of the immense powers of the unconscious mind.

If Stan will release these powers at the suggestion of a hypnotist, then he will release them at the suggestion of the conscious mind. We can see this in the case of Kirk Allen's psychiatrist, Robert Lindner; here it released them—in response to his request to allow him to empathize with the patient's delusions—so effectively that it nearly scared the life out of him.

Yet what is so significant about this case is that, unlike his patient, Lindner was not in a state of neurotic desperation when he sent his request for assistance; he was simply prepared to expend a great deal of mental energy to empathize with the patient. It was the amount of effort he expended that brought results. In Lindner's case, these results were admittedly more than he bargained for; like Jung (whose bang on the head nearly resulted in permanent invalidism) he had paid more than he intended for his lesson in the terrifying powers of the unconscious.

This merely makes us aware that the unconscious must be approached with caution, like any other powerful natural force. But the major insight that arises from the case of Lindner is that the unconscious is susceptible to gentle persuasion. It will respond to the conscious mind just as to the suggestion of a hypnotist. The real problem lies with Ollie (i.e., the "you"). He lacks self-confidence, and the knowledge of how to persuade Stan to collaborate. Yet we are all intuitively aware of the answer.

When I am tense and mistrustful, things tend to go wrong because I am behaving as if Stan did not exist. When I am relaxed and confident, things seem to go right, and this is because Stan is responding to my optimism.

This is clearly the answer to the problem of Wells's "amphibians." It is not true that they have fins instead of legs. They possess legs, but they are not aware of them. Our "legs" are invisible; yet they work nevertheless.

Wells's amphibians analogy might be improved by saying that man is still at the Kitty Hawk stage. He thinks that about twelve seconds is the normal time for a flight. Yet within six or seven decades of that first lift-off at Kitty Hawk, jumbo jets were flying the Atlantic, and man had traveled to the moon. The possibilities for human evolution, once we recognize the existence of the "two streams," and the importance of learning the trick of lift-off into the second stream, are equally enormous.

Let me clarify the point with a personal anecdote.

On New Years Day, 1979, I was trapped by snow in a remote Devon farmhouse, where I had gone to lecture to extra-mural students. After twenty-four hours we decided we had to make an effort to escape. It so happened that my car was the only one that would climb the slope out of farmyard. After several hours hard work with shovels, we finally reached the main road.

The snow on the main road had been churned up by traffic, but was still treacherous. And in places where the snow was still untouched, it was hard to see where the road ended and the ditch began. So as I began to make my way home, I was forced to drive with total, obsessive attention.

Finally back on the main Exeter road, where I was able to relax, I noticed that everything I looked at seemed curiously real and interesting. The hours of concentrated attention had somehow fixed my consciousness in a higher state of awareness. There was also an immense feeling of optimism, a conviction that most of our problems are due to vagueness, slackness, inattention, and that they are all perfectly easy to overcome with determined effort. This state lasted throughout the rest of the drive home. Even now, merely thinking about the experience is enough to bring back the insight and renew the certainty.

Total attention had closed all my "inner leaks," allowing consciousness to build up a pressure far beyond its normal level. Dr. Samuel Johnson demonstrated that he understood the process when he said: "When a man knows he is to be hanged in a fortnight, it concentrates his mind wonderfully." What we call depression is simply a low level of inner-pressure, due to a kind of inner leakage. But no one deny that a bucket or a tire that leaks has something wrong with it. It is functioning below the level for which it was intended. The same is true of consciousness; what we call normal consciousness is actually subnormal. Before we can become normal human beings, we must learn the trick of closing the leaks. The first person to learn to do this permanently will be the first truly human being on this earth.

Since that drive in the snow, I have experienced "non-leaking" consciousness on a number of occasions, once lying awake all night in a Japanese hotel, and alternately concentrating and relaxing deeply. It also happened once after hours of concentrating on a train on the way to a British city, and again when being driven down a Japanese freeway. It has not happened often, but frequently enough to convince me that this is not some kind of visitation, but a state that can be achieved by directed effort.

It is non-leakage that enables the mind to build up the speed that causes it to take off into the second stream.

This effort, I repeat, is the kind of focused attention we achieve when some disaster has almost taken place, almost but not quite. Its essence is the sheer concentrated effort we summon to force ourselves into total alertness, and to make sure that it doesn't happen again. When Ollie summons such heightened alertness, Stan hastens to reinforce it with the support necessary to lock it in focus—in other words, to make heightened attention the kind of habit we need to transform the nature of daily consciousness.

When I began this study of rogue messiahs, I had no expectation that it would lead me, with such inevitability, to the solution of problems I had explored forty years earlier in *The Outsider*. It seemed then that it was basically a study in self-delusion and power-mania. Yet even at an early stage, I began to feel that the paranoid behavior of David Koresh or Jim Jones or Brother Twelve could not be explained in terms of mere opportunism or self-deceit. What was involved here was an overwhelming need to transform the reality presented to them by their senses. This is the same longing that destroyed so many Outsiders of the nineteenth century. Yeats felt that same desire, but was too much of a skeptic to believe that it was any more than a compulsion to tell beautiful lies. But prophets like Sabbatai Zevi and George Fox, and even John Humphrey Noyes, felt a compulsion to create their own society of believers, to serve as an example to the rest of the world.

Such a compulsion has its dangers, as we can see in the case of Jeffrey Lundgren, Ervil LeBaron, or Rock Theriault. The desire to impose one's own vision on the rest of the world leads to ruthlessness, brutality, and eventually paranoia. But the problem here is plainly an element of weakness that forms the rogue messiah's Achilles heel.

The question of this longing to transform reality led me to the three Christs of Ypsilanti and Kirk Allen's jet-propelled couch, which led in turn to the recognition that what messiahs are trying to create is a transformational system that can alter their vision of reality. Ibsen's Peer Gynt is willing to enter into a pact of mutual self-delusion with the Trold king; he is willing to see the Trold king's repulsive daughter, riding on a pig, as a beautiful princess on a white horse, if she will accept his mother's broken-down hut as a palace. But when the Trold king proposes to slit his eyes, so that he will actually see these things as he pretends to see them, he decides that the price is too high to pay.

We see this kind of mutual self-deception in the case of messiahs and disciples, who are perfectly willing to have their eyes slit if it will allow them to see the world as they would like to see it.

But the most important insight of all is the recognition that the unconscious mind has such extraordinary powers that it can "slit the eyes" so as to transform reality. Of course, I had known for a long time that the shaping faculty can transform reality; yet it had never struck me that it can secure the cooperation of the unconscious mind so as to literally replace one reality with another.

Yet I should have seen it. I had written about Freud's case of Bertha Pappenheim in a biography of Abraham Maslow twenty-five years ago, and again in a biography of Reich ten years later. What had misled me is that Bertha's delusions came about through the trauma of her father's death, and therefore it seemed a purely pathological case.

But Freud had understood it, and had recognized it as an example of the tremendous power of the unconscious mind to transform reality. Unfortunately, Freud had also allowed the case of Bertha to mislead him into believing that all neurosis is sexual in origin, and had gone on to defend this notion, which to us seems so obviously exaggerated, with all the harsh aggressiveness of a Right Man.

This in itself was a central insight, leading me to recognize that messiah psychology has a far wider application than I had realized.

One of its most basic mechanisms is the creation of a mask, which can be seen in individuals as diverse as Yeats, Crowley, Manson, and Mishima.

That is to say, the major lesson that emerges from the study of messiahs is that we are not faced with a bleak choice between self-deception and a reality that frightens and depresses us. What they teach us is that the unconscious mind can transform reality without self-deception.

For there is no obvious reason why these powers should respond only to self-delusion. The simple truth seems to be that they respond to a form of self-hypnosis or persuasion. If Van Gogh had understood the implications of "The Starry Night," he would have been able to induce the insight at will, and the threat of madness and suicide would have disappeared.

The faculty I am describing is not, of course, the "next development in man" that Wells talked about. This would involve more than occasional flashes of such intensity, as well as the ability to pass it on to our children genetically. Yet such states, I have no doubt whatever, foreshadow the more highly controlled states of consciousness of which human beings are capable.

It would be a pity if the messianists who declare our civilization on the brink of destruction are correct; there has never been a more exciting time in human history.

INDEX

Hampton Roads Publishing Company

. . . for the evolving human spirit

Hampton Roads Publishing Company
publishes books on a variety of subjects,
including metaphysics, health, integrative medicine,
visionary fiction, and other related topics.

For a copy of our latest catalog, call toll-free
(800) 766-8009, or send your name and address to:

Hampton Roads Publishing Company, Inc.
1125 Stoney Ridge Road
Charlottesville, VA 22902

e-mail: hrpc@hrpub.com
Website: www.hrpub.com